THE
EXPENDABLES

Also by Jeff Rubin

Why Your World Is About to Get a Whole Lot Smaller

The End of Growth

The Carbon Bubble

THE EXPENDABLES

HOW THE MIDDLE CLASS
GOT SCREWED BY
GLOBALIZATION

JEFF RUBIN

RANDOM HOUSE CANADA

PUBLISHED BY RANDOM HOUSE CANADA

Copyright © 2020 Jeff Rubin

www.penguinrandomhouse.ca

Random House Canada and colophon are registered trademarks.

Library and Archives Canada Cataloguing in Publication

Title: The expendables : how the middle class got screwed by globalization / Jeff Rubin.
Names: Rubin, Jeff, 1954- author.
Identifiers: Canadiana (print) 20190158425 | Canadiana (ebook) 20190158492 | ISBN 9780735279391 (hardcover) | ISBN 9780735279407 (HTML)
Subjects: LCSH: Middle class—Economic conditions. | LCSH: Globalization. | LCSH: Equality.
Classification: LCC HT684 .R83 2020 | DDC 305.5/5—dc23

Text design: Andrew Roberts
Jacket design: David Gee

Printed and bound in Canada

MIX
Paper from responsible sources
FSC www.fsc.org FSC® C016245

10 9 8 7 6 5 4 3 2

Penguin
Random House
RANDOM HOUSE CANADA

To all those left behind.

CONTENTS

FOREWORD

THEN AND NOW

You could see the pandemic coming. It wasn't as though there was no warning. The virus emerged in China but arrived in North America before we were ready, and it landed with the destructive force of a tsunami. Record-setting consumer spending hit a brick wall as shoppers stayed home. New car sales went over a cliff. And following just like clockwork, unemployment went through the roof as shops and factories shut down. An unprecedented bull run on the stock market quickly turned into panic selling, and the Dow cratered, seemingly overnight. The S&P 500 dropped over 20 percent into bear market territory, and the result was a global recession that seemed to come out of nowhere. More than 116,000 people died in the United States.

Elvis Presley appeared on the *Ed Sullivan Show* that year, the Frisbee was invented, Ford introduced the Edsel with great fanfare, Canada unveiled the Avro Arrow jet fighter, the USSR launched *Sputnik*, and Dwight D. Eisenhower was sworn in as president of the United States. It was 1957.

By the way, the world recovered almost immediately from the Asian flu, as that pandemic was known. After a staggering 10 percent decline in gross domestic product (GDP) in the first quarter of 1958, by the third quarter growth had spiked to 10 percent—a 20 percentage-point swing. So, no big deal, right? The economy got the flu, it took some time off, and it went right back to churning out jobs and profits. In fact, when economists and historians talk about the "Eisenhower Recession," they seldom even mention the Asian flu as a cause.

It would seem to follow, then, that we have a model to help us predict what the recovery from COVID-19 will look like. Just look at 1958, and then wait for the jobs and the markets to return to form and the good times to resume—not quite the catastrophe we feared.

But if you're thinking that what was true in 1958 is true today, this book is for you. Because while consumer spending, consistent GDP growth and a record-breaking bull run on the stock market may make it feel as though we've wandered into the Eisenhower (or Diefenbaker, if you live in Canada) era, that is a dangerous illusion, especially if you're a member of the rapidly shrinking middle class. Because consumer spending, GDP growth and stocks have almost nothing to do with your economic health.

In fact, as you will see, those things measure only *rich* people's economic health. And of late, these folk haven't been getting rich by making more Edsels or engineering more Arrows. Those cars and planes belong to a different world, a world in which factory jobs paid a middle-class wage and products on the shelves came from factories down the road. A world in which local labour was so essential that their jobs were secure. And a world where taxes were so progressive that the rich actually paid their freight. That was a long time ago.

Looking backward in politics is usually considered poor form. It's much safer to be considered *progressive and look ahead*. But the fact is that the late 1950s and early 1960s may have marked the greatest economic equality in history. And that economic health was like immunological health. The economy got better quickly because it was already healthy.

But two other things happened in 1957 that give us some sense of why the recovery from the COVID-19 recession might be a lot harder than shaking off the Asian flu.

First, the Treaty of Rome was signed in March of that year, establishing the precursor of the European Union (the European Economic Community). Though the tight political and economic integration of a "United States of Europe" was still just a dream, the Treaty of Rome was an important step in creating a common market. Up until that point, each country had the ability to impose tariffs to protect key industries and the associated jobs. From that moment on, France, West Germany, Belgium, the Netherlands and Luxembourg would give up that ability in exchange for the right to sell in each other's markets without facing tariffs. The hope behind lifting tariffs was that in a world of economic expansion, workers and industries wouldn't *need* protection: there would be so much wealth to go around that everyone would be better off.

In other words, it was a form of free trade and a precursor of what was to follow. Free trade was an idea that was sweeping the world. As we will see, the General Agreement on Tariffs and Trade (GATT), a treaty designed to increase international trade by removing protections for industry and labour, had been signed into law in 1947, and went through several rounds of updates, each slashing more tariffs. In 1956, the so-called Geneva Round (because it was negotiated in Geneva), eliminated $2.5 billion of protections between twenty-six countries. So, globalization was swirling in the air as the Asian flu was making its way across the Pacific.

The Asian flu could have cratered the global economy, but it didn't. By coincidence, there was another near miss that year that most people didn't even notice at the time. In 1986, it was revealed that a United States Air Force B-36 bomber had accidentally dropped a hydrogen bomb on New Mexico in May 1957. It was, it turned out, the most powerful nuclear bomb ever built. At ten megatons, it was bigger than anything in today's nuclear arsenal, and about 625 times more powerful than the bomb that was dropped on Hiroshima. Though the forty-two-thousand-pound bomb did not detonate, it left a crater three and a half metres (12 feet) deep and more than seven metres (25 feet) wide. If it had gone off, it would have vaporized the air base where the bomber was scheduled to land.

An investigation revealed that a safety mechanism had been removed.

You would think the Air Force would have been a little more careful with warheads by 1957. They'd already jettisoned one bomb off the coast of British Columbia, and another in the St. Lawrence River, in addition to crashes of nuclear bombers in the Atlantic and in the mountains of New Mexico. Another two nuclear bombs fell out of the sky in 1961 over North Carolina. Removing protections when so much is at stake, even to increase efficiency, can be more than dangerous. It can be apocalyptic.

None of those bombs detonated, but the slow-fuse-burn of GATT and globalization has left an industrial landscape every bit as cratered as the destruction left by a nuclear warhead. If a worker from 1957 could see Detroit today, what would he think? The shuttered factories across North America, the boarded-up main streets, the empty union halls—the physical toll of globalization would be inescapable.

Which brings us back to the flu.

Early on in the COVID-19 crisis, the scale of the required government response was often compared to that needed during the Second World War. It was time for our ingenuity and industrial might to be put to good use and mobilized, much in the way it had been a couple of generations ago. The United States built more than twenty-seven hundred Liberty-class freighters between 1941 and 1945. That's two fourteen-thousand-tonne ships every three days (or more than thirty-nine million tonnes of ship.) Surely, the world's biggest economy could make some N95 masks.

Well, not really. On March 19, 2020, Taiwan announced it could spare 100,000 masks per week for the United States (their sole military ally, which has been protecting them from Communist China for generations at immense cost). That's out of a weekly output of 7 million masks. So the Taiwanese were willing to set aside 1.4 percent of their mask capacity for their much larger ally.

The EU also adopted a policy of "every man for himself." In March, Brussels banned the export of medical equipment, even to other European countries, before eventually relenting in the face of pleas from member countries like Italy which were hit particularly hard by the pandemic. Exasperated Serbian president Aleksandar Vučić stood in front of television cameras and said, "European solidarity doesn't exist. That was a fairy tale on paper." Shortly thereafter, Serbia shut its borders. The only foreigners allowed to enter the country? Chinese doctors. Vučić called China "the only ones who can help."

He did have a point (though Russia also sent several transport planes full of equipment and medical personnel). Before the crisis broke, half of the world's masks were made in China. Since then, the country has increased production twelve-fold. By the end of March, factories in China were pumping out 115 million a day (which puts the Taiwanese gift in perspective). But there's more to the story than Chinese manufacturing output.

Many of those Chinese factories are making masks for international companies. On paper, Canadian company Medicom was making 3 million masks a day at its Shanghai factory. But rather than being shipped to Canada, they were all claimed by the Chinese government. American chemical giant 3M also has mask plants in Shanghai, but according to American trade officials, the factories had effectively been "nationalized." They may have been under contract to the American company, but when push came to shove, the Chinese government had priority. According to Canadian entrepreneurs on the ground in China, government officials had been posted to factories producing medical equipment like ventilators and protective suits to police where those items were being shipped.

So sure, our companies still make things. It's just that the factories are somewhere else. And the jobs are somewhere else. And, when we need them, the masks are somewhere else too.

While the Chinese government is busy controlling the world supply of crucial commodities, Canadian diplomats are reduced to sending out messages on social media, hoping that Chinese alumnae of Canadian universities will be willing to help find a few boxes of gloves and masks. Hardly the commanding heights of the global economy that globalism promised.

What the COVID-19 crisis has shown us is that questions of economic theory aren't just about economic health. They're about health. Period. Because it's not just masks and protective gowns the Chinese government effectively control. For years, lax regulatory control and low wages have made China a major source for the majority of component chemicals that go into generic drugs—that is, nearly all of the drugs Canadians and Americans are prescribed.

The same goes for antibiotics. In the 1980s, the United States had far-ranging emergency-response readiness, including antibiotic manufacturing capacity spread across the continent. The US produced 70 percent of the world's supply. Now it is dependent on imports from China. North Americans face the same dependency for a wide variety of health-related products, from vitamin C to chemotherapy drugs.

In a world frequently described as "globalized," that's not supposed to matter. The magic of just-in-time-delivery, combined with efficient labour markets and economies of scale, is supposed to provide us with whatever we need, in abundance and at the best prices. That may work for flip-flops and lawn furniture (or whatever globally sourced product you buy at Walmart), but, as it turns out, it doesn't work in an emergency. It doesn't work when you absolutely need it to work.

It shouldn't have taken a bat peeing on a pangolin in Wuhan to teach us this lesson. The evidence has been piling up around us for years. But tragedy has a way of focusing one's attention. Global deregulation was always a bad idea. It was always set up to benefit a small number of people at immense cost to everyone else. Exactly what that cost is becomes clear when we compare today's economy with 1957's.

INTRODUCTION

A s they watched the news in November 1999, the mayors of Dallas, Detroit, San Diego and Honolulu must have been feeling as though they'd dodged any number of bullets. They were the runners-up in the bid to host the first Ministerial Conference of the World Trade Organization (WTO) ever held in the United States. The winner was Seattle.

In no small measure, Seattle's selection was due to the fact that no other American city was as economically dependent on foreign trade. Trade ministers from more than one hundred countries were gathering at the aptly named Washington State Convention and Trade Center to negotiate a new "Millennial Round" agreement that would open up even more of the world to the free flow of capital and goods, and there was a relatively new word in circulation for this economic experiment: *globalization*.

Over the previous decade the world had steadily been crystallizing into free trade zones. The Maastricht Treaty, signed in 1992, had only recently brought a common currency to most of Europe. On the other side of the Atlantic, Canada and the United States had signed the Free Trade Agreement in 1989, and then, in 1994, invited Mexico to join what became the North American Free Trade Agreement, or NAFTA.

Since the days of Adam Smith, David Ricardo and John Stuart Mill, economists have been pretty much unanimous in the opinion that free trade between countries is the only way to make sure that capital is used efficiently. And they can make a pretty compelling case. Deregulated trade has a great track record of boosting gross domestic product (GDP), the standard measurement of a country's economy. And it doesn't seem to hurt stock prices or corporate profitability either. What's not to like?

So when Seattle won the bid to host the WTO's globalization talks, the organizers probably didn't expect the more than forty thousand protestors who assembled in the city. It turned out to be the most violent demonstration the United States had seen since the street riots that broke out during the Democratic National Convention in Chicago in 1968. Back then, the Vietnam War was dividing the nation like few other issues before it ever had. This time around, the topic of globalization was not even on most Americans' radar screens. Few had ever questioned the widely presumed benefits of globalization, including their president at the time, Bill Clinton.

The people on the street came from a broad coalition of labour unions and environmentalists, with the usual sprinkling of anarchists who typically made their presence felt at such events. Labour decried the loss of American jobs to overseas sweatshops and demanded that labour standards be part of any new trade deals that the WTO might sanction. For their part, the environmentalists insisted that trade deals had to uphold pollution standards so that production couldn't just be moved to jurisdictions that had lax standards or no standards at all.

Both groups argued that without such safeguards, globalization meant nothing more than a vicious race to the bottom in a chase for ever-greater profits for the world's largest corporations. As for the WTO itself, the protestors considered it a bureaucratic supranational power that had no accountability to the electorate of any of the countries it represented.

Of course, as an unaccountable supranational body, the WTO had no reason to pay attention to the protesters' concerns. The organization's mandate wasn't to prevent the use of child labour in the production of textiles, or to stave off the ecological disasters that so often accompanied third-world mining projects. They were there to protect and further promote the free movement of goods and capital.

Many of the protestors were peaceful, including the American Federation of Labor and the Congress of Industrial Organizations (AFL-CIO) and its member unions—including the United Steelworkers of America, the Teamsters, the Machinists union and the International Longshore and Warehouse Union—which organized a large permitted rally and march. But other protestors, particularly the so-called black bloc variety from the anarchists' ranks, were not. It didn't take long before the violence escalated, with thousands of the protestors flooding the downtown streets and battling local police and the two National Guard divisions that Washington governor Gary Locke called in to restore order.

Needless to say, not much was accomplished at the ministerial meeting. As chaos reigned in the streets, most delegates were barricaded in their hotel rooms. The three-day conference adjourned early, and most of the delegates couldn't wait to get out of town. The collapsed trade negotiations weren't resumed until a meeting two years later in Doha, Qatar, where the authorities, determined to prevent another Seattle-type protest, prudently sealed off a three-kilometre (2-mile) radius around the meeting site.

At the time, the Seattle protestors were almost universally condemned by the American media. *The New York Times* even went so far as to fabricate a story about how protestors had tossed Molotov cocktails at the police. All the media wanted to focus on was masked protestors smashing in the windows of upscale Seattle storefronts, or protestors scuffling with police. But the even more damning accusation against those who had shown up to demonstrate was that they were naive and backward-looking. The consensus among those with skin in the game was that globalization was the future.

SO WHO WAS RIGHT?

Twenty years have passed since those protests rocked both Seattle and the news cycle. Passions on all sides have cooled. It seems fair, now, to ask who was right. The results should be in. Did globalization deliver on its promises?

Well, global trade grew nicely in the years after that ministerial conference. Apart from a crater in 2008, the global economy has been expanding steadily. Stock markets are up, corporate profitability is up, and unemployment is down to historic lows.

It sounds like a complete victory for the globalists. In fact, hardly anyone questions the importance of global free trade these days. Even political constituencies that were against it

4

when it was a new idea have come around. In Canada, for example, the Liberals campaigned vehemently against the original Canada–US Free Trade Agreement in the 1988 election, but Justin Trudeau's Liberal government recently defended its successor, the North American Free Trade Agreement with equal tenacity when Donald Trump threatened to rip it up. Meanwhile, that same government has been quietly expanding free trade agreements with the European Union (EU) and less quietly courted China. They've clearly made peace with the idea that globalization is profitable. It's hard to argue with a success story.

But there is more than one way to define success in a trade deal.

If the American unions protesting in Seattle back in 1999 thought the WTO's trade rules were costing their membership their jobs, they hadn't seen anything yet. A scant two years later, the WTO admitted China into its fold, and the exodus of North American manufacturing jobs went into overdrive. Between 1999 and 2015, the American economy alone had lost almost 5 million manufacturing jobs.[1] The Canadian economy, roughly one-tenth the size of the US economy, lost over half a million manufacturing jobs, or over a quarter of the country's industrial workforce.[2]

And the warnings of the protesting environmentalists have more than come to fruition. The mass movement of manufacturing production overseas has led to the mass movement of the industrial pollution that accompanied it. Less than a decade after Seattle, China overtook the United States as the world's largest carbon polluter, with much of that pollution coming from the production for export of the goods that

Americans once made.[3] And to make matters worse, China's antiquated state-supported factories in migrating industries like steel were pumping out a lot more carbon emissions per ingot than anything that had once come out of Pittsburgh. But carbon emissions didn't matter to the WTO, or to the companies sourcing Chinese steel. The only thing that mattered was that Chinese steelworkers were getting paid a fraction of what American, Canadian or European steelworkers once earned, and hence could produce steel, as well as most other manufactured goods, a whole lot cheaper.

Since 2006, China's emissions, like its industrial production, have skyrocketed, dwarfing the improvements in North American emissions that have come about through the loss of manufacturing industries and the substitution of renewables and gas for coal in power generation. By 2015, China's carbon emissions were 80 percent higher than those of the United States.[4] Air pollution in the country got so bad that many of its residents in cities like Beijing and Shanghai wear masks before venturing outside. And the impact of anthropogenic emissions on climate change, which was still a hotly debated and controversial theory back at the time of the Seattle demonstrations, is today an acknowledged fact.

In light of those developments, you might think that there would be new standards and regulations to protect labour and the environment in the so-called rules-based trading system that the WTO governs and promotes. Guess again. The WTO and the governments that support it are no more willing to listen to their critics today than they were two decades ago.

THE SAME OLD STORY

As contentious and violent as the protests in Seattle were, the two sides were never really disagreeing. The question was not whether globalization would work; the real question was, *Who benefits?*

Nobody ever frames it quite that way, certainly not politicians or newspaper columnists. Maybe not even you. But the message is there all the same. Fans of globalization have always had good news to share, and GDP growth and bull markets make great headlines. But there is no such thing as a free lunch. Someone is picking up the bill, and it could very well be you.

Among mainstream neoclassical economists there is virtual unanimity on that subject. Free trade and free markets boost growth, and any attempts to deviate from that path will hurt our collective economic well-being. Only economic illiterates would fail to understand that, or so we are told.

What we are *not* told is why we should care about GDP. GDP is a measure of the value of all the goods and services produced in the economy. It would be nice to think that living in a country that's getting richer means that you're getting richer too, but that's not the way it works anymore.

What mainstream economists don't get is that, while they may be right about the effect of global trade on GDP, that measure has less and less significance for you—particularly if you happen to belong to the rapidly shrinking middle class. What these economists fail to look at is the *distribution* of the benefits from stronger growth. The gains from trade have become so skewed that while in theory everybody should be better off, many are now faring much worse. For these folks, free trade

has been impoverishing, not enriching. But most of the economists extolling the virtues of free trade don't concern themselves with distribution. All that matters to them is that GDP
is bigger than it would otherwise have been.

While economic experts are quick to remind us that without growth, GDP per capita cannot rise, that statistic is a
fictional measurement of our true economic well-being. No one
takes home per capita GDP. If your boss gets a raise, the average
salary at your company goes up, but you are no further ahead.
That's how much good gains in per capita GDP do you. The
same experts who remind us we are living in one of the longest
running economic expansions on record talk as if everyone is
getting an equal slice of that growing pie. But at best, most of
us are getting crumbs. So why should we care what happens
to GDP growth or, for that matter, GDP per capita?

What holds true for GDP growth also holds true for job
creation—another one of those sacred economic tasks that
governments around the world have pledged to their elector-
ates. In most places, as our economists constantly remind us,
employment is booming. Governments congratulate themselves on the fact that the jobless rate in many countries is now
at the lowest mark in decades, telling workers they've never
had it so good. But rest assured that those telling you how good
you've got it have it that much better themselves.

What they're not telling you, of course, is that having a
job doesn't mean what it used to—not by a long shot. Of
course, you don't need some high-powered economist to tell
you that. Your own experience speaks loud and clear on the
subject. Today, you often need to hold down multiple jobs to

get by, because you typically don't earn enough at any one of them to pay the bills. And benefits have become as much an anachronism as a decent wage.

It used to be that having a middle-class job meant you owned a home, went on an annual family vacation and put away a few dollars each year for the kids' education. But that was a long time ago. In today's global economy, things are different—very different. Getting a job once offered many people a route out of poverty. Today, most of the jobs being created are a gateway *into* it. And once you cross through that gateway, chances are you aren't crossing back.

So, sure, in one sense the economists are right. Globalization has led to greater competitiveness and efficiency. But if greater global efficiency means you are being left further and further behind, then maybe it's not really something you want. Maybe all of the poor, foolish economic illiterates out there are the ones who really understand how—or, more importantly, *for whom*—the economy works. Because it's certainly not working for you, and it hasn't been for quite awhile now.

So maybe it's time to tune out all the condescending lectures from economic experts who endlessly extol the virtues of concepts like comparative advantage and international competitiveness, and the wonders of today's global supply chains. They constantly warn us that there are other countries nipping at our heels, so we'd better not let down our guard or slacken our pace. Regardless of the cost, we must protect our position in the all-important global marketplace.

As it turns out, most of those countries chasing us have low-wage economies in which workers are only too happy to take your job. And, for the most part, the companies you work for are only too happy to let them steal it, given that they can make more money by building supply chains on the back of cheap labour. That may be good for shareholders, but unfortunately you don't own any shares. And that leaves you wondering about your future in the global economy. It seems the more internationally competitive your economy becomes, the less room there is in it for you.

Maybe it's time to see the world economy for what it has really become: a giant auction where jobs go to the bidder offering the lowest wage. And if you're not willing to work for the same pay that some overseas sweatshop offers its workers, you suddenly become an expendable cog in some far-flung global supply chain.

Maybe it is time to focus instead on your own circumstances, and to understand the factors that have brought you here. Do this, and you'll soon stop caring about growing the pie and start focusing on carving yourself a larger slice. And if the pie shrinks in the process—as the experts continually warn us it will—it's not you who will notice but rather the few who have engorged themselves on the spoils of growth.

The irony is that while globalization is often heralded as a tide that lifts all boats, it is also trotted out as an explanation for why some boats can't be lifted at all. Go ahead and ask your government to curb the flow of cheap imports that cost you your job, or to raise the minimum wage that so many of us now earn, or to make rich people and corporations pay more tax so that it doesn't all have to come out of your paycheque. The response is always the same. Calls for a fairer economy are readily dismissed as hopelessly naive. Governments routinely claim that if they were to enact any of these admittedly well-intentioned policies, their efforts would ultimately backfire and hurt the very people they were trying to help. We are constantly warned against the dangers that would come from letting social workers manage our economy. We are told that attempts to redistribute income or wealth or to protect local industries with tariffs would undermine our economy's international competitiveness and take a heavy toll on economic growth and employment.

So what if the experts are right? What if they are absolutely correct when they claim that measures that would help improve your daily life—like earning a decent living wage with proper benefits—would hurt your country's chances for economic growth? Who cares? Maybe those benefiting from the current system do, but you certainly shouldn't. GDP growth is doing just fine. It's you who is hurting.

Economic growth might as well be taking place in some distant galaxy, because it's taking light years for its benefits to trickle down to you. Why not let the gilded one percent of our population—those who are the true beneficiaries of an expanding economy—worry about growth? The rest of us just need to get paid a living wage.

SEATTLE'S POSTSCRIPT

Looking back over the two decades following the ill-fated WTO ministerial meeting in Seattle, it would seem that the ragtag group of tree huggers, union members, socialists and anarchists pretty well got everything right. The WTO's trade rules have squeezed the middle class of every country in the Organisation for Economic Co-operation and Development (OECD).[5] And the shift in production to low-wage countries has also shielded producers from environmental regulations—like the need to limit climate-changing carbon emissions—they might have had to contend with if they'd remained in an OECD country.

The protesters had a good run. There were memorable riots in Washington, DC, and Montreal in 2000, the year after Seattle, as well as in Quebec City in 2001. Similar protests sprang up around the world whenever the International Monetary Fund (IMF), World Bank, WTO, G7, G20 or other supranational groups gathered to talk about deregulating trade. For a variety of reasons, however, the urgency gradually drained away from the anti-globalization movement. It flared up again in 2011 as a coalition of activists representing a variety of interests set up camp in New York's Zuccotti Park and touched off the Occupy movement, which called for regulation on banking and debt forgiveness, and measures against greed and corruption. It inspired left-leaning and anti-capitalist protest camps across the continent, but without a clear agenda or leadership, the movement stalled and tents were cleared away by police in dozens of cities.

But what the protestors in Seattle would have never imagined is who, sixteen years later, would step up to champion their cause—and has done so, no less, with a gusto and fervour that has left their nemesis, the WTO, on life support and the world trading system it so carefully constructed on the verge of collapse.

CHAPTER 1

THE NEW POPULISM

The protesters in Seattle and in Zuccotti Park thought they had billionaires all figured out. Billionaires use their power to shape institutions such as Wall Street, the WTO, and even governments so that those institutions work to their benefit—and against everyone else's. People were sick and tired of billionaires having their own way, and the protesters could see that things would only get worse. What they couldn't foresee was the arrival upon the scene of the next great advocate for the working class. Turns out this wouldn't be a bearded socialist firing up crowds of fellow travellers in an Occupy tent city, as one might have expected, but one of the most flamboyantly gold-plated billionaires on the planet.

Billionaires who worry that middle-class wages aren't growing enough don't come along every day. It was back in 1992, during the presidential election campaign, that Ross Perot made the case against NAFTA. He was one of the first US politicians to warn Americans of what would happen as a result of that trade deal, claiming that the "giant sucking sound" they were about to hear was the rush of middle-class jobs draining away into low-wage Mexico.[1] Although that turned out to be prophetic, Perot took home only 19.7 million votes. More than

two decades later, a guy named Donald Trump wasn't interested in losing.

The world in which Donald Trump found himself campaign-
ing, ahead of the 2016 presidential election, was very different
from the one Ross Perot had experienced—and Trump himself
was a very different sort of billionaire from the earnest former
Boy Scout. When it came to shaping his political persona,
Trump took cues from one his earliest political mentors, Jesse
"the Body" Ventura, whom Trump first met through his involve-
ment in promoting World Wrestling Entertainment Inc. (WWE).
In 1998, the famous wrestling star walked away from the ring to
run for governor in his home state of Minnesota. He ran as a
Reform candidate, choosing to join the party Perot had founded.
(Neither the Republicans nor the Democrats were particularly
keen on the prospect of a hulking bully who had made a wrestling career as a cheater and a heel representing them on the
campaign trail.)

In what would turn out to be a pattern repeated around the
world, the establishment parties got it wrong. They were either
unwilling or unable to sense that change was in the air. Ventura
carved out a sizeable niche among the Minnesota electorate,
who were tired of the endless parade of professional politicians
that both parties insisted on trotting out year after year.
Claiming to have a direct line to the people, Ventura triumphed:
"the Body" became the thirty-eighth governor of Minnesota.
And since he wasn't beholden to any political party apparatus,
Ventura could pretty well take whatever positions he felt like
on the issues facing the state legislature. It turned out that
a heel could not only beat both establishment candidates but

also be a pretty good governor. When Ventura left office in 2003, he ended up a fellow at the John F. Kennedy School of Government at Harvard. That's a long way from the ring.

Donald Trump was watching. He'd been mulling over a run at the presidency for the better part of a decade, and had publicly mused that 2012 might be the year. For a time, he considered running as an independent, hoping the Ventura approach could work for him in Washington. He would position himself as an outsider—not a professional politician sullied by the swamp that Washington had become, with its cesspools of special-interest groups and lobbyists with their chequebooks always at hand.

Trump surely recognized that running as an independent would be a daunting task. Andrew Jackson—whose portrait adorns the US twenty-dollar bill and space on the wall in Trump's Oval Office—was the last president of the United States to win as an independent, and that was back in 1829. It wasn't that others hadn't tried. Many did, but they all lost. These days, it takes a vast organization and party machinery to win a US presidential election. For Trump, this meant that winning the White House as an independent was going to be a lot more difficult than Ventura's quest to become a state governor. So, despite having described himself as more of a Democrat than a Republican over the years, and in fact having registered as a Democrat, Trump announced his intention to run in the primaries for the leadership of the Republican Party. Of course, being a billionaire didn't hurt. Unlike other contenders, Trump didn't have to worry about raising campaign funds, although it turned out he was no slouch in that department.

He also didn't have to pen weighty op-eds in *The New York Times* or *The Washington Post*, like other aspirants for party leadership did. He had other ways to get his message out. His exploits—negotiating huge Manhattan real estate deals; writing bestsellers like *Trump: The Art of the Deal*; promoting Miss Universe pageants; and, of course, starring in his own blockbuster reality TV show, *The Apprentice*—all gave him a huge following in the tabloid press. And he was betting there were a lot more people reading the tabloids than the newspapers of the country's elite.

More importantly, he was also betting on the fact that many Americans were fed up with the status quo and convinced that nothing much ever changed for them, regardless of whether a Democrat or a Republican was sitting in the White House. He figured that's why many of them no longer bothered to vote. He addressed those underlying sentiments of frustration and apathy by borrowing, and later even trademarking, the "Make America Great Again" slogan from the last American populist president, Ronald Reagan.

That message resonated with the millions of Americans who were feeling anything but great about themselves or their futures. And as would soon be revealed at the polls, there were a lot more of those folks out there than the political pundits had recognized. What Trump understood and capitalized on was a growing undercurrent of resentment in American society, a resentment felt by those who saw themselves being left behind. The "Make America Great Again" message tapped into nostalgia for a not-so-distant past when most Americans still had middle-class jobs. Trump has been accused—often—of cynical opportunism, but on this key issue he has been very consistent. As far back as the time of the Seattle riots, Trump was on record as saying that America was getting ripped off by China in trade deals and needlessly losing valuable manufacturing jobs.[2]

In the aftermath of what seemed like an improbable victory for Trump, analysts and commentators who were unhappy with the outcome immediately pointed their fingers at "angry old white men," the embittered victims of globalization—as though unemployment turned middle-aged men Republican. What they forgot was that Bernie Sanders, the most progressive Democratic candidate in decades, had run for the nomination on a very similar platform to Trump's.

Trump and Sanders might not have agreed on much, coming as they did from polar opposite ends of the ideological spectrum, but what often gets lost in the narratives on their respective campaigns is that they were on the same page in terms of how they viewed the world trading system and its treatment of American workers. And both directly sought the support of those workers. Sanders relentlessly attacked Hillary Clinton, his establishment opponent in the Democratic primaries, for her unqualified support for globalization and the free trade deals that did nothing but increase its sprawl. He dismissed the so-called progressive idea of "open borders" on the grounds that it would lower wages and increase unemployment—the same issues Trump was capitalizing on in his campaign.

Both Sanders and Trump bucked the established positions of their respective parties in denouncing the global trading system as fundamentally unfair to American workers. Global trading rules, they argued, gave huge commercial advantages to low-wage countries such as China at the expense of American workers (and workers from other OECD countries). Trade deals like the recently negotiated Trans-Pacific Partnership (which the Obama administration had signed) or even the long-standing NAFTA were destroying factory jobs in the United States and, with them, America's shrinking middle class, once the backbone of the nation's economy and the heart of American society. Most of all, both Trump and Sanders questioned China's unfair trade practices and the country's massive trade surplus with the United States, which had cost American factory workers millions of jobs.

But challenging global trade rules wasn't on the agenda of either the Democratic Party establishment or the Republican Party elite. And neither considered American industrial workers to be part of their vision of the country's future, which was all about fintech, robotics, artificial intelligence and investment banking. Factory workers were the expendables—an unfortunate but necessary casualty in the battle to stay on top of the fast-moving world of economic progress and technological change.

Making the plight of America's long-forgotten and politically disenfranchised industrial labour force the centrepiece of an election campaign not only held little appeal to either party's establishment, the message also didn't resonate well within corporate America, which for the most part strongly favoured global free trade.

Many American companies were benefiting from trade

agreements promoting ever-greater levels of global trade. Apple, for example, had vast supply chains in China, along with a vast number of iPhone sales.[3] At the same time, however, most American workers were being left behind, seeing few if any real-income gains over decades running. And they weren't alone. Workers across OECD countries were in the same boat, either losing their factory jobs or taking huge pay cuts to keep them. The unrelenting offshoring of factory jobs and the associated undercutting of wages were, in fact, shrinking the middle class in pretty well every developed economy in the world. Across the OECD their share of the population has declined and their share of national income has fallen even more.[4]

Little wonder, then, that politicians looking for an issue on which to hang their hat might settle on the very same conflict that spurred on those protestors in Seattle in 1999. In a time when the rich were getting ostentatiously richer and the middle class was evaporating before our eyes, the age-old battle between the "people" and the "elite" seemed primed and ready for another round. Populism—which had been hanging around as a school of political thought since the nineteenth century—once again started to sound appealing, and this time, it promised to do something about the fallout from globalization. Both the Sanders camp (on the left wing of the Democratic Party) and the Trump campaign (on the right wing of the Republican Party) argued that further globalization was neither desirable nor inevitable. In fact, both candidates vowed to turn the clock back to a time when most things sold in the US economy were actually made by Americans, and when those making them enjoyed a steadily rising standard of living.

Trump's message may have struck a chord with voters, but it didn't resonate well with the media. His controversial views on trade and immigration were ridiculed in the mainstream press, and his campaign chances were essentially dismissed by every major news network in the country. But to their shock and dismay, "The Donald" beat out sixteen other candidates in the most widely contested Republican primaries ever to grab the nomination of the Grand Old Party. (The same media outlets were almost equally dismissive of Sanders's attempt to secure the Democratic nomination, even though he ended up capturing 46 percent of delegate votes at the party convention.[5])

The Republicans rolled the dice and won the election. The Democrats played it safe and lost. The difference was that the Democratic Party machinery was able to ensure that Sanders never got on their ticket. While Sanders's surprisingly strong campaign captured twenty-three primaries, the party closed ranks around status quo candidate Hillary Clinton and did everything it could to prevent a Sanders nomination. On the other side of the aisle, the Republican establishment failed in its similar attempt to prevent a rogue outsider from hijacking the party and its platform. But it could just have easily been a two-outsider race.

Despite his shocking win in the primaries and then at the party convention, Trump still wasn't convincing the mainstream media, who didn't give him any better a chance of winning the election than they had of getting the Republican nomination. As a result, the GOP stunned the world when its improbable candidate took the White House. After all, the political novice was going head-to-head with wily veteran

Hillary Clinton, the very well-versed, well-informed and politically connected senator, former First Lady and former secretary of state. The media projected an overwhelming victory for Clinton. Polls gave her between a 70 and 99 percent chance of winning. But like the sixteen other Republican candidates who ran against Trump in the primaries, Hillary Clinton learned you can't always believe the polls, and you can't always believe what you read in the news.

BREXIT AND THE RISE OF POPULISM

One of the ironies of globalization is that it has made the recent uptick in populist sentiment global too. After all, if middle-class American voters left behind by free trade eventually got frustrated enough to dig in their heels, it stands to reason that the disenfranchised in other developed countries would feel the same way.

In fact, if the Clinton campaign had been paying attention, they might have noticed the warning delivered by the Brexit referendum in the United Kingdom: people were reaching the end of their rope when it came to tolerating the status quo. As unlikely as it had seemed that a huckster real estate tycoon might become president of the United States, it was almost equally unimaginable that voters in Great Britain would decide to leave the European Union. London was, after all, doing quite nicely as part of the trading bloc. But a few months before the American election, that's just what they did.

Of course, it wasn't the investment and banking communities of London's famous financial district, the Square Mile, that voted to leave. They were solidly in favour of maintaining the status quo and remaining in the European Union. After all, they were its financial centre. Members of these communities issued a steady stream of warnings that Brexit would be disastrous for the British economy. In other words, they argued, what was good for the financial sector was good for everyone else.

But everyone else wasn't buying it. Support for Brexit was the greatest among those left behind in the hollowed-out ruins of the country's once-mighty industrial areas. Although Brexiters were typically white middle-class males who had become increasingly marginalized in the now globally integrated British economy, support came from across the ideological spectrum. The vote to leave was hailed in publications as politically disparate as *Socialist Worker* and the *Daily Mail*—both of which rightfully claimed that it was a vote against the country's ruling elites.[6]

The people who voted for Brexit were the same type of folks who voted for either Marine Le Pen (of the far-right party the National Front) or Jean-Luc Mélenchon (the Communist Party candidate) in the 2017 French elections. Both argued for France to leave the European Union for the same reasons espoused by UK Independence Party leader Nigel Farage and former London mayor (and current prime minister) Boris Johnson.

At the heart of these protest votes—whether cast from the left or the right—were the continual loss of factory jobs and the subsequent immiseration of the industrial working class. At one point, even the governor of the Bank of England, Canadian Mark Carney, referred to the "Dickensian" conditions in which the English working class now found themselves. During the French presidential election, the loss of the 295 remaining jobs at a Whirlpool dryer factory in Amiens, in Northern France[7]—a region that had been gutted by factory closures—served as a rallying cry for those calling for France to leave the European Union (production moved to Poland), in much the same way that the scheduled movement of a Ford assembly plant from the United States to Mexico had played out during the Trump presidential campaign.

While Emmanuel Macron, a former Rothschild investment banker, easily won the French presidential election, the status quo is far from being assured in the EU's second-largest economy (once the United Kingdom leaves). Voter turnout was the lowest since 1969, and among those who did turn up, 4 million cast spoiled ballots in protest against what they saw as an impossible choice between the far right and the billionaires' party.[8] Just over a year after Macron's inauguration, protesters against new energy taxes levied on the poor took to the streets and rioting broke out. While the new taxes were shelved, the *gilets jaunes*—or Yellow Vests—named for the high-visibility vests required by French law to be carried in all vehicles, had more grievances to air. The movement has quickly morphed from a protest against higher fuel costs into a broader revolt against the French elite and the government that is widely considered to be representing its interests. The Yellow Vests are now demanding the reintroduction of the wealth tax eliminated by the Macron government and a minimum-wage increase, among other things. They are the longest-running anti-government street protest movement in France in over a decade.

While these political upheavals all have their own national flavour, they also share some common ground. The Brexit vote, the electoral strength of radical parties on both the left and the right in the French election and the subsequent yellow vest movement, and, of course, the improbable election of Donald Trump to the presidency of the United States all represented a resounding rejection of globalization and the economic status quo. As well, these upheavals drew their support from the men and women left behind by the economy. Contrary to the message most economists and politicians had been delivering, globalization had created a lot more losers than its advocates acknowledged. You would seldom (if ever) hear about those losers in the speeches made every year at Davos, where the global elite and so-called thought leaders gather to pontificate on the world's economic problems over champagne and canapés. Nor would you read much about them in the pages of *The Wall Street Journal* or *The Economist*. But that didn't mean they didn't exist—or that their ranks weren't swelling. It just meant that they were ignored in the media, and that they had no real voice in what their governments were doing. But now, all of a sudden, they did. Whether autoworkers in America or Yellow Vests in France, they would be silent no more.

It is surely one of the great ironies of modern American politics that the person who took up the cause on behalf of these losers—these expendables—is a man who probably never worked a day in a factory in his entire life. Yet in a novel and uncompromising manner, President Donald Trump has shaken the world trading system to its very core. In his inauguration speech, Trump vowed that America's globalist policies were about to change. And unlike most politicians who promise their voters change, this one wasn't kidding.

CHAPTER 2

CHANGING THE RULES

Nineteen sixty-two was a busy year for C. Douglas Dillon, even by his own impressive standards. Dillon had graduated from Harvard magna cum laude with a varsity letter for football. He was a decorated naval veteran of the Second World War who in 1946 took over as chairman of his father's investment firm, Dillon, Read & Co. Within seven years, he had doubled the firm's investments. In 1953, Dillon was appointed the American ambassador to France. In 1959 he was named undersecretary of state by President Dwight D. Eisenhower, and in 1961 he took on the role of secretary of the treasury for the incoming president, John F. Kennedy (despite being a committed Republican). He was also extremely rich. Dillon's father had been named one the wealthiest men in the United States by *Forbes* magazine in 1957, and Dillon himself was good friends with John D. Rockefeller III.

It was Dillon who proposed the fifth round of negotiations under the umbrella of the General Agreement on Tariffs and Trade (GATT). The GATT countries had met four times before, going back to 1947, and each round of talks resulted in billions of dollars of tariff reductions. That was the whole point of GATT—to increase international trade by negotiating cuts to tariffs and quotas.

The small group of countries that signed the original GATT agreement in the aftermath of the Second World War has grown to encompass almost the whole global economy. In 1995, GATT was superseded by the World Trade Organization that the protesters in Seattle found so objectionable. It now has 164 members and twenty-three observer governments. The WTO sets the rules for the vast bulk of international trade, and is integrated into a network of international bodies that came into being as the Second World War wound down, including the International Monetary Fund and the World Bank. The WTO is based in Geneva, Switzerland; the IMF and World Bank in Washington, DC. Together they have provided relative stability and dizzying economic growth. They have made a lot of people richer.

C. Douglas Dillon started rich and knew a thing or two about getting richer (the negotiations he led certainly weren't undertaken to make him poorer). He was so influential that the fifth round of GATT negotiations—which took place between 1960 and 1962 in Geneva—has since been known as the "Dillon Round." You don't have to have an investment bank named after you to also have an international trade negotiation named after you, but it doesn't hurt.

Dillon had much more to accomplish in 1962. In addition to leading the GATT talks to completion, he also had a hand in drafting the Revenue Act, a piece of American legislation that offered tax incentives to companies investing in domestic production while granting tax exemptions to companies that chose to invest in "less developed" countries. According to Senate hearings at the time, while only seven cents of every dollar invested in a developed country flowed back to the United States, forty cents of every dollar invested in the undeveloped world found its way home.[1] The bill was meant to spur domestic growth, but it was also explicitly designed not to interfere with the high returns yielded by "less developed" countries. Tax breaks at home and investments abroad—Dillon had seen the future.

And he wasn't done yet. Dillon also played a role in concentrating unprecedented trade negotiating power in the president's hands with the Trade Expansion Act. At the next GATT negotiations—which took place between 1964 and 1967 and became known as the Kennedy Round—the American president used those powers to cut $40 billion in tariffs, ten times the cuts that had been negotiated at the Dillon Round. The Trade Expansion Act also gave the president the power to *impose* tariffs, though that privilege has rarely been used. In fact, it had not been used at all since 1995, the year GATT was replaced by the World Trade Organization—that is, until Donald Trump dusted off his copy of the Trade Expansion Act in 2018.

FROM WTO TO FART

In the eyes of President Trump, making America great again would require movement on many fronts. For one thing, it meant making US corporate taxes competitive with other jurisdictions so that American firms would no longer be at a disadvantage. With the help of an initially Republican-controlled House and Senate, the Trump administration introduced the largest tax reform package since Ronald Reagan's day, slashing US corporate tax rates.

Making America great again also meant that the United States was no longer going to be taken advantage of by its military allies. President Trump made it painfully clear to the other members of the North Atlantic Treaty Organization (NATO) that things were about to change. Washington (and hence the American taxpayer) wasn't going to continue picking up the tab for the massive defence expenditures required to protect Europe from Russia, particularly when some countries, such as Germany,[2] were signing huge commercial deals to import natural gas from this supposedly mortal threat. Similarly, Trump openly questioned what America was getting in return for militarily guaranteeing Japan's security. The messaging coming out of the White House shocked America's allies, who saw it as an affront to their integrity and an encouragement of Russian or Chinese aggression. Regardless, only seven of NATO's twenty-nine countries were spending 2 percent of their budgets on defence as recommended by NATO guidelines.[3]

But the two issues that most defined Trump's America-first vision were the renegotiation of trade deals and the construction of a wall along the entire length of the US-Mexico border—a wall that would, he promised, stem the flow of illegal migrants crossing into the country. Restoring the integrity of the American border—be it against cheap foreign goods or illegal migrants—was the signature issue of Trump's campaign and his subsequent administration.

Trump's critics claim the president has never read a history book in his life. That may or may not be true, but his instincts for trade policy tap into his country's time-honoured history of protectionism. While it's true that the United States has pursued a policy of free trade and globalization during most of the postwar period, this has not always been the dominant ideology in Washington. Far from it.

The use of tariffs as a cornerstone of American trade policy has a long history. In fact, it dates all the way back to Alexander Hamilton, the country's first secretary of the treasury, who initiated the "infant industry" argument in defence of using tariffs to protect newly emerging manufacturers in the United States.[4] Hamilton feared that without the aid of tariffs, the US economy would be consigned to producing only agricultural products and raw materials.

The United States stuck to protectionist trade policies even when the major European powers were dramatically cutting tariffs over most of the latter half of the nineteenth century. American tariffs on imports of manufactured goods ranged around 40 to 50 percent, four to five times higher than tariff rates in continental Europe at the time. And contrary to the narrative around tariffs today, those high tariffs didn't seem to hurt the US economy very much at all. From 1871 to 1913, the average American tariff never fell below 38 percent, while US GDP growth was twice that of the pace in free-trading Great Britain over the same period.[5]

American protectionism spiked with the advent of the Great Depression. In 1930, in an effort to protect American workers and farmers, the Republican administration of Herbert Hoover passed the Smoot-Hawley Tariff Act, which hiked the tariff rate to 59.1 percent on dutiable goods, second only to the 61.7 percent rate passed back in 1830.[6] As an effort to alleviate the Depression, it was certainly a failure, though it's not clear what lessons can be drawn from that, given the huge structural and political problems that beset the global economy in the wake of the First World War, as well as monetary policy errors made by the Federal Reserve Board at the time. By the time the tariffs went into effect, international trade had already been decimated by the deepening recessions sweeping across the world's economies.

In the decades since, the pendulum of US trade policy has swung decidedly in the other direction. When the Democrats came to power in the mid-1930s, Franklin Roosevelt negotiated more than thirty separate bilateral trade agreements under the Reciprocal Tariff Act that reduced tariffs with each of America's major trading partners in exchange for equivalent tariff cuts against US exports. The bilateral approach gave way to multilateral trade agreements, and the result was GATT.

Reagan and George H.W. Bush each pushed harder on the free trade agenda than any other postwar president, and their efforts ultimately resulted in the 1987 signing of the Canada-US Free Trade Agreement. President Clinton followed suit and, ignoring the objections of US labour, pushed the North American Free Trade Agreement through Congress in 1993, extending the tariff-free continental zone to low-wage Mexico. When Al Gore debated Ross Perot on *Larry King Live* that same year, he presented the anti-NAFTA Perot with a photo of Smoot and Hawley—a smug threat that failure to embrace free trade would lead to economic stagnation or even another depression. Thereafter, the Clinton administration lobbied hard to admit China into the WTO.

But there were signs both in the United States and elsewhere among OECD countries that governments were starting to shun unfettered free trade flows and turning to more protectionist policies. By 2016, world trade growth was at its lowest point since the 2008–09 recession, growing at half the pace it had in previous decades. That same year also saw the largest number of trade restrictions imposed by G20 countries (the world's largest economies) since the recession.[7] And, of course, the United States, which had been the principle driver of globalization and world trade, was about to have an abrupt about-face on the issue.

Renegotiating or, if necessary, abrogating existing trade deals was the first order of business for the new Trump administration. Harkening back to Roosevelt's original bilateral deals, Trump called for fair and reciprocal trade deals. "Fair and reciprocal": that key phrase kept popping up every time Robert Lighthizer, the United States' hard-nosed chief trade negotiator, spoke. In fact, one of the first pieces of legislation the new administration drafted was the Fair and Reciprocal Trade Act (or FART, to the endless amusement of the Twittersphere), which would mandate US trade policies in direct conflict with existing WTO rules.

Among other things,[8] FART would allow the United States to impose different tariffs on different countries. The WTO explicitly forbids treating one country differently from another; whatever terms you grant one, you must grant to all. This is the "most-favoured-nation" principle, and it applies even to domestic products—WTO members must agree to treat their own products the same as they do imports. There is no way to square FART with the most-favoured-nation rule.

The new legislation would also require the United States to charge reciprocal tariffs—that is, the same tariffs that its exporters were being charged by other countries, even if they were developing countries. This is another no-no under WTO rules, which grant developing countries tariff privileges denied to wealthy countries. While FART does not explicitly call for the United States' withdrawal from the WTO, it would allow Washington to effectively ignore the world trade body and its regulations. As such, it set a powerful precedent: national governments could henceforth feel free to override rules established by the global trade regulator. In fact, they were almost forced to if they wanted to sign any new trade deals with the largest economy in the world.

It wasn't that the new administration in Washington was anti-trade, per se. They weren't. But they were certainly against how most of the trade agreements that the United States had signed were structured and were operating. Unlike past American administrations, both Democratic and Republican, the Trump administration argued that the WTO rules were basically unfair to US workers.

And they were right.

Trump and Lighthizer argued that if we were going to have a rules-based world trading system, as advocated by the world's trade cop, the WTO, the rules needed to be the same for all players. To most people, that might seem a very reasonable and straightforward request. But what most people don't realize is that it's not actually how the rules laid down and enforced by the WTO work.

Let's say you're a car company operating in a country that

has most-favoured-nation status with the United States, and you want to sell your vehicles into the US market. Under WTO rules, you need pay only a 2.5 percent tariff. But if you manufacture the same car in the United States and want to sell it in China, you will need to pay a tariff as much as ten times that under the same rules.[9] You see, under the WTO, there are different rules for different countries. If you're designated a "developing" country, you get to protect your own industries with tariffs that are a multiple of those that developed economies are allowed to use to protect their workers.

When China first entered the WTO back in 2001, there was justification for granting the world's most populous country certain trade advantages to help it industrialize and pull hundreds of millions of its citizens out of abject poverty. Back then, no one in the G7 ever considered the possibility that China might one day become an economic threat. Nor did anyone expect that billions of dollars of investment would pour into China, turning what used to be a backward agrarian economy into an export platform for the world's manufacturing industries.

But that is exactly what has happened. Since the 1970s, China's share of world manufacturing output has risen almost sevenfold, from 3 percent to 20 percent. By 2010, a mere nine years after its inclusion in the WTO, the country had surpassed the United States to become the world's largest manufacturing economy. As Chinese economic growth shifted into overdrive, this poor developing country suddenly became the second-largest economy in the world, and was growing at a pace that put it on track to overtake the United States as the world's largest by 2030.[10]

Yet the WTO continues to allow China to operate with domestic tariffs that are a multiple of those permitted for developed countries like the United States.[11] Meanwhile, the World Bank continues to provide China with over a billion dollars a year in low-interest loans. As US National Economic Council director Larry Kudlow put it, "China is a first-world economy, behaving like a third-world economy."[12] And WTO rules allow it to do so.

For the millions of industrial workers in the United States, Canada, the United Kingdom, France and beyond who have seen their jobs moved to China and taken by workers making a fraction of their wage, this system seems egregiously unfair. It does to Donald Trump and, for that matter, to Bernie Sanders as well. But to many companies, including those from the United States and other G7 economies who moved their supply chains to China, the WTO rules are extremely attractive. They allow for huge cost savings that make their products much more price-competitive while simultaneously furnishing much greater profit margins. Cheaper prices for consumers and richer profits for producers are the powerful economic calling cards of globalization. But, of course, lost jobs and stagnant wages for American (and other OECD) workers were the flip side of that same coin.

China isn't the only so-called developing country that trade rules turned into a destination for jobs. If you're an auto-worker who has lost your job in either the United States or Canada, odds are that it's someone in Mexico, not China, who now has it. Since NAFTA came into effect in 1994, Mexico has been the landing spot for most of the auto industry's jobs.

Autoworkers are among the over 950,000 American expend-ables who have lost their jobs because of NAFTA and qualified for Trade Adjustment Assistance (a federal program to reduce the damaging impact of imports on effected sectors of the US economy).[13]

Of course, in this case the WTO wasn't to blame; the governments that had negotiated and administered NAFTA bore that responsibility. President Trump called NAFTA the worst trade agreement the United States had ever signed, and he singled out its impact on the American autoworker as an example of why. Autoworkers across North America would wholeheartedly agree with him, which is why most American autoworkers voted for him in the 2016 election and states like Wisconsin, Pennsylvania, Michigan and Ohio suddenly swung red.[14] If, however, you happen to be a shareholder in General Motors or Canadian auto parts giant Magna, you probably think Trump is dead wrong. Both perspectives are valid. It's just that capitalists and workers use very different yardsticks for measuring success.

CHAPTER 3

TODAY'S WORKER:
I AIN'T NO FORTUNATE ONE

For more than a year, it was one of the most hyped stories in the business press, and an announcement that had every municipality in North America fine-tuning a pitch. American e-commerce giant Amazon announced in September 2017 that it was on the hunt for a second headquarters.

The buzz was, of course, understandable. The worldwide tech giant employs more than half a million people. It's the second-largest private-sector employer in the entire American economy, behind only retail king Walmart.[1] Amazon sold more than $258 billion in goods in the United States in 2018, capturing almost half of the entire e-commerce market in the country. Amazon doesn't just dominate e-commerce; it pretty much invented it.

With its business based on consumers ordering goods online, Amazon is listed on the NASDAQ, where most American high-tech companies trade. In fact, next to Apple, it's the largest stock listed on the index. With its industry-leading advances in warehouse automation and robotics, Amazon enjoys that high-tech billing.

In the fall of 2018, when Amazon's stock price briefly hit $2,035 a share, its market capitalization touched $1 trillion. To put that number in perspective, only sixteen countries in the world had a gross domestic product larger than Amazon's market cap.

It's easy to understand, then, why every mayor in the United States and Canada was dreaming about the shiny new office towers the global e-commerce giant would occupy in their city.

SOLOMONIAN WISDOM: THE SEARCH FOR TWO SECOND HEADQUARTERS

Why exactly did the company need a second headquarters? As it turns out, Amazon seemed to be wearing out its welcome in its hometown—none other than Seattle, where our story began. In 2017, Seattle's city council approved a new municipal income tax targeting those making more than $250,000 a year.[2] In addition, the city was levying a tax on its large businesses to fund more homeless shelters and affordable housing, a move that the company publicly opposed.[3] It seems all those well-heeled Amazon executives were pushing Seattle home prices out of reach for many of the city's less fortunate residents.

There was certainly no shortage of places for the company and its head office jobs to go. More than three hundred municipalities across the United States and Canada put in a bid. Some offered the land for free. Others offered a holiday from paying municipal taxes. Some offered both. After all, this was a once-in-a-decade opportunity for a city to secure no less than fifty thousand high-paying head office jobs. Roughly a year later Amazon announced a short list of twenty finalists.

When every city in North America is trying to bribe you to look their way, why take one bribe when you can get two? With Solomonian wisdom, Amazon decided to cut its planned second head office into two—with one branch to be housed in Arlington, Virginia, not far from Washington, DC, and the other in the Queens district of New York City. Not one head office with fifty thousand jobs, but two head offices with twenty-five thousand jobs each.

Interestingly, Amazon wore out its welcome in New York City before the company and twenty-five thousand of its head office staff even arrived. (Actually, only seven hundred jobs were coming—the highly publicized twenty-five thousand referred to jobs over the next decade.) New Yorkers had already been grumbling over the $3 billion in tax breaks and other financial incentives the city was offering the company, but the tipping point was the plan to construct a helipad on the roof of Amazon's headquarters on the East River—presumably so that the company's elite wouldn't have to rub shoulders with the plebs on the city's perpetually crowded subways. Despite entreaties from state governor Andrew Cuomo and city mayor Bill de Blasio to stay, Amazon sensed the building resentment of New Yorkers like congresswoman Alexandria Ocasio-Cortez[4] and cancelled its plans. Instead, it contented itself with its second head office in Virginia, where the state legislature rubber-stamped $750 million in incentives while the county of Arlington offered the nearly trillion-dollar-valued company millions of dollars more in incentives to locate there.[5]

Back in its original home base in Seattle, Amazon was intervening in the 2019 municipal elections like never before.

They spent more than $1.4 million, a staggering amount for a municipal election, in a failed attempt to unseat Councilwoman Kshama Sawant, who represents the Capitol Hill neighbourhood where many Amazon workers live. She has been a constant critic of the company and was instrumental in Seattle adopting a fifteen-dollar-an-hour minimum wage back in 2014.[6]

THE BEZOS ACT

So exactly what kind of jobs does Amazon offer these days? Since they are a high-tech company, it would stand to reason that they'd be offering high-tech jobs—positions in, say, software development, application engineering or systems architecture.

But it would be difficult to hire any of those folks at the wages Amazon pays most of its workforce. In fact, it was only in 2018 that Amazon raised its hourly wage to a minimum fifteen dollars. It was no coincidence that the move came after Senator Bernie Sanders introduced legislation to tax corporations for every dollar that their low-wage workers receive in government health-care benefits or food stamps. That legislation was called the Stop BEZOS Act, in honour of Amazon's founder and CEO Jeff Bezos, reportedly the richest man in the world.[7] In the wake of the bill's introduction, more than 250,000 of Amazon's regular employees, as well as 100,000 seasonal employees, got a much-welcomed raise.[8] Even so, the new rate is still a little over half the average hourly wage in the private sector, according to the US Bureau of Labor Statistics.[9]

Low wages and growing income inequality are typically associated with technologically backward industries and poorer areas of the country—like Appalachia, for example. But these issues are not just experienced by warehouse workers at Amazon or cashiers at Walmart. We're also talking about employees in Silicon Valley, supposedly the innovation hub for America's world-leading high-tech sector, where no less than a quarter of the workforce is employed by high-tech companies.

GETTING POORER IN SILICON VALLEY

For sought-after tech talent, Silicon Valley pays more than anywhere else in the world. But if you are not a software genius, it's not the greatest place to work.

While Silicon Valley's tech sector has grown by leaps and bounds since the 1980s, the same can't be said for the real incomes of most people who work there. According to a study by the University of California Santa Cruz, 90 percent of Silicon Valley workers earn a lower real wage today than they did twenty years ago. Middle-income earners in the Valley, as elsewhere in America, have lost the most ground. Their real wages are down a whopping 14 percent.[10]

Back in the 1980s, even janitors at computer giants like IBM could become millionaires thanks to the stock allotments given to employees over lifetime careers at the company. Today, services such as janitorial and security, as well as the work performed by cafeteria staff and drivers, are all contracted out to low-wage-paying suppliers. It's become so bad that in 2017 more than five hundred cafeteria workers who dole out food at Facebook's sprawling California campus unionized in order to get better wages and benefits from their contractor.

Rents in Silicon Valley have risen by 50 percent since 2011, while home prices have doubled. That may be okay with the world's highest-paid software engineers, but it's not okay with the legions of minimum-wage service workers who cater to those well-paid tech employees. Homelessness in Silicon Valley, supposedly housing America's engine of economic growth, has surged 30 percent, with more than 30,000 service-sector workers now being forced to live in cars and recreational vehicles.[11] Considering that high-tech industries create more employment for local services than they do for their own work-forces,[12] their overall impact on wage growth and income distribution is hardly positive.

If things are that tough for workers in the richest industry in one of the richest countries in the world, what are they like for everyone else?

I suppose the good news is that these folks pretty much all have jobs—as do most workers across the OECD countries. Unemployment rates are now as low as, if not lower than, they were before the 2008 global financial crisis. In fact, in some cases they are much lower. In that regard, the United States leads the way. Its 3.5 percent national unemployment rate (as of December 2019) is the lowest in half a century. Canada is not far behind, with its jobless rate sitting at a low not seen in forty-plus years. And the United Kingdom's jobless rate is the lowest since 1974.

The bad news is that low unemployment doesn't pack the same punch for wage growth that it once did. Wage rates are growing at about half the pace they were before the last recession—a figure that holds for the United States and Canada as well as countries in the European Union, Japan and Australia. When it comes to getting ahead, the last decade has been a lost one for most workers, marking an unprecedented period of wage stagnation in the world's developed economies. And the longer that wage stagnation persists, the more we've come to accept it as an intrinsic part of the new economic order that globalization has brought.

The German Institute for Economic Research in Berlin noted that in 2017, when the country reported near-full employment, about 9 million German workers were on low-wage contracts, earning less than two-thirds of the median hourly wage.[13] That was nearly a quarter of all jobs in the German economy.

Things haven't been any better for British workers. While the United Kingdom's unemployment rate is the lowest it's been in over a generation, median wages after inflation are below where they were in 2008, with millennial workers posting the greatest declines.[14] Everywhere you look these days, wages are either frozen in time or moving backward—which explains what on the surface appears to be an odd contradiction: even though a greater proportion of the population in OECD countries is employed than was the case a decade ago, so too is a greater proportion of these populations living in poverty. Having a job ain't what it used to be.

The lack of wage growth is a puzzle to economists, including Jerome Powell. The Federal Reserve Board chairman is wondering why real-wage gains have been missing in action despite a postwar record-low unemployment rate. His counterparts at other central banks are asking their computer models the same question.

It's certainly not because runaway inflation has robbed wages of their purchasing power. Economists used to worry that raising wages would raise the price of everything in the economy, arguing that earning more money would actually make workers effectively poorer once the inflationary impact was considered. But economists can't make that argument today. Inflation has seldom been lower, in no small measure due to the impact that lowered global trade barriers have had on price movements over the last decade. Things are cheaper, not more expensive. Rather, it is nominal wage growth itself— or, more precisely, the lack thereof—that has been the principal culprit in the mystery of why so many workers today make less in inflation-adjusted terms than they did in the past. They're not poorer because they're being paid too much. They're poorer because they're not being paid enough.

NOT ALL JOBS ARE CREATED EQUAL

During recessions and periods of economic slack, when job losses are piling up, it's normal for wages to stagnate. But what has Powell and other central bank governors scratching their heads is why so many wage earners have seen little if any real-income gain during a time when their economies have been pumping out so many jobs. The competition to hire scarce workers should have pushed wages up—but it hasn't.

And that runs counter to both economic theory and economic history.

If you consider what today's jobless rate would have meant in the past, wage gains for North American workers should be at least double what they are today. For example, before the last recession, wages of US production workers were growing at over 4 percent. Until Trump's election, they were growing at around 2 percent.[15] But full employment doesn't mean what it used to—at least, not as far as wages are concerned. In 2018, American workers eked out their first real-wage gain in a decade, while the wages of Canadian workers barely grew at 2 percent, once again yielding no increase in workers' purchasing power once inflation was taken into account.

As it turns out, real wages haven't grown for a very long time in North America—or in any other OECD countries, for that matter. Your average American worker's real wage packs basically the same purchasing power as it did more than forty years ago. In current dollars, average real wages peaked back in 1975. That's a long time to go without an increase in your purchasing power. The only part of the labour force that has seen significant real-wage growth is—you guessed it—the top 1 percent of all wage earners. The one-percenters probably didn't vote for Donald Trump or Bernie Sanders. But when you look at what's happened to the purchasing power of the other 99 percent of the workforce, it becomes a little clearer why so many of those folks did.

Normally, strong job creation and low unemployment denote the kind of economic environment where most people are getting ahead. But not all jobs are created equal. Some leave people falling further and further behind—and those are precisely the types of jobs our economies seem so good at pumping out these days.

Virtually all of the jobs that have been created in North America over the last two decades have been in the service sector. And that applies to pretty much all of the OECD countries too. Employment on the goods-producing side of the economy hasn't grown in years. Of course, it's no coincidence that the goods sector has been the most vulnerable to global trade patterns, and has borne the brunt of the massive movement of production and jobs to cheap-labour-market supply chains around the world.

Goods-sector employment peaked in the United States economy around the year 2000, at just over 24.6 million. Up until the Trump presidency, it had been on a one-way trend—down. By 2017 it had fallen to 19 million, with almost half of the job losses occurring in manufacturing industries. During the same period, service-sector employment rose from 107.5 million to just over 127 million, accounting for all of the net job creation in the American economy.[16]

The story isn't any different north of the border in Canada. As a share of overall employment, the current goods-sector workforce is the lowest it's been during the entire postwar period.[17] Barely two in every ten workers are still employed in making things today. While the Canadian economy has pumped out more than 3 million jobs over the last two decades, there hasn't been a single net job created in the goods sector in the past eighteen years. Since 2000, Canada's manufacturing sector has shed some 600,000 jobs, or about a quarter of its workforce.[18] Most of those jobs were lost in Ontario, the country's industrial heartland.

Of course, what has happened to manufacturing employment in the United States and Canada is also reflected in the factory output in those economies. You don't need to hire workers to produce what you're no longer making. Manufacturing's share of employment has been cut in half since 2000. No great mystery why. As is the case in other G7 economies, the share of global manufacturing output in the United States and Canada has been cut by a similar proportion as trade barriers against everything from textiles to cars have either been eliminated or dramatically reduced.

There is nothing intrinsically wrong with working in the service sector. I was employed for two decades as the chief economist at an investment bank, and I made a pretty good living doing that. But for the most part—and outside of financial services, which are often given an exaggerated importance—the service sector is where the lowest-paying jobs in the economy are found. There are a lot more people flipping burgers at McDonald's than there are investment bankers at Goldman Sachs.

Yet there seems to be a stigma today associated with factory work, particularly among millennials, who often consider those jobs to be unskilled and low-wage work. In reality, the opposite has been true. For most of the postwar era, goods-sector jobs paid significantly higher than service-sector jobs. Back in the early 1980s, average hourly earnings in private-sector goods jobs in the United States were more than 20 percent higher than average hourly earnings in private-sector service industries. Roughly the same wage premium held in the Canadian goods sector as well.[19]

Over time, however, that premium has been steadily whittled down. By 2006 the wage premium of goods-producing jobs over service-sector jobs in the United States had been halved, to around 10 percent. By 2017 it had shrunk to as little as 6 percent. It's a bit of a double whammy for workers: not only is the goods-producing part of the economy that generated higher-paying jobs not providing those jobs anymore, but the once considerable wage premium that those jobs offered has steadily fallen. In other words, there are fewer good jobs to go around, and those that are still out there pay less.

But these comparisons capture only half of the story behind what's happened to your paycheque. Average hourly earnings don't tell you how many hours you are actually working, which, of course, is vitally important in determining just how much you earn. Nor do those earnings necessarily capture all the non-wage benefits that used to come standard in most goods-producing jobs. Bring those additional factors into the discussion, and things look even worse for today's workers.

Whereas goods-sector jobs like factory work are mostly full-time, jobs in the service sector are often temporary or part-time work—and more so all the time. This is not good news for wage growth, since the wage gap between part-time and full-time employment has widened steadily in the United States and in the labour markets of most other OECD countries.

JOBS IN THE GIG ECONOMY

Self-employment, temporary employment, on-call work, home-based work and telecommuting are becoming more and more common in today's service-based economy. In some countries, such as Australia, nearly *half* of the workforce falls into one of these categories.

The growth in these types of employment opportunities is often attributed to the rise in app-based gig employers like Uber or Lyft. The employment contract signed by those working in the gig economy is very different from what workers in goods-producing industries had come to expect during most of the postwar era. Back then, for example, you knew when you were working. There were regularly defined work hours (normally forty hours a week, assigned at a fixed time). These days, your gig employer practises just-in-time labour, putting you on perpetual standby. The company will call you when they need you, thanks. And they might need you for only ten to fifteen hours in a week.

And don't count on receiving much in the way of the non-wage benefits unions negotiated for most industrial workers in America. Get sick or need dental work as a part-time employee in the gig economy? Sorry, companies don't pay health-care benefits to part-time workers or "independent contractors," as gig workers are classified by so many of their employers. Vacation pay? Let one of your other part-time employers cover that. And as for a pension? That's something your government should provide.

Uber and Lyft have both been hit with numerous lawsuits over the legal status of their drivers,[20] but they claim that the independent-contractor status of their workers is essential to the viability of their business model. The state of California has recently passed legislation that requires these companies to treat its so-called independent contractors as actual workers. Labour groups are pushing for similar legislation in other states.[21]

It's debatable just how robust that business model is, however, since neither company, despite the billions they've raised from investors, has made a profit. Nevertheless, it's certainly worked out for those in the C-suite. Uber's five top executives pocketed $143 million between them last year. And their former CEO, Travis Kalanick, became an instant billionaire when the ridesharing company made its debut on the New York Stock Exchange.[22]

The independent-contractor business model embraced by Uber and Lyft has been decidedly less lucrative for its drivers. As their businesses have grown, these companies have adjusted their payment algorithms in ways that have left less money in their drivers' pockets. The Economic Policy Institute calculated that Uber drivers earn on average an hourly wage of $9.21 after deducting expenses such as fees and commissions.[23] In most of Uber's major markets, that's below the statutory minimum-wage rate, but since the drivers are classified as independent contractors, they are not covered by minimum-wage requirements. And since the average Uber driver doesn't last for more than three months on the job, how they feel about their paycheque is a non-issue; they are totally expendable.

With more and more employment contracts following this model, it's not hard to understand why we haven't seen much wage growth in the service sector over the past few decades—and why an ever-greater reliance on the booming gig economy points to even weaker wage gains from the sector in the future.

This is especially bad news for millennials—now the largest segment of the labour force, and the cohort most likely to work in the gig economy. Roughly half have a second job to make ends meet. They are the most college-educated generation in history, raised by parents who were convinced that higher education was a pathway to success. But all that education hasn't translated into higher wages.

The average salary of American millennials is disproportionately lower than the national average. They are doing a lot worse than most of their parents did at the same age—earning about 20 percent less—and their college education has left them with a record $29,000 in student loan debt on average, which costs $351 per month to repay. In Canada, according to the OECD, only 59 percent of millennials had attained the minimum salary threshold for middle-class status, defined as $29,432 (or 75 percent of the median national income). Sixty-seven percent of their parents had reached the middle class by the same age. In other words, millennials are falling behind, even though they're working harder than their parents did.

WHY DON'T WORKERS STRIKE ANYMORE?

What's happening to millennials, and indeed all workers, is not supposed to be happening, according to economic theory—and not because it seems unfair. Economic theory has nothing to say about fairness, but it has plenty to say about the relationship of wages to unemployment rates. And what it says is that something is wrong. Stagnant wage growth in the face of low unemployment is an anomaly; it flies in the face of what economists used to refer to as the Phillips curve. The Phillips curve is a standard macroeconomic theory. On one axis is the unemployment rate; on the other is the rate of wage increases. The higher the unemployment rate, the lower the rate of wage increases. The lower the unemployment rate, the higher the rate of wage increases.

What the Phillips curve tells us is that during economic good times, employers are more willing to pay higher wages to hire additional labour. Why? Because profits are higher, and strikes become more costly when business is booming. But when sales slump during an economic slowdown or a recession, businesses don't need to hire as much labour and are less likely to grant large wage increases to attract it. For their part, workers are less likely to demand them, knowing that they're lucky to have a job.

So, with unemployment rates at or near record lows, why aren't workers striking to demand larger wage increases in the way they've done in the past? If you want the answer to this question, head down to your local union hall and ask some of the angry old men hanging out there. Their tale pretty well explains why the Phillips curve is no longer working in today's labour market.

For the most part, the angry men are blue-collar workers who used to have well-paying jobs in industries like autos or steel and belonged to unions like the United Automobile Workers (UAW) or the United Steelworkers. In the old days, they would have voted Democrat (if they were American), but the leadership of the Democratic Party since the Clinton presidency has abandoned them in favour of global trade treaties that rendered them expendable. Until Donald Trump came along and courted them, many had stopped voting altogether.

They had good reason. To them, it didn't matter if Congress was Democratic or Republican, or who was sitting in the White House. Nobody cared about them or their concerns. When it came to the new trade agreements being negotiated, they were the first to lose their jobs, and they would be the last to be rehired, if such a thing ever came to pass.

What made them a primary target of the new trade deals? Those union-won wages and benefits. That was, after all, the whole idea behind organizing a union in your plant—union action got workers higher wages and better benefits. Unions set the market price for labour by forcing companies to bid as high as they could pay.

But globalization changed the rules. Now companies could buy labour wherever they wanted, and what was once a virtue for workers suddenly turned into a vice. Once trade barriers fell, unionized plants were the first to be shut down in favour of the new global supply chains that were being forged with cheap labour markets all around the world. Job losses in unionized plants have been double those in non-union (and generally lower-paying) shops.

It shouldn't come as a surprise to anyone that as union membership shrank, so too did workers' wages. The right to collective bargaining, which in the past covered as many as a third of all private-sector workers in the US economy, now plays a marginal role in the labour market. In addition to falling trade barriers, you can also credit right-to-work legislation— enacted in twenty-eight states as of 2019—that enables workers in unionized plants to opt out of paying union dues, hence undercutting a union's ability to finance itself. Take unions out of most workplaces and you get a different dynamic than in days gone by: the firm sets the wage, and you can either accept it or not work there.

Union membership hasn't just fallen markedly in the United States. Union membership as a percentage of the labour force has declined across OECD countries, even in those that traditionally had the highest rates of unionization.[24] And it's not just "angry old men" who have lost their union jobs to cheap overseas labour; women are affected too. Still, the job losses for male union workers have been far more severe than for their female counterparts.

The reason is largely sectoral. Male union members have tended to work in goods-producing industries, like manufacturing, that have been on the front lines when it comes to the invasion of cheap imports from low-wage countries. For example, three-quarters of US manufacturing jobs are held by men. Female union membership is heavily concentrated in the health and education sectors, much of it in the public sector, where in sharp contrast to the goods sector, employment is still growing and union membership is still relatively strong. It's harder to offshore a teacher or a nurse than it is a welder.

Elsewhere, the story of declining union membership is much the same. Union membership as a percentage of the labour force in the once highly organized United Kingdom has fallen by about a third. More or less the same reduction has been seen in Germany. In Canada, union membership as a percentage of the labour force has declined by about a quarter. But nowhere in the OECD has union membership fallen more than in the United States, where less than 10 percent of the labour force now belongs to a union.[25]

But even that economy-wide number, which includes government workers, understates the true extent of the decline in union membership in the private sector. During the 1950s, at the zenith of the labour movement, one in every three American workers in the private sector belonged to a trade union. Today, just one in twenty private-sector workers still does.

That precipitous decline has had widespread implications. Unions didn't just raise wages and benefits for their own membership; they also had a big influence on raising wages for unorganized workers who were employed in highly unionized industries or regions.[26] That was particularly true for manufacturing industries operating in the highly unionized northeast and midwest parts of the United States. Back in the day, if you didn't want your workers to organize a union, the best way of keeping one out was to closely monitor collective bargaining agreements and, if need be, match union rates. So, when 50 percent of truckers belonged to a union like the Teamsters, their settlements had a big impact on what the unorganized 50 percent were getting paid. But today, when less than 10 percent of truckers are unionized, the other 90 percent can't expect to get much of a pay lift from their wage settlements. And that 10 percent is not exactly going to be throwing its weight around. If you own a factory today, you're pretty much in the clear. As union membership declined, so did the unions' leverage.

All of this explains why you rarely hear about workers going on strike anymore, no matter how tight labour markets appear to be. You can't go on strike for a pay raise if you don't belong to a union—and even if you're one of the few workers who still belong to one, your union's bargaining tactics today are very different from what we used to see in the past.

With the threat of plant closures hanging over such negotiations like the sword of Damocles, union priorities have shifted from bargaining for wage increases to bargaining for job and pension security. Strikes have become virtually suicidal. What invariably happens on the rare occasions they do occur is that a fleet of trucks rolls into a plant after midnight on a giant repo operation to cart away all the machinery they can remove before padlocking the factory gates. And the next thing you know, the firm has opened a new plant in Mexico and has sold the factory to some developer who is going to build luxury condominiums on the site.

That, in a nutshell, is why the Phillips curve no longer works. If companies weren't so easily able to offshore production, there would be more workers to organize *and* it would be a lot easier for unions to sign them up. And if unions didn't have to worry about wage gains leading to plant closures, they would be more likely to go on strike to achieve those gains—at least when the economy was strong and tight labour markets permitted them to do so. It's quite possible that the venerable Phillips curve may never work again—no matter how low the unemployment rate falls, or how long job-vacancy lists grow—unless something changes to give workers more bargaining power, like trade rules for example.

If the old WTO trade rules led to the demise of industrial unions and jobs, will the new FART trade rules that Washington is creating and enforcing give rise to their rebirth? It's no coincidence that wages in the US economy are suddenly growing at their fastest pace in years, as President Trump imposes more and more tariffs on imports, particularly from China. If the WTO hollowed out America's manufacturing sector, and in the process its middle class, FART-type trade policies seem to be bringing it back.

CHAPTER 4

LEFT BEHIND

You'll never hear a politician say anything bad about the middle class. That's because most of us believe we are middle class (whether we are or not), so when a politician promises to "help the middle class," they are speaking to a pretty wide audience—one they hope will turn up at the polls in droves. Most of us think of the middle class as being defined by its values. A commitment to education. A strong belief in democracy. Saving for a rainy day. Family. That sort of thing. It's all motherhood. Who wouldn't be in favour of that?

The OECD, however, has a different definition. For them, the middle class is defined by a range around the median income in the economy.[1] If you earn between 75 and 200 percent of the median income, you're middle class. In Canada, that means between $29,432 and $78,485 (the median being $39,237). In the United States, the range is $23,416 to $62,442. In the United Kingdom, £15,856 to £42,283.[2] So, while most of us think we're middle class, only about 60 percent of us in the OECD countries actually are. If you earn less than the lower threshold, you are not, from the OECD's point of view, middle class.

But you are far from alone. All over the developed world, the middle class represents a shrinking percentage of the population.

That is particularly true in the United States, where for the first time in more than four decades the middle class comprises a minority of Americans. And it accounts for a steadily shrinking percentage of income in the economy.

Moreover, those still fortunate enough to call themselves middle class are far more vulnerable to being thrown out of it than ever before. For the better part of the postwar era, membership in the middle class was for life. Today, staying in the club is a lot harder. Middle-income households are slipping down into the lower-income classes at an alarming rate. According to a recent OECD study, one in seven earners from the lower middle class slide down that income ladder every four years. In the United States, it's one in five.[3] And for every middle-class earner who climbs up the income ladder, twice as many fall down into the ranks of the working poor.

Even more noticeable than the middle class's downward mobility is the decline in its share of national income, which has been shrinking at about twice the pace of the decline in its share of the population. In the early 1980s the middle class accounted for over 60 percent of the income in the American economy. Today, it accounts for barely over 40 percent.

The upshot is that some people are falling out of the middle class because they're too poor to belong. But the group as a whole has also grown poorer. In the United Kingdom, more than a third of middle-income households "report having difficulty making ends meet."[4] Belonging to the middle class isn't what it used to be.

Between 2007 and 2016, middle-class incomes in the OECD countries grew at less than a fifth of the rate they had grown in

the preceding decade and at only a third of the rate seen during the mid-1980s or mid-1990s. In many countries, middle-
class incomes haven't grown at all in a decade; in several, they
are actually lower. Meanwhile, over the last decade, the
incomes of the top 10 percent of the population have grown at
three times the pace of middle-class incomes.

And while more and more people are dropping out of the
middle class, it is simultaneously becoming harder for others
to get in. Each generation that has followed the baby boomers
has found it increasingly difficult to earn a middle-class income.
Seventy percent of boomers were already in the middle class
in their twenties. That's dropped to 60 percent for millennials,
and even less for Generation Z. Over time, then, the middle
class is not only getting smaller but older as well.[5] It is showing
signs of going extinct.

THE AMERICAN DREAM

When it comes to defining national identity, no other country
in the world has been more identified with the middle class
than the United States. Throughout the postwar era, the
middle class was as good a benchmark as any for measuring the success of the American dream. For the most part, the
middle class worked in the goods sector of the economy, making the very things they consumed—cars, houses, televisions,
dishwashers and the other goods that signified membership
in their class. And they made a good and steadily rising living.
As their incomes and numbers swelled in the postwar economic boom, their taxes supported the social security blanket

that governments provided through welfare and unemployment insurance, and funded essential public services such as education and health.

But as trade agreements pried open their home markets to a flood of low-wage imports, middle-class workers suddenly found themselves competing for jobs with workforces in developing countries who made a fraction of their wage. They were ill-equipped to do so, and they began to lose their jobs. Those who were fortunate enough to stay employed were forced to make huge wage concessions to prevent their factories from closing up shop and moving to cheap labour markets overseas. As this scenario repeated all across the United States, the industrial jobs that remained were no longer able to furnish workers with the middle-class lifestyles to which they'd become accustomed.

The same pattern played out north of the border in Canada, a country that considers itself to be far more egalitarian than its southern neighbour. Between 1990 and 2015, 80 percent of Canadian households saw few if any income gains. But as in the United States and the United Kingdom, the top 20 percent of households realized significant income gains, and the top 1 percent saw the greatest gains of all.[6]

No wonder, then, that rich people support globalization pretty much everywhere you look. It has made them a lot richer. They are the only strata of the population that has seen incomes grow—and grow handsomely, at that. Everybody else's income seems frozen in time.

THEIR HANDS ARE TIED

During the leaders' debate ahead of the 1988 federal election in Canada, Conservative leader and incumbent prime minister Brian Mulroney offered both carrots and sticks as he tried to convince Canadians to embrace his platform of further free trade with the United States. On the one hand, he said, prosperity makes us "better able to finance social programmes for those who need our care," which sounded pretty appealing. On the other hand, he growled, "In today's economy, Canada can compete and grow, or it can retreat . . . and shrink."[7] In other words, Canadians couldn't expect decent social programmes if they didn't sign on for free trade.

David Ricardo first postulated his theory of comparative advantage in the nineteenth century.[8] Since then, most economists have agreed that there are net welfare gains that accrue from free trade, potentially bettering everyone's lot. At the same time, though, economists have always recognized that free trade would also create losers.

And it wasn't hard to figure out who those losers would be. In fact, modern neoclassical economic theory predicted exactly who they were.[9] A country's comparative advantage was determined by what are called its "factor endowments." Countries that were rich in agrarian land were well suited to be major agricultural exporters. Countries with vast labour forces found their comparative advantage in exporting labour-intensive goods. And countries that were capital-rich exported either their capital or capital-intensive goods like machinery. Hence, farmers in land-rich countries, capitalists in capital-rich countries and labourers in labour-abundant countries would all support free trade. The more foreign markets these folks had access to, the better off they would be.

It was those on the other side of the comparative advantage equation who would oppose free trade. Farmers in land-scarce countries would oppose opening up their domestic markets to foreign food imports because those imports would bring down prices for the crops they grew—and their incomes along with them. Manufacturers in capital-scarce countries would oppose dropping tariffs against imports of manufactured goods because they couldn't compete with them and would be displaced in their home market. And workers in labour-scarce countries feared a flood of cheap-labour imports (or swarms of immigrants from labour-abundant countries) because they knew it would drive down their wages. It should be clear by now why C. Douglas Dillon was such an advocate of GATT, and why unions opposed the WTO in Seattle. Opening up markets creates winners and losers, and they wanted to be the winners. Who doesn't? You just have to pick your fights.

In theory, at least, governments could always redistribute the economic gains from trade by raising taxes on trade's winners and redistributing those revenues through transfer payments to the losers. That way, no one would have to be left behind.

But in practice the very opposite has happened.

In the early postwar decades most governments in OECD countries, including the United States and Canada, played a key role in redistributing income through taxes and social security payments. There was a broad social and political consensus to build a safety net to protect the least fortunate.

And indeed, over the first three decades following the Second World War, that was exactly what happened. The public sector in most industrial countries rose from an average of 27 percent of GDP to 43 percent, while transfer payments more than doubled from 7 percent of GDP to 15 percent.[10] Taxes and transfer payments reshuffled incomes, and income distribution in the United States and most countries in Western Europe was relatively equal by any historical benchmark. But around the mid-1970s things began to change.

Two oil shocks led to an economic condition that required a new word: *stagflation*. Until the Organization of the Petroleum Exporting Countries jacked up the price of a barrel of oil by boycotting countries supporting Israel in the Yom Kippur War, economists had assumed that you could have inflation or you could have high unemployment with economic stagnation, but you couldn't have both. The belief was that inflation was caused by higher-demand growth: higher demand for goods and higher demand for labour. A bit of inflation was not a bad thing at all, since it indicated demand for labour was high and hence most people were employed.

But a lot of inflation was a bad thing. It turned out that higher oil prices could drive inflation sky high—what economists call a "supply shock." When oil prices rose from three dollars a barrel to thirty dollars a barrel, both the inflation rate and the unemployment rate in the United States and most other OECD economies jumped three times what they had averaged over the previous thirty years.[11] And when wages started chasing oil-fuelled inflation, it created a wage-price spiral that made everybody poorer.

Suddenly, the old Keynesian prescriptions weren't working anymore. John Maynard Keynes was perhaps the most influential and brilliant economist of the twentieth century, and the chief architect of the Western welfare state. His idea was that the economy is driven by aggregate demand. If the economy is flagging, and unemployment is rising, the government can step in and halt the downturn by increasing demand; that is, the government can stimulate the economy and create jobs by spending money. The trouble in 1973 was that, on the one hand, high energy prices meant that creating jobs would worsen inflation. But on the other hand, slowing inflation would cost jobs. Stagflation proved to be the nemesis of Keynesian economics.

The situation left the door open for a challenge to the social consensus behind Keynesianism—and it didn't take long to materialize. Monetarism, an approach espoused by Milton Friedman and other free-market economists, took the position that it is not the government's job to use monetary and fiscal policy to manage the cyclical gyrations of the economy. All the government has to do is manage the money supply (to avoid inflation), and then deregulate trade and get out of the way as capital works its magic in the market. This is sometimes known as supply-side economics (in contrast to Keynesian demand-side management of the economy).

What does all of this have to do with the middle class? It was the Keynesian consensus that led to the emergence of the middle class across the OECD. It is still very much alive and well in Scandinavia and other parts of Europe, and it has not entirely disappeared in North America. But the middle class has retreated since the mid-1960s, when President Lyndon B. Johnson's "Great

Society" programmes redistributed wealth to eradicate poverty and racial inequality, promote the arts, and build public infrastructure. A couple of decades later, British prime minister Margaret Thatcher felt comfortable saying "There's no such thing as society. There are individual men and women and there are families. And no government can do anything except through people, and people must look after themselves first."[12] That's the difference between Keynes and Friedman.

Since Thatcher spoke those words in 1987, the social safety net has been shrinking—just as falling trade barriers were throwing more and more workers its way. The circumstances created by globalization called for governments to play a larger role in redistributing market incomes just as governments, for the most part, were retreating to the sidelines.

Defenders of globalization are quick to argue that we shouldn't blame trade agreements for the failure of governments to look after their economic casualties. They note that falling trade barriers do not in themselves prevent governments from helping those adversely affected. But what this defence fails to take into account is the mobility of capital and production that those trade agreements encourage and make possible.

When capital and production are highly mobile, as they are today, they can readily move elsewhere when they don't like what they see. The more mobile capital is, the harder it is for government to tax and regulate it. And the more mobile production is, the harder it is for government to keep businesses— and the jobs they create—from moving as well. That's what the "free" in "free trade" really means.

In today's integrated global economy, governments are under continual pressure to keep their tax rates, as well as their labour and environmental regulations, closely aligned with those of their trading partners, lest their policies induce an even greater exodus of industries and jobs than is already occurring. Attempts to raise corporate taxes, or taxes on capital gains or dividends, or wealth taxes, or to impose taxes on large inherited estates, are routinely thwarted by arguments that such measures will drive investment away and, over time, render the country's economy uncompetitive at the expense of future job creation.

In order to keep in step with its trading partners, a country dares not raise its own taxes—and it better make damn sure that it follows suit if another country lowers theirs. The goal is always to remain in line with the competition. For example, when President Trump slashed US corporate tax rates in 2017, Canada's corporations very quickly started clamouring for similar changes. If Prime Minister Trudeau didn't match those cuts, went the argument, industries would soon be packing up and crossing the border.

The same logic applies for any proposed increases in the minimum wage. They are immediately condemned as job-killers that will hurt the very workers they are intended to help. In the US, for example, that argument has stood in the way of an increase in the federal minimum wage, which has been frozen at $7.25 an hour since 2009, when it was hiked from a little over $5 an hour. Of course, those condemnations are coming from the employers who would have to absorb the added cost at the expense of their own profit margins.

But those tax and wage measures are precisely the type of policies that would need to be adopted in order to protect or reimburse those on the "loser" side of the globalization equation. What to corporations are simply the imperatives of global commerce are to labour a race to the bottom. And it's getting pretty crowded down there as more and more people who used to belong to the middle class take the plunge.

So why isn't the middle class complaining? Why aren't its members insisting that their governments take measures to prevent this downward spiral from continuing? When you lose your economic clout, you often lose much of your political leverage along with it. Today's shrinking middle class doesn't pack the same political punch that it did when parties across the political spectrum used to actually heed their concerns instead of just paying lip service to their cause. The middle class is no better treated when it comes to tax policy than it is with trade policy. While middle-class citizens in most OECD countries still get the lion's share of government transfer payments, they are also the ones largely paying for those programmes through their taxes. On a net basis, they are not really any better off as a result of the government intervention.

Taxes and transfer payments still reduce income inequality across the OECD, but their redistributive impact has been falling steadily for decades. One culprit behind government's reduced role in redistributing income is less generous transfer payments, particularly for employment insurance. In most OECD countries, eligibility rules have been tightened, benefits reduced and the duration of payments shortened. Declines in personal income taxes as well as social security contributions have steadily denuded government's redistributive role.

That is clear enough from Gini coefficients. The Gini coefficient is a tool economists use to measure income distribution both before and after taxes and transfer payments. Its value ranges from zero to one.[13] A Gini coefficient of one indicates extreme inequality, where one person (or household) owns all of the national income. Alternatively, a Gini coefficient of zero indicates perfect equality, where national income is shared equally by all members of the economy. Gini coefficients that measure the distribution of after-tax income have been moving steadily in the same direction as those that measure only market incomes—upward.[14]

Most governments that profess to be concerned about equality and income distribution want to decrease the Gini number, especially if their trade policies have played a hand in creating winners and losers in the economy. And that just hasn't happened in countries like the United Kingdom and the United States, which have seen some of the largest jumps in market income coefficients among OECD countries, or in Canada, whose government claims that protection of the country's middle class is one of its primary objectives.

Canadians like to think that they have a far more progressive tax and social security system than their more laissez-faire southern neighbour. In fact, they might be surprised to learn how little their governments have done to halt growing income inequality. The wealthiest Canadians have done even better on an after-tax basis than on a pre-tax one. For example, average income for the top 20 percent of Canadian households between

1994 and 2016 grew faster on an after-tax basis than on a pre-tax basis (44 percent versus 38 percent).[15] That's right: Canadian tax policy *exacerbates* income inequality. And Canada is by no means unique in that regard.

There are several reasons why progressive tax systems— where the richest taxpayers pay proportionately the most in tax—don't have the redistributive effect that they once did. First, income taxes in most OECD countries used to be a lot more progressive than they are today. There used to be much higher top marginal tax rates and a number of different high-income tax brackets. For example, the top US marginal tax rate is currently 37 percent. The top marginal tax rate was as high as 91 percent during the Eisenhower Republican administration in the 1950s.[16] Moreover, a number of high-income tax brackets ensured that the richer you were, the higher the rate at which your income was taxed. Today, the top marginal tax rate of 37 percent is one-size-fits-all for household incomes above the $600,000 threshold.[17] That's chump change for many American millionaires.

A second reason for the tax system failing to redistribute income is the growing importance of capital gains and dividends to high-income taxpayers in what has been a record run for stock markets over the past decade. In most OECD countries, capital gains are taxed at about half the rate of top marginal tax rates, or less on labour income. In the United States, the maximum capital gains tax on assets held for longer than two years is 20 percent, roughly half the top marginal tax rate. In Canada, the effective actual capital gains tax is also about half that of the top marginal tax rate on other income.

So people who work for a living are subsidizing those who let their money do their work.

And, of course, what is not captured in Gini coefficients that measure either market inequality or after-tax inequality are the trillions of dollars that the world's wealthiest households park offshore. Not only do these households escape having their wealth measured, more importantly they escape taxation too.

THE PANAMA AND PARADISE PAPERS

Relying on the favourable tax treatment of capital gains and dividends is one way that top earners escape the consequences of progressive taxation. But for the wealthiest among us there is an even more enticing route: moving their wealth to tax havens where there are no taxes on investment income—or, for that matter, on any income at all. For the world's plutocracy, it's nothing short of paradise.

Moving their wealth to offshore tax havens allows the world's wealthiest to avoid paying any tax on the income they generate from their vast fortunes. In the old days, everyone from billionaires to dictators to drug lords would go to Zurich or Geneva to park their money and let it earn a sizeable return. There were no questions asked and, more importantly, no disclosure of your offshore accounts to foreign tax authorities.

These days there is a whole atlas of countries offering the same services as Switzerland—and with much better climates as well. Tropical paradises such as the Bahamas, Belize, Bermuda, the British Virgin Islands, the Cayman Islands and Panama all make the list. In many cases, the actual ownership of the accounts is opaque, hidden behind personal holding companies or shell companies, trusts and foundations.

Offshoring wealth skews income inequality because the practice is so concentrated among such a small percentage of the population. More than half of all offshore accounts are held by the richest 0.01 percent of the world's population. If these accounts were captured in Gini coefficient measurements, global income distribution would be even more skewed to the super-rich than it now appears to be. More importantly, offshoring is no small contributor to inequality in its own right.

Hidden from view, this stashed-away wealth has always been hard to estimate—at least it was until hackers found their way into the confidential files of two law firms that specialize in arranging such accounts. The so-called Panama Papers consisted of some 11 million computer files from law firm Mossack Fonseca detailing the activity of more than 120,000 offshore accounts, including some eye-popping names such as Deng Jiagui, Chinese President Xi's brother-in-law.[18] Another 13.4 million confidential electronic documents were leaked when someone hacked into the computer files of Appleby, a Bermudian bank. The Panama Papers and the Paradise Papers, as the documents were dubbed by the media, provided an unprecedented perspective on the scope of tax avoidance by the world's wealthiest individuals and families.

So just how much wealth is socked away in those places? In a highly revealing study that mined much of the hacked data, the National Bureau of Economic Research (NBER) found that there was a lot more cash stashed away than economists had estimated. The NBER estimated that more than $5 trillion was held in opaque offshore accounts in 2007, equivalent to 10 percent of global GDP.[19] Updated estimates for 2015 peg offshore holdings at $8.7 trillion, or 11.7 percent of global household wealth, depriving governments around the world of $170 billion in tax revenue.[20]

The use of offshore tax evasion has risen alongside the growing concentration of world wealth in the hands of the very few. And just as the free movement of goods under globalization allows companies to arbitrage between different countries' wage rates, the free movement of capital allows arbitrage between different countries' tax rates. Hence, it is yet another race to the bottom that globalization is only too happy to oblige.

Not only do offshore accounts conceal inequity, but they also create more of it by shifting the tax burden onto those much less capable of bearing it. The fiscal consequences of the super-rich not paying tax on the streams of investment income generated by their vast wealth are far from trivial. For example, the Canada Revenue Agency estimates that wealthy Canadians are dodging up to $3 billion worth of federal tax on the investment income generated from an estimated $240.5 billion in offshore accounts every year. That's $3 billion in forgone tax revenue that far less fortunate Canadian taxpayers have to make up for. An even greater amount—an estimated $22 billion—is lost from corporations doing the same.[21]

WHAT'S GOOD FOR BILLIONAIRES IS GOOD FOR APPLE AND GOOGLE

Clearly, it's not just the wealthiest .01 percent of the world's population that resorts to offshore accounts to escape taxation—some of the world's largest corporations use the same playbook. However, unlike many of the people who hide their wealth in offshore accounts, corporations do it legally. And instead of stashing their cash in Caribbean paradises, companies often send their profits to the frigid North Atlantic—or at least book them there.

At first glance, Dublin might not strike you as a corporate capital, but if you knew the dollar figure of the profits booked there, you'd be forgiven for thinking we were talking about New York or London instead. Then again, you need only look at Ireland's corporate tax rate to know why it is brimming with corporate filings; its 12.5 percent rate is about a third of the corporate tax rate in most other European Union countries. And it has a special 6.5 percent rate for intellectual property, which has caught the eye of a few tech giants. If you're a multinational firm with revenue streams generated across a number of countries, it's not hard to figure out where you want to declare those revenues for tax purposes.

Tech giants Apple and Google are at the head of a long list of multinationals that have established residency in Ireland to take advantage of its enticingly low corporate taxes. Apple channelled most of the revenues from its European operations into its Irish subsidiary, resulting in a tax savings of €13 billion (US $14.3 billion). That led the rest of the EU to accuse Ireland of stealing corporate tax revenue from other member states.

Google did much the same with some €16 billion (US $17.6 billion) of European revenues. By booking those revenues in low-tax jurisdictions like Ireland, the Netherlands and Bermuda, using such tax avoidance schemes as the "Double Irish" or the "Dutch sandwich," the company saved $3.7 billion in taxes that it would have had to pay if it had filed the earnings in the countries in which the income was generated.[22]

If you are shareholder in either company, these are good-news stories. Those billions of dollars in tax savings flowed directly to the companies' bottom lines and to the price of your shares. But if you happen to be a taxpayer in any of those EU countries where Apple and Google chose not to declare their income, guess who's on the hook for those revenue shortfalls?

Apple and Google are not doing anything illegal—nor, for that matter, are any of the other companies filing their taxes in Ireland, the Netherlands or Bermuda. The corporate executives guiding those decisions are simply doing what they get paid to do, which is to minimize the amount of tax their firms have to pay and hence maximize after-tax earnings. If you can achieve that by shifting revenues to the lowest-tax jurisdiction, that is what shareholders want you to do. In Apple's case, Tim Cook, who vigorously defended his company's accounting practices in front of both a US Senate subcommittee and EU regulators during his tenure as chief operating officer, got promoted to CEO when founder Steve Jobs died. If I had been an Apple shareholder, he certainly would have gotten my vote.

And it's not just declared earnings that companies shift around to better their tax positions. The transfer of asset ownership to offshore subsidiaries—be it Nike's Swoosh trademark, Uber's app or Facebook's database and platform technology—allows many of the world's largest corporations to avoid paying tax on their global earnings. Facebook's user database, as well as rights to use its platform technology (together worth billions of dollars), has been traded through companies resident in the Grand Cayman.

Back in 2015, the OECD conservatively estimated that the transfer of intangible assets such as intellectual property to tax havens cost governments around the world as much as a quarter of a trillion dollars a year in lost tax revenue.[23] According to one estimate, the Netherlands, Ireland and Bermuda, three of the favourite destinations for multinational corporations to declare their global revenues, account for 35 percent of all profits that US multinationals reported earning overseas in 2016.

When trillions of dollars of personal wealth or corporate income is sheltered from taxation by offshore accounts, it creates huge gaps in a country's tax revenues. Who do you think ends up filling those gaps? It falls to personal income-tax payers to make up for any shortfalls in corporate tax collections. And we aren't talking about taxpayers who have their money stashed away in offshore tax havens. We are talking about you.

It's not Apple's or Goggle's job to make sure that the countries where they operate get to collect tax on the revenue they generate there. That's the job of the governments in the countries where these multinationals set up shop—the governments that are supposed to be looking after their taxpayers' interests. If taxpayers around the world want to stop having to backfill the huge gaps in their country's tax collections due to corporate avoidance, the rules need to change.

Of course, that's precisely why protesters took to the streets in Seattle—to stop people like C. Douglas Dillon from creating rules that benefit themselves at the expense of others. Turns out, once those rules are instituted, they are hard to change—but it can be done. One of the first things Donald Trump did when he assumed office was kill the opaque Trans-Pacific Partnership, which Barack Obama had negotiated and Hillary Clinton strongly endorsed. Trump tore up the deal because it put American workers at a disadvantage. But he was not criticized for thwarting the interests of the global investor class, which such trade and investment agreements served. Instead, he was taken to task for his willingness to turn his back on the world's poor, who were counting on free trade to lift them out of poverty.

CHAPTER 5

GREATER GLOBAL EQUITY (FOR THE RICH)

"Working for a world free of poverty": that's the motto of the World Bank, a key part of the Bretton Woods plan to shape the global economy after the Second World War. The bank's president is always an American, and its membership comprises the world's biggest economies. It is divided into the International Bank for Reconstruction and Development, and the International Development Association. "Development" is obviously important to the World Bank.

And most people are in favour of it. Allowing international trade flows to redistribute income from rich countries to poor countries sounds like a welcome and long-overdue process to those who care about global equity. And most advocates of globalization at least profess to care.

Since the Industrial Revolution some 250 years ago, world wealth has been ever more concentrated among a handful of advanced industrial economies, principally in North America and Western Europe. As the first countries to industrialize, they acquired what seemed like an insurmountable lead over everyone else. The countries that today make up the G7 saw their share of global income soar from around 20 percent in the early years of the nineteenth century to around 50 percent by the late twentieth century.[1] Over the last two decades, though, the G7's share of global income has been falling—and falling fast.

That sudden reversal of fortune is the mirror image of what has lifted hundreds of millions of people out of poverty through the emergent economic strength of countries like China and India. As incomes in those countries rose rapidly, international income disparities started to narrow for the first time in two and a half centuries.[2] At long last, that much-sought objective of greater global equity appeared to be within reach.

However, if you are a farmer in Bolivia or one of the estimated forty thousand child labourers mining cobalt and other metals in the Democratic Republic of the Congo, you probably haven't noticed this great convergence in global incomes. Life is just as hard as it's always been. And, as it turns out, you have lots of company. The narrowing in the income gap between people in the developed world and people in the developing world is attributable to impressive income growth in a relatively small number of countries. Most of the developing world has been left out of the process.

Admittedly, the two big developing countries that have seen impressive growth, China and India, have between them over 2 billion people, or some 30 percent of the world's population, so their weight is certainly felt in the global statistics that measure international income differences. Aside from these two behemoths, the other countries that have seen the greatest income gains in the developing world are mostly Asian (South Korea, Taiwan, Indonesia and Turkey). Exclude this handful of big winners, though, and the gap between the world's richest and poorest countries remains pretty much as it's always been—huge.

CHANGING TRADE RULES LEAD TO A MASSIVE MOVEMENT OF FACTORY JOBS

Where income gaps with the developed world have shrunk dramatically, as in the cases of China and India, the trend has primarily been driven by the massive movement of manufacturing industries and jobs to their economies. In the aftermath of the Industrial Revolution, high-paying manufacturing jobs were typically concentrated in G7 economies. That's what made them so wealthy in the first place. But these days, those countries are no longer the home of the world's factories. In the span of several decades, we have witnessed one of the greatest industrial migrations in history, with manufacturing moving on an unprecedented scale to China and a number of other developing countries. As we've seen, dramatic changes to world trade rules facilitated this shift. Those rule changes severed the umbilical cord that had linked where goods were produced with where they were ultimately sold.

Of course, it was China's low-wage labour force that ultimately made it the ideal location for most of the world's factories. But China has always held that advantage. In fact, the country's wages used to be a lot cheaper than they are today. But back then, capitalizing on the situation was a different matter altogether.

Let's say you were running an American company back in the 1970s. You couldn't just move your factory to China and substitute dirt-cheap Chinese wages for the wages you'd have to pay American workers back home—at least, not if you wanted to sell anything made there back in the United States. If you did, and if you tried to export what you produced in your low-wage Chinese factory back to your North American or European market, you would face huge tariffs, if not out-right quotas. And with incomes so low in China, there would have been no domestic market there for whatever it was you were producing. So despite the huge wage incentives that moving production to China offered, there was really no over-all economic rationale to go there once tariffs or quotas were taken into account.

But as GATT and then its successor, the WTO, guided multiple rounds of trade liberalization, everything changed. Brick by brick, tariff walls around the world crumbled, and as they did, you actually could move your factory overseas—or, even better, just arrange for someone local to produce your goods and then load them onto a big container ship bound for Los Angeles or Rotterdam. Tariffs were now so low in the rich markets of North America and Western Europe that you could supply them from just about anywhere in the world, provided that the labour was cheap enough to offset the freight costs.

And so manufacturing jobs moved. And wherever they went, income growth followed.

Wages in the new Chinese factories might be considered sweatshop rates compared to what workers were being paid in developed countries (at least before the factories moved). But those sweatshop rates were still a multiple of what wages were in the rest of the Chinese economy. The country quickly urbanized, with millions of peasants leaving their fields to work on the shop floors of the factories that were sprouting up like ripening rice stalks. Over time, the rapidly rising incomes of these new industrial workers provided a market for the products that were originally produced only for much richer export markets overseas.

Apple offers a good example of this process in action. America's largest tech company initially went to China in 2007[3] for the assembly of its iPhones. Since then, China has become one of Apple's most important smartphone markets, and as of the first quarter of 2019, represented almost a fifth of the company's total revenue.

Of course, there was a flip side to booming industrial employment in countries like China: imploding industrial pay-rolls and abandoned factories in the G7 economies and through-out most of the rest of the OECD nations. By 2014, factory employment in G7 countries had shrunk to a quarter of the levels found in developing countries. Manufacturing employ-ment throughout the OECD has declined by over 20 percent in the last two decades.[4]

As it turns out, though, most of that shift in factory employment landed in one country: China. While the share of factory jobs in advanced countries has fallen from roughly a quarter of the labour force in 1970 to barely over 10 percent today, China's share has risen by a comparable amount. Interestingly, in the rest of the developing world, manufac-turing's current share of employment in the labour force is about the same as it was nearly fifty years ago.[5]

So, has the middle-class dream of more leisure, disposable income and democratic governance arrived in China?

INCREASING INCOME INEQUALITY WITHIN COUNTRIES

While the international income gap between the developed world and the developing world (or at least countries such as China) started to narrow, the gap between the incomes of the rich and the poor *within* individual countries widened—yet another example of globalization's race to the bottom.

For the last two decades, Gini coefficients in most countries have been more or less moving up, indicating greater inequality across the income spectrum. Among the OECD economies, the United States and United Kingdom have seen the greatest increases in income inequality. But even those increases take a back seat to what's happening in China.

While China has seen impressive income gains in a rapidly expanding urban labour force and the emergence of a burgeoning middle class, the country's Gini coefficient has risen by a whopping 40 percent, from .35 to .50, between 1990 and 2015. And that has left China with one of the world's most unequal distributions of income[6]—not exactly a distinction that a still officially communist country can be very proud of.

While capitalist and communist countries officially espouse radically different ideologies about income distribution, when you get right down to it, the income stratum that is doing the best in either type of economy is the same—the gilded one percent. They've never had it so good. This global plutocracy (which comprises roughly 70 million people) has captured almost a fifth of all the gains in global income since 1988.[7] And they have accounted for a far greater share of the increase in global wealth. Statistics from 2017 estimate that the top 1 percent of the world's population captured an astounding 82 percent of the new wealth created that year around the world.[8]

China has been particularly adept at contributing to that plutocracy, creating more billionaires every year as its economy turns away from its agrarian roots to become the world's factory. According to *Forbes* magazine's annual list of the world's billionaires, China now has 324 such individuals, second only to the United States' 607.[9] The vast bulk of that new wealth is in the hands of a tiny number of people in a tiny number of countries.

BLOWBACK

Sometimes its funny the way things work out. Part of the justification for the project of globalization is the need to make developing countries like China more closely resemble the liberal democracies of the West—and yet, what seems to be happening is that Canada and the United States are beginning to more closely resemble the People's Republic, at least when it comes to income distribution and a highly stratified plutocracy.

In the United States, of course, the concentration of income and wealth isn't just in the hands of the top 1 percent. Even that percentile is a far too broad a category to capture the full extent of the concentration of wealth in today's American society. The income share of a very small subset of that group—the top 0.1 percent of the population—has more than tripled from 7 percent of total household income in 1978 to 22 percent.[10] No wonder Bill Gates and Warren Buffett are so generous with their money. These days, they and their fellow billionaires have a lot to give away.

Globalization has brought about a third trend in income distribution—a pronounced and almost universal shift in the distribution of what economists call "factor income" (as in factors of production, such as labour, capital and land) from wages to profits. The trade flows that have accompanied ever-greater economic globalization are the primary culprit. A Brookings Institution study, for example, found that the decline in labour's share of US national income, which has fallen to the lowest level in decades, was chiefly due to the offshoring of labour-intensive production to cheap labour markets like China.[11] That is, those who advocated for globalization and free trade back in the 1980s and 1990s were right: their policies did create a lot of wealth. It's just that almost all of it went to a small number of people.

Of course, if you own a lot of stock, you are not complaining. The reason we've had such a record run of bull markets around the world is principally because profits have never been so good. The share of national income going to profits is sitting at a postwar high in virtually every OECD economy today. However, this has largely come at the expense of a steadily declining share of national income that has historically gone to wages.[12]

Growing inequality in household incomes and a shift in factor income from wages to profits are not unrelated trends, as they might first appear to be. In fact, they are conjoined twins, attached at the hip. The ownership of profits is highly concentrated in the hands of the top income stratum, whose members receive the bulk of the dividends and capital gains that profits pay and create. It shouldn't come as a surprise, then, that the rising fortunes of that top stratum have gone hand in hand with a major redistribution of factor income from wages to profits. That's how your country gets richer while you get poorer: wages may not be growing, but investment returns sure are.

But doesn't the tide from a rising stock market lift all boats? You might think that in the midst of the longest-running rally in the history of the S&P 500, more and more of us would own publicly listed stocks. But the opposite is true. Whereas 65 percent of American households owned stocks before the last recession, today barely over 50 percent do. Instead, stock ownership has become more concentrated in the hands of the wealthy. According to estimates by Goldman Sachs, the wealthiest 1 percent of American households own significantly more stocks than the other 99 percent of the population.[13] In fact, the wealthiest 1 percent own half of all equities held by American households, while the top 10 percent own more than 80 percent of all publicly listed shares.[14] Hence, the better the stock market does, the better rich people do.

While globalization has led to worsening income equality in both the developing and the developed world, it is largely in the latter that its distributional effects have been challenged by growing populist movements. The reasons seem clear enough. Whereas worsening inequality in places like China has occurred against the backdrop of rising income for virtually everyone, growing inequality in the OECD countries has coincided with stagnant incomes for most of the population. And the explosive growth of the middle class in China and India has coincided with the decline of the middle class in most OECD economies, most notably in the United States.

Moreover, the slowdown in economic growth in OECD countries has been the counterpart to the economic boom in China and India, just as the OECD's hollowed-out industrial sectors are the flip side of China's sprawling global supply chains. It is no surprise, then, that globalization's gains are being questioned the most throughout OECD countries—and nowhere more so than in the world's largest economy, the United States.

The sudden grassroots rejection of the prevailing ideology of globalization has shocked American politicians as much as it has shocked economists. At first, the economics profession argued that trade with developing countries was far too small to act as an effective brake on manufacturing workers' wages in G7 economies, or to lead to shrinking manufacturing employment. That was their natural instinct, since most economists are, in principle, supporters of free trade. Instead, they blamed labour-saving technological changes for industrial job losses in America and other G7 economies.

Many still do. The prevailing view is that automation is the prime culprit behind the loss of all those jobs in the manufacturing sector, and that robots and artificial intelligence will ultimately replace human labour. But so far, at least, widespread automation hasn't stopped economies from pumping out record numbers of new jobs. And it's not like factories today don't hire millions of workers around the world. It's just that those factories aren't in the same countries that they once were—and they sure don't pay anywhere close to the same wages that they once did.

As trade volumes have mushroomed with the growth of global supply chains, it's become harder and harder for economists to deny that the massive outsourcing of jobs to low-wage countries has had a profoundly negative impact on both factory employment and wages in the G7 economies. Even some of globalization's greatest advocates are having sober second thoughts on the subject, including *New York Times* columnist and Nobel Prize laureate Paul Krugman, and former US treasury secretary and Obama economic advisor Lawrence Summers.[15] The more exposed an industry was to imports from cheap labour markets, the more employment and wages declined for American workers.[16] One study estimated that between 1999 and 2011, growing import penetration of the American market by Chinese goods cost American workers between 2 and 2.4 million jobs, most in competing domestic manufacturing industries and their upstream suppliers.

That adverse impact on American workers' wages was quickly translating into economic stagnation for a growing number of households. Unlike the members of the wealthiest stratum of the population, who rely on capital gains and dividends for their income, most households in North America depend on wage income to pay their bills. As wage gains became harder to achieve, at least for lower- and middle-income workers, more and more households found themselves being left further behind—so much so that they fell right out of the line of vision of most of America's establishment politicians.

But now, as the wealth spectrum becomes more and more polarized, they are suddenly coming back into view.

THE NEW ROBBER BARONS

At the end of the nineteenth century, the American economy was dominated by a small group of monopolists that history has dubbed the robber barons. Some of the group's more illustrious members were Cornelius Vanderbilt, John Rockefeller and Charles Mellon. Each of these men amassed a giant fortune through what many regarded at the time as unscrupulous and ruthless business tactics, gaining for their businesses a privileged monopolistic position in the American economy. The robber barons' domination of American commerce and the massive amounts of personal wealth they acquired in the process ultimately led to the Sherman Antitrust Act of 1890, which was eventually used to break up Rockefeller's Standard Oil in 1911. History warns us that when monopolistic control falls into the hands of the few (who make massive fortunes as a result), someone is getting screwed.

Some commentators have suggested that the CEOs of today's tech giants—Apple's Tim Cook, Facebook's Mark Zuckerberg and Amazon's Jeff Bezos, to name a few—are the robber barons of our age.[17] Their modern-day uniform of jeans and T-shirts may not scream "money" the way the three-piece suits and top hats of Rockefeller and his cohort did, but their enormous wealth dwarfs the riches of their nineteenth-century predecessors.[18]

And the companies they manage dominate their markets just as surely as Standard Oil did at the dawn of the twentieth century. Google, for example, controls 92 percent of the global search engine market—more than the 90 percent control Standard Oil had of US refinery capacity before it was forced to break up. And with more than 2 billion users, Facebook similarly dominates social media networks.

All of these CEOs are good at what they do. And what they do best is manipulate public governance in ways that the early twentieth-century global oil industry could only dream of. In the United States, where most of them are based, they have supported the establishment wing of the Democratic Party—the same wing that was in power for eight years under President Obama. They've been outspoken on climate change, racial intolerance, gender equity, and all of the other hot-button issues of American liberalism. But at the same time, the efforts to prove their liberal bona fides have helped protect this group from something they care far more deeply about: government regulation of the monopolies that have made them all multibillionaires.

CHAPTER 6

THE NEW ECONOMY: NON-INCLUSIVE GROWTH

On September 1, 1966, Canada became the third country in the world to enjoy television broadcasts in colour. The second was Japan. The first, the United States, had been watching colour TV since the *Colgate Comedy Hour*'s broadcast on November 22, 1953. Canadians who tuned in on that day in 1966 could watch bucking broncos at the Calgary Stampede. (There had been a test broadcast earlier in the year—an NHL playoff game between the Toronto Maple Leafs and Montreal Canadiens.)

The thing is, there was hardly anyone to watch those bucking broncos; at the time, only 1 percent of Canadians had colour televisions. With a price tag of more than $850— upward of $6,000 in today's currency—they were just too darned expensive for most people (plus, you needed a new antenna, which tacked on another $200). Buying a TV used to be a big deal. People used to fix them when they broke. People used to steal them. Now they're not worth the trouble. Black Friday mayhem aside, the cost of a television has come down about 96 percent since they were first introduced.[1]

If you like watching TV, that's great news. Falling prices are great for consumers. But the prices of most things don't fall unless the wages of workers making them fall as well.

Wage stagnation may sound really awful for economic growth, but it isn't all bad. If it were, our economies would have stopped growing a few decades ago. Fortunately, wage stagnation—whether in the United Kingdom, Australia, Japan or North America—brings with it some valuable economic rewards. They sure aren't distributed equitably, but they've become vital to how our economies now grow.

By far the most important benefit stagnant wages bring to the economy is a check on inflation. Short of an oil price shock, it's difficult to have inflation if wages aren't growing. For all of industry's talk of automation and artificial intelligence, labour is still far and away the most important cost when it comes to making most things. And if stultifying domestic wage growth isn't applying a big enough brake on inflation, consider the impact that the continual replacement of high-priced domestic goods by cheaper imports is having (not to mention the offshoring of some business services as well). Globalization provides an unrelenting upstream current against which inflation has to swim. At best, prices simply tread water.

Once the principal nemesis of Western economies, inflation has all but vanished. Central bankers typically take credit for the victory, claiming that their skilled and careful management of monetary conditions has vanquished this menace. In reality, their role has been much less vital. Trade negotiators are the real architects of today's low inflation environment. They seldom get the credit, but they and the trade treaties they've negotiated have done most of the heavy lifting when it comes to putting inflation to bed.

LOW INFLATION BOOSTS PURCHASING AND BORROWING POWER

The mass movement of production to low-wage countries has dramatically lowered the cost of making most things—like, for example, the colour TV. Thanks to globalization, everything that was once produced domestically is now imported more cheaply from some distant low-wage market. In the process, inflation has been buried. But that's not all globalization has done. It has also boosted the purchasing power of consumers all around the world, and particularly in places like North America, where there has been such wide-scale substitution of cheap imports for locally produced goods.

Of course, the irony here is that many a Western worker has used that increased purchasing power to shop themselves right out of their own job. Walmart parking lots are filled with people who once made the things they are there to buy. Those bargain-priced goods now come from a distant low-wage supply chain. If they came from the factories where many of those shoppers once worked, Walmart wouldn't be selling them at the prices it does today.

Low inflation doesn't just stretch your paycheque; it also stretches your borrowing capacity. How much you can borrow depends critically on the cost of money. The fact that a lid has been kept on inflation is directly responsible for today's low borrowing rates—the same rates, it's worth mentioning, that have been so critical to the recovery and economic expansion that have followed the world financial crisis and Great Recession of 2008.

In most OECD economies, interest rates have been at or near record lows ever since. In some European Union countries, the long-term interest rates embedded in bond yields have actually become negative—the result of what is called "quantitative easing," which occurs when a central bank, such as the European Central Bank, buys so many of its member governments' bonds that the interest rate dips below zero. Those low interest rates have certainly helped to soften the blow that stagnant wages have dealt to household spending, the largest part of our economy.

First, the low interest rates have encouraged consumers to spend almost everything they make. And, then, as interest rates declined, so too did savings rates. Over the past two decades savings have been significantly lower than in previous decades during the postwar period.[2] In some countries, Canada for instance, the household savings rate (household savings as a percentage of after-tax income) has fallen to near six-decade lows.[3] When you aren't earning any interest, why bother to save?

Less saving at least partially compensates consumer spending for the lack of wage growth. And consumer demand is what usually drives economic growth, since around 60 percent of GDP in most OECD economies is attributed to personal consumption.[4] While wages aren't growing anywhere close to historic norms, most of the population isn't saving anymore—other than through forced pension contributions (and there are fewer and fewer workers who have pension plans to contribute to). Instead, everybody spends everything they make. Some do more than that and, in the process, rack up increasing loads of household debt. And why not, since the cost of carrying it is also so low at today's borrowing rates?

The middle class has strapped on the most debt. With less money than in the past, this income group is nevertheless trying to maintain its standard of living. Stagnating incomes have made it harder to pay the bills. Rising housing expenditures, among other necessities, have left more than one in five lower-middle-class households across the OECD spending more than they earn—a pathway to ever-greater debt loads.[5] This is also true for low-income households. The difference in debt load comes down to access. The middle class still has the recourse of borrowing from financial institutions, whereas the creditworthiness (or lack thereof) of lower-income workers closes those doors. In other words, the middle class has more rope with which to hang themselves.

While some households borrow to purchase a car or even to pay their monthly bills, by far the biggest reason that households borrow is to buy a place to live. Mortgage rates in North America are at one of their lowest levels in decades, which translates into savings of hundreds of dollars on a typical mortgage. The average cost of a home in Canada is now $455,000. If interest rates today were where they were back in 1981—18.45 percent—and you had put down 20 percent, the monthly mortgage cost would be $5,558. Not many Canadians could afford that. But at today's rates, the market is much bigger, and therefore more accessible.

Not surprisingly, then, the housing market is far and away the most leveraged part of the economy—the biggest winner in the low-borrowing-rate sweepstakes. And homeowners are the principal beneficiaries. The benefits have even trickled down to construction workers. In fact, they are the only workers on the goods side of the economy who have seen any job growth. But then again, unlike factory workers, the construction trades don't have to compete with what carpenters and bricklayers get paid on the other side of the world.

Historically, home ownership was the cornerstone of a typical middle-class lifestyle. That is much less the case today. Housing prices throughout the OECD countries have risen at a multiple of middle-class incomes, which for the most part have been stagnant. In the mid-1980s it would have taken a typical middle-income family with two children less than seven years of income to save up to buy a home; it now takes more than ten years. At the same time, housing expenditures that accounted for a quarter of most middle-class household incomes in the 1990s now account for a third.[6]

But while mortgage rates are much lower than they were in the past, qualifying to get a mortgage has become much harder. The days of being approved for a mortgage with little or no income to pay for it disappeared with the collapse of the subprime mortgage bubble. Today, qualifying for a mortgage is mostly about how much you earn. And as we saw in the last chapter, for most middle-class citizens of the developed world, earnings haven't grown. If you are a low- to middle-income household, your income may no longer meet the bar—in which case, home ownership is no longer an option for you.

CATERING TO THE SPENDING POWER OF THE RICH

If you look, you'll see signs of income polarization everywhere. It can certainly be seen on the signs and storefronts of today's

retail world. As wealth and income become increasingly concentrated in the hands of the rich, so too does consumer
spending power. More and more, it's the spending habits of
the wealthy that are driving consumer demand. The two, after
all, go together. The top 5 percent of earners in the United
States drive almost 40 percent of all consumer spending. These
are the kind of shoppers you want in your store.[7]

It's not just that rich people account for a greater proportion of consumer spending than ever before. To a retailer, the
real significance is in what they buy—because rich consumers
purchase very different types of goods and services than poor
or even middle-class shoppers do. If you're a retailer, or a bank
that is financing a retailer, you tend to notice these things.

Whether you're talking about where people shop, where
they stay or where they eat, the growing polarization of incomes
is having a profound impact on which goods and services are
selling and which are not. There is a lot of growth at the top
end, reflecting the booming spending power of that narrow
stratum of the population. And there is growth at the bottom
end as well, since more and more households have fallen into
its ranks. It's the middle-class shopper who is getting squeezed.
First, there are fewer of them. Second, those who are left have
less money to spend. So their shopping habits change.

Take department stores, for example. Upscale chains like
Nordstrom are doing well, while stores targeting traditional
middle-class buyers, like Sears and JCPenney, are scraping
by. In fact, Sears, the 125-year-old retailer that was once America's largest, finally declared bankruptcy in 2018 after closing
stores over the course of several years. JCPenney, with its

share price trading below $1 dollar recently, seems headed in the same direction.

But commercial success in an increasingly polarized retail market isn't all about catering to the spending power of the rich. Retailers can also enjoy success by catering to the rapidly growing ranks of the poor. The downwardly mobile middle class, with its ever shrinking incomes, has turned toward stores that target austerity, like the plethora of dollar and ninety-nine-cent stores that have sprung up across North America. As the American middle class continues to shrink, chains like Family Dollar have grown by more than 60 percent during the last decade, to over eight thousand stores across the United States, although it now faces pressures from other discount chains.[8]

In the past, these stores targeted only the very poor. Now, however, their doors are wide open to people whose spending budgets once allowed them to shop at middle-class retailers like Sears or JCPenney. Little wonder these folks are shopping at very different outlets than they once did. More than 40 million Americans now receive some form of food assistance, almost double the number of recipients a decade ago.[9]

The growing gap between rich and poor shoppers is not purely an American phenomenon. The same polarization is apparent north of the border, where income distribution has pretty well moved in the same direction as it has in the United States. Stores that have traditionally sold to middle-income Canadian shoppers—Target Canada, Petcetera, Esprit and Tip Top Tailors, for example—have seen nationwide closures. But retailers who have targeted either the rich or the poor have done well. At the lower end, Montreal-based Dollarama has seen the same success that Family Dollar has seen stateside. Discount stores like Costco and Winners are also thriving. And at the booming luxury end of the market, Prada, Dior, Ermenegildo Zegna and Saks Fifth Avenue have all moved across the border and established a presence in the Canadian retail marketplace.

GROWTH DOESN'T MEAN WHAT IT USED TO

Looking back at the economic expansion over the last decade, it's certainly the case that you no longer need wage gains to drive economic growth. The purchasing power of the rich, coupled with that of the growing ranks of the poor, will drive consumer demand, although for very different products than those sought by a once more affluent middle class. And the benefits that low inflation has brought to both purchasing and borrowing power have proven to be important drivers of economic activity.

But at the same time, and for most people, economic growth doesn't mean what it used to. GDP growth used to be inclusive; now it's become increasingly exclusive. A growing economy still translates into rising GDP per capita, but most of the gains are accruing to a very narrow slice of the population. In a nutshell, the average income is going up, but no one earns the average income. And looking at averages hides a climbing Gini coefficient and a level of polarization not seen in generations. Per capita GDP tells us almost nothing about how most people in the economy are doing.

Within OECD countries, the incomes of the top 10 percent have grown at over three times the pace of median incomes. In some more extreme cases, like the United States, the top 1 percent of the population has captured roughly half of all income growth in the economy over the last three decades, in the process doubling their income share from 11 percent to over 20 percent.[10]

The economy may no longer depend on wage increases to support growth, but the corollary of that condition is that economic growth doesn't equate into rising living standards for most wage earners. GDP growth used to be as good as any measure of our economic welfare. Strong GDP gains used to mean a rapidly growing economy was pumping out a lot of well-paying jobs. And the creation of those jobs boosted income gains for everybody.

Today, for the most part, GDP growth means the economy is pumping out a lot of low-paying jobs. While politicians still strut strong GDP growth numbers like a badge of honour, economic growth has become an abstraction for an increasing number of workers across the OECD. To them, it doesn't really matter if GDP is growing at a rate of 1 percent or 3 percent, any more than it seems to matter if the national unemployment rate is sitting at 3 percent or 6 percent. Neither the traditional benefits of GDP growth nor the perks of a decades-low jobless rate have trickled down to them in the form of solid wage growth.

If you're an older worker, you haven't seen a real-wage gain in decades, even with today's low inflation rate. You wake up every morning wondering whether today is the day you'll finally receive notice that your factory is closing and moving to some cheap labour market abroad. If you're a millennial or Generation Z worker, you're probably juggling several minimum-wage jobs in the booming gig economy to make ends meet. And with that tenuous income stream, you might be trying to pay off the student loans you racked up getting a university education in the hope that you could earn a decent living after you graduated.

From the demise of inflation to the demise of workers' pay, from income polarization to its retail consequences, from the types of jobs being created to those that no longer are—so much of what we have come to take for granted about today's economy has been shaped by globalization and the shifting contours of world trade. But laying it out in this way also provides a sense of how much could change if the ground rules governing how our economy operates were suddenly torn up and replaced with a new set of rules—ones that championed the interests of those left behind.

CHAPTER 7

GLOBALIZATION AND THE DIGITAL REVOLUTION

f you ever have an urgent need for a toilet while taking in the sights in France or Italy, you are likely to find yourself inside a chapter of the ancient history of what economists call "technological unemployment."

You see, the Italian word for "public toilet" is *vespasiano*; in French, it's *vespasienne*. Public toilets are a Roman innovation introduced by Titus Flavius Vespasianus, also known as Emperor Vespasian. He devoted himself to what might be called Keynesian building projects. Those public toilets are such a good example of the work he undertook that they bear the emperor's name to this day. His most ambitious public project also bore his name: the Flavian Amphitheatre, known today as the Roman Colosseum. Despite the ravages of time—almost two thousand years of wars, earthquakes and barbarian invasions—the Colosseum is still standing. It's an impressive feat of architecture and engineering, but it turns out that the Romans had an ambivalent relationship with their advanced technology.

Like us, the Romans worried about their workforce. They were well aware that slaves put Roman labourers out of work and created political tension, and they thought of technological advancements in much the same way: "An engineer offered to haul some columns up to the Capitol at moderate expense by a simple mechanical contrivance," the historian Suetonius tells us, "but Vespasian declined his services: 'I must always ensure,' he said, 'that the working classes earn enough money to buy themselves food.'" Vespasian recognized that technology created as many problems as it solved. It may have made life easier for some, but it put others out of work.[1]

We tend to think of history as the story of relentless technological progress, but there is a parallel history of inventions that were ignored or suppressed because of their likely effect on employment levels. You may recall reading about the Luddites, who made a name for themselves in Britain back in the early days of the Industrial Revolution. They were the workers who, fearing that their jobs would be automated, took sledgehammers to the machines that were about to replace them. The term "Luddite" is still used to describe those resistant to progress and technical change. What is sometimes forgotten, though, is that it's not just the expendables who occasionally dig in their heels. Hundreds of years before the Luddites gave a bad reputation to anyone who resists technological progress, Queen Elizabeth I denied a patent to an inventor who had designed a knitting machine, on the grounds that it would create unemployment.[2] Leaders always worry about putting their subjects out of work; it can be dangerous. At points during the twentieth century, people were concerned that subway ticket machines and concrete mixers would displace jobs in the transportation and construction industries.

The question is, did those fears prove to be right? With all of the hype about the coming age of artificial intelligence, concern over future technological unemployment has never been more in vogue. An OECD study claims nearly half of the jobs in the developed world are vulnerable to some form of future automation.[3] The McKinsey Global Institute warns that as many as 73 million jobs in the US economy could disappear due to automation over the next decade.[4]

In the meantime, the economy is pumping out a record number of jobs. Nevertheless, this paradigm holds sway over much of the world's business community and among the think tanks it so generously sponsors. And more often than not, economists use it as an explanation—or rather a justification—for what has happened to wages and the middle class. It is misguided to focus on trade policy and global supply chains, pundits argue, when the digital revolution is the real underlying cause of what is happening to labour markets throughout the OECD.

Of course, advocates of that argument conveniently ignore some crucial connections between the digital revolution and the new global trading order. On closer inspection, it turns out that those booming digital industries are not only affected by global supply chains but are also critically dependent on them. In fact, few industries have taken greater pains to fit the contours of today's highly integrated global economy than the electronics industry has. The story of the digital revolution is as much about globalization as it is anything else.

When you get right down to it, the digital technology that is transforming the economy and, in the process, disrupting so many traditional industries isn't some amorphous force. Rather, digital technology is embodied in equipment, just as the Industrial Revolution's steam engines and weaving looms were. Digital signals may travel at the speed of light through the atmosphere, but they are sent and received by devices. Those devices are a mass of copper wires, aluminum alloys, a lithium battery, and trace amounts of gold, palladium and rare earths, all encased in glass. The price of those electronic devices represents a critical gateway through which consumers must pass to enter the digital world.

Without smartphones, iPads or laptop computers, we wouldn't be able to use all of those wonderful new apps that allow us to function in the online space: shopping, booking hotels or pensions on the other side of the world, or hailing a cheap ride from Uber or Lyft. The cost of those electronic goods is critical to their users—and to workers like retail sales clerks, travel agents, and taxi drivers, whose jobs are disrupted by the services now provided by digital apps. Entire economies depend on the price of phones. The cheaper the devices, the more people can access their apps—and the more disruptive they can be to established industries. It is at that critical cost threshold where globalization and the digital revolution meet.

ELECTRONIC SWEATSHOPS

While the use of smartphones often displaces labour, the production of those same phones—and other electronic devices like tablets—involves an enormous amount of labour. That's one aspect of the electronics industry we seldom hear about. We don't know much about the labour that goes into creating our smartphones because they are built and assembled in far-off places where labour is a fraction of the cost that it is here. Globalization allows for the price of labour to be arbitraged—which is precisely why smartphones are assembled and manufactured by cheap labour all around the world.

If you stop to consider how much labour goes into a smartphone's assembly, you'll realize that it's a lot more than you might initially think. First, the chipset containing the android software technology must be manually installed into the phone's casing. Next, it must be manually fitted with the peripheral connections that will be attached to the digital display, camera and speakers. Once that is complete, it must be manually sealed. The only part of the entire production process that is automated is stamping the phone's back plate to the main casing. The smartphone must then be taken on and off the assembly line several times to fit the lens of the camera on the housing before it is finally resealed.

And the actual assembly of the phone is only half of the process. Testing it at the factory is the other half, and that process is just as labour-intensive. The unit must be manually tested using an external power source and then again using its own power. Smartphones may be disrupting old ways of doing business, but the way they're built—by workers toiling away on long production lines—is decidedly old-fashioned.

Smartphones and iPads and the like may be designed in Silicon Valley, but they sure aren't produced there. Over time, major smartphone manufacturers like Apple have got out of the manufacturing business altogether. Instead, they rely on far-flung global supply chains to build and assemble their devices. Out of sight, out of mind—at least as far as Apple's customers are concerned. The California-based electronics firm that the stock market briefly valued at $1 trillion is the acknowledged industry leader when it comes to global supply chains. Today, almost all of the componentry and assembly of its flagship smartphones takes place offshore.

Apple's CEOs—from founder Steve Jobs to current boss Tim Cook—have defended the company's offshoring practices by claiming that it's no longer about accessing cheap labour in China. Instead, they argue, their offshore supply chains are all about the rare combination of a flexible and skilled workforce that China supplies.

It's hard to know how Tim Cook defines "low wages," but $1.85 an hour would seem to fit the bill.[5] That's what China Labor Watch—a not-for-profit organization that monitors the working conditions of Chinese labourers—found when it infiltrated one of Apple's major Chinese suppliers, the Pegatron Group. It had a discernably different perspective on the company's global supply chains than the one routinely described in the company's corporate headquarters in Cupertino, California.

The Pegatron Group, whose massive plant in Shanghai employs as many as 100,000 workers, churns out millions of Apple's latest iPhone models. China Labor Watch found that its employees were often asked to work eighteen days straight without a day off. Those highly skilled and flexible workers Jobs and Cook were referring to were falling asleep on the production line during shifts that lasted anywhere between twelve and sixteen hours.[6]

Apple's rival Samsung is no different when it comes to the use of cheap labour. The world largest smartphone manufacturer started out producing its phones in South Korea. But Korean wages were too high to remain competitive, so it outsourced some of its production to Vietnam. Vietnam now produces more than half of Samsung's phones, compared to the 8 percent still being produced in South Korea.[7]

Vietnam isn't the only place smartphone manufacturers are heading in the never-ending pursuit of cheaper labour. The newest smartphone-producing country is India, which offers manufacturers even cheaper labour than China, South Korea or Vietnam. Chinese tech companies such as Xiaomi, Huawei and Lenovo/Motorola have all set up manufacturing facilities in the country, where they have lots of company. Samsung is the largest smartphone manufacturer in India, but others who have set up production there include LG, Microsoft, ASUS and Micromax.

And it's not just the production workers on the assembly line whose wages subsidize the profits of Chinese corporations. Wage stagnation in Silicon Valley notwithstanding, if you are employed in the high-tech industry, you would still rather work in the Golden State than across the Pacific in China. In China's booming high-tech sector, workers are expected to do what's called "the 996"—meaning they work from 9 a.m. to 9 p.m. six days a week. The seventy-two-hour workweek has become standard in the country's tech industries. It is vigorously defended by many of China's high-tech billionaires on the grounds that it's the only way China's tech sector can remain internationally competitive.

Jack Ma, the billionaire founder of Alibaba, not only defended the practice but also referred to it as a blessing.[8] (No one has asked Alibaba's nearly seventy thousand employees how they feel about being so blessed.) Richard Liu, another Chinese billionaire who made his fortune in the high-tech sector, referred to workers who complain about the practice as "slackers" and claimed that his firm, JD.com, would not remain commercially viable without its workers adhering to a 996 schedule.[9]

The practice is originally linked to Huawei, which has been China's most successful and internationally recognized high-tech company. The long hours Huawei demands from its employees are widely seen in the industry as an important commercial advantage that allows the company to undercut the prices of competitors like Ericsson.

The cutthroat economics of globalization shape the lifecycle of consumer technology from beginning to end. A typical smartphone contains as many as eight rare-earth materials. (Actually, rare earths aren't that rare. They are more common than precious metals like gold or silver, but are difficult to extract in commercially viable concentrations.) In addition to rare earths, a typical smartphone also contains lithium and cobalt. Sixty percent of the cobalt used to build the rechargeable lithium ion batteries that power smartphones comes from the Democratic Republic of the Congo, where an estimated forty thousand child labourers scavenge for it in what are euphemistically called "artisanal" mines.[10] Once mined, the raw cobalt is refined and assembled into smartphone components in factories in Vietnam. Those components are then sent to the assembly plants in China that turn out the latest Apple and Huawei phones.

From there, the phones are shipped all over the world,

destined to become trash in about two years. It's ironic that the digital revolution is credited with saving millions of trees. Though virtually every bill you receive implores you to pay electronically in the name of the environment, and the digitization of the economy has indeed cut down on the use of paper, it has also left mountains of electronic trash in its place. A study by the United Nations University found that in 2016 the world produced no less than 433 million tons of electronic waste.[11] It was by far the fastest-growing type of refuse in the world, increasing at double the rate of plastic garbage.

The sheer number of smartphone users around the world is in itself a powerful driver of the growing electronic trash heaps. (In 2018, global sales of smartphones were over 1.5 billion units.[12]) But what makes those trash heaps grow even faster is that most of the equipment, like the workers who make it, is expendable. Falling prices and enhanced technological capability (as well as engineered obsolescence) encourage customers to continually upgrade. That means the world's stock of billions of smartphones churns steadily.

Many outdated phones end up back in the very same countries in which they are manufactured, and not merely by coincidence. It's all part of the virtuous cycle of interlinked supply chains that encircles today's electronic industry. And like all global supply chains, it's based on the same thing—cheap labour.

The Basel Action Network (a non-governmental organization working to combat the export of toxic waste from industrialized countries to developing ones) estimates that as much as 50 to 80 percent of the electronic waste directed to recycling in the United States is put on container ships and sent to places like Guiyu, in the Shantou region of China, or Delhi and Bangalore in India.[13] And what happens there isn't what typically comes to mind when most people think of recycling plants. The discarded smartphones are pulverized by hand to extract the precious and other valuable metals they contain. Batteries are smashed to recover cadmium, while circuit boards are cooked in open baths of lead to remove the slivers of gold and silver inside.

Guiyu has long enjoyed the distinction of being the world's largest e-waste site. There are thousands of workshops in the area that dismantle and extract valuable material such as lead, copper and gold from discarded electronic equipment. The industry employs thousands of people of all ages and dismantles more than 1.6 million pounds of electronics such as cellphones, computers and electronic home appliances each year. On average, workers earn barely $1.50 a day, with an average workday of sixteen hours.[14] If cheap labour is behind the production of electronic devices, even cheaper labour lies behind its disposal.

It's funny how closely Chinese billionaires agree with the Seattle protesters. The rewards of globalization go to the winner in the race to the bottom.

CHEAP LABOUR DRIVES THE DIGITAL ECONOMY

For the sake of argument, let's suppose that instead of farming out the manufacture of its smartphones to an overseas company like the Pegatron Group, Apple decided to assemble the phone at home in California.

If Apple had to pay its workers $12 an hour (California's minimum wage) instead of the less than $2 an hour foreign labourers command, the company's smartphone would no longer be retailing at the same price. By some estimates, Apple's top-of-the-line smartphone, which typically retails in the United States for around $1,000, would sell for double that. And if that smartphone now sold at $2,000, it's a safe bet that there would be a lot fewer people buying it and using all the apps we can download to it. So it turns out the app economy is as dependent on globalization as everything else. And what applies to Apple also applies to all the other smartphone producers.

Apple claims that it can't afford to reshore production of its smartphones and computers if its competition continues to access cheap and abundant global labour. And it is, of course, right. But what would happen if the whole industry was forced to reshore as a result, for example, of the United States applying punitive tariffs on Chinese electronic exports? Initially, firms could shift production to other low-wage countries to escape the US tariffs, as they are already doing in the face of the ongoing trade war between the United States and China. But if the intention behind the tariffs was to bring production home, those countries would ultimately be targeted too. Then, all of a sudden, the playing field would be levelled for American workers. If smartphone manufacturers insisted on hiring sweatshop labour, the wage advantage that cheap labour afforded would largely be eaten up by the tariff. And if they chose to produce the phones where they were selling them, the wage bill would spike. The cost of a smartphone or similar device would soar, and as it did, fewer and fewer people would be using them to book a lift, a room or a dinner reservation.

The digitization of the economy isn't an alternative explanation for what globalization has done to Western wage earners and the middle class. It's simply another guise that globalization has taken. The new digital technologies are disruptive of traditional industries precisely because they offer comparable services to consumers at a much cheaper price. But what ultimately makes them price-competitive is cheap labour—labour that trade rules say can be sourced anywhere in the world.

CHAPTER 8

DUELLING GIANTS:
THE TRADE WAR WITH CHINA

The digital revolution owes a huge debt to the planet-shrinking supply chains of globalization. But you don't need to be in the electronics industry to benefit from globalization. Just ask Harley-Davidson.

Back in the 1920s, Japan was a big market for American motorcycles. Harley had been exporting to the United Kingdom, but the British erected tariff walls to protect industries rebuilding after the First World War. So the Americans had to look elsewhere to expand their global market. Rival American company Indian Motorcycle had been selling big bikes in Japan for years, so it seemed like an obvious opportunity for Harley.

For a while, it worked well, but the stock market crash of 1929 marked the beginning of the end for the Japanese market. As the yen dropped in value against the dollar, Harleys became too expensive for Japanese riders.

It was a British entrepreneur who came up with the idea of getting around the currency problem by building the bikes under licence in Japan. Alfred Child brokered a deal between Harley-Davidson and a Japanese company called Sankyo, which transferred blueprints and technology one way, and sent royalties back the other way. Those royalties helped Harley-Davidson weather the Depression, when their factory in Milwaukee was operating at a fraction of full capacity. And production of the Japanese Harley, known as a Rikuo, began in 1935.

Fast-forward nearly a hundred years and things look eerily similar. In 2018, the EU raised tariffs on Harley-Davidsons from 6 percent to 31 percent in retaliation for Trump's tariffs on their aluminum and steel exports.[1] The move came just as the motorcycle manufacturer was looking at Asian markets. They already had a factory in India (and another in the Free Economic Zone of Manaus, in Brazil), and had announced another in Thailand. It was a lot cheaper to build motorcycles with foreign labour than with an American workforce.

But the interesting wrinkle was their partnership with the Quianjiang Motorcycle Company, a subsidiary of Geely (the company that bought Volvo from Ford after the last recession, and that has a joint venture with Daimler to build Mercedes in China). Quianjiang already builds 1.5 million motorcycles a year, about six times more than Harley, so scale won't be a problem. Together, they are developing a cost-competitive smaller bike for the Asian market.[2] At 338 cc, the "baby Harley" is laughably small compared to classic Hogs, but there could be a lot of them. Harley is looking to increase international sales to 50 percent of its annual volume.[3]

There's a flip side to this scenario, of course. Increasing your international sales and manufacturing is another way of saying that you're cutting back on domestic operations. And, in fact, that's exactly what's happening. Harley's sales have been dipping steadily in the United States, and the company recently shuttered its factory in Missouri. So it's looking a lot like the

1930s. The company has found a way to take advantage of global markets, but the services of its American workers won't be required. The same forces that drive companies from OECD countries to import from the developing world also bar them from exporting to them.

One result is certainly layoffs. But economy-wide, the loss of potential exports also shows up as a trade deficit. That is, rich countries are importing more than they export, and it's the expendables (and not their bosses) who pay the price with their jobs. Nowhere is this more apparent than in the United States.

The US trade scorecard has never looked worse. The country is running a record trade deficit, and by far the largest component of that figure is its bilateral trade balance with China, where the deficit topped $400 billion in 2018.[4] And 2018 wasn't just a one-off, as President Trump has been only too eager to remind voters. The trade deficit with China averaged more than $300 billion a year for more than a decade, totalling upward of a staggering $3 trillion. The situation remained the same over a number of different administrations; not one was inclined to do much about it.

For the most part, these administrations bought into what their high-powered economic advisors were saying. Typically, those gurus would tell their president that the trade deficit wasn't something Washington needed to worry about—or, for that matter, anything the White House or Congress could actually fix. To try to do so would be misguided, since the deficit itself was in large measure driven by a huge gap in the savings rates between the two countries, along with other macroeconomic forces. As such, it wasn't amenable to trade actions like the imposition of tariffs.

In large measure, the argument goes, the trade imbalance reflects the fact that Chinese households save way too much of their incomes and spend way too little. If Chinese households spent proportionately as much of their incomes as their American counterparts, their economy would be drawing in many more imports than it does today, and China's huge trade surplus with the United States would consequently shrink. Moreover, economic advisors would confidently predict, the Chinese economy would over time evolve toward exporting less and consuming more. Until then, America just had to patient.

Mathematically, the argument is sound enough. The less people save, the more people spend—it's a zero-sum proposition that holds as true in China as it does throughout the world. And there is no debating the huge gap between the two countries' savings rates. China has one of the highest savings rates anywhere in the world, at around 30 percent; the United States had an 8 per cent rate in 2018, roughly a quarter of China's.[5]

Even if Chinese households threw caution to the wind and started to spend like drunken sailors, they wouldn't necessarily be buying US-produced merchandise. America might end up selling China more oil or soybeans, but most of the additional goods a falling savings rate would allow Chinese households to buy aren't even made in the United States anymore. And the few that still are face huge Chinese tariffs.

Economic advisors also cautioned the White House against worrying too much about the job losses that usually accompany large trade deficits. Those jobs, they believed, would be replaced by new and much-higher-value-added jobs. Instead of assembling cars and producing their components, for example, American engineers would do the high-value-added design work on the autonomous and electric vehicles of the future. So, as David Ricardo postulated two centuries ago in his theory of comparative advantage, everyone was going to be better off.

While President Obama basically bought into that carefully triangulated story (as did Presidents Bush and Clinton), President Trump wasn't buying it for a moment. For decades Trump had believed China was ripping off American companies and workers—and now he was in a position to do something about it. He certainly wasn't going to wait around and watch American workers continue to lose their jobs until the Chinese savings rate dropped. And he had no intention of trying to retrain laid-off autoworkers (most of whom had no more than a high-school education) to become engineers and coders. Instead, he was determined to help them keep their existing production-line jobs—the ones for which they were well suited. The best way to do that, he believed, wasn't by staking their livelihoods on negotiations with the WTO, which allowed China to have tariffs that, in the case of autos, were ten times what they were in America. No, the best way to keep automotive jobs, not to mention the jobs of all American factory workers, was through direct—and hard—bargaining with the country that was taking those jobs away.

HIGH NOON AT MAR-A-LAGO

In April 2017, Trump engaged China directly in high-level bilateral talks. He went straight to the top, speaking directly to President Xi Jinping. Not only did this approach steer clear of the WTO bureaucracy and its "rules-based trading system," but it also gave Trump the chance to show off his highly touted skills as a master deal-maker, honed during his career as a Manhattan real estate developer. In a one-on-one meeting at Trump's palatial Mar-a-Lago resort in Palm Beach, Florida, the two men spoke about how to reduce the United States' enormous trade deficit with China.

While the nitty-gritty details of trade negotiations are inherently complex, the reduction of a huge trade imbalance is, in principle, pretty straightforward. When you get right down to basics, there are only two ways for America's trade deficit with China to shrink: either China ramps up the amount of goods it's buying from the United States, or the United States cuts down on the amount of goods it's buying from China. Trump offered Xi the first option, but he threatened to impose crippling tariffs on Chinese imports if the second option were needed.

Enormous as it was, the record trade deficit wasn't the only commercial beef President Trump had with China. Trump reminded Xi, as had other US presidents before him, that China was stealing billons of dollars in intellectual property from US firms. And it was no longer just an Asian factory building knock-off Harley-Davidsons. According to a seven-month study ordered by President Trump and conducted by United States Trade Representative Robert Lighthizer, Chinese firms were stealing between $250 and $600 billion of US intellectual property every year—a sum that, at the top end, was larger than the annual trade deficit.[6] Unlike previous American presidents, however, Trump was prepared to do something about it. He tied the resolution of that issue to any new trade deal China and the United States might negotiate.

While most American businesses, particularly those with supply chains in China, were against the imposition of tariffs on Chinese imports, virtually all businesses were supportive of Trump's initiative to stop Chinese firms from ripping off their technology. The practice is mandated by the very restrictive conditions imposed by the Chinese government on foreign companies that want to do business in the world's second-largest economy. In fact, it's one of government's signature trademarks when it comes to managing the economy. China's regulations compel foreign companies to engage in joint ventures with Chinese partners, and to transfer their technology to them at no cost. For foreign firms, the practice had become an integral cost of doing business in China. In essence, Chinese companies have been allowed to leverage their low wages not once but twice—first to take jobs from the expendables, and again to take technology from Western companies. As with the trade deficit, Trump vowed that intellectual property theft had to be stopped.

THE WAR BEGINS

Despite the personal chemistry the two leaders quickly displayed, Trump and Xi failed to come to terms on a new trade deal. True to his word, Trump followed up on his ultimatum by signing a series of executive orders throughout 2017 and 2018 that slapped tariffs on no less than $250 billion worth of Chinese exports to the United States—covering roughly half of what China exported to the United States every year. Fifty billion dollars' worth of Chinese tech goods—including aerospace, automobiles, communications and robotics—were hit with a crippling 25 percent tariff. A 10 percent tariff was applied to another $200 billion of Chinese imports.

This opening salvo was the largest trade action the United States had ever taken against its Asian rival. In fact, short of the Smoot-Hawley Tariff Act back in 1930, it was the largest trade action that the country had ever taken, period. And President Trump threatened there was a lot more to come if the initial round of tariffs did not elicit a satisfactory new trade deal. He targeted another $267 billion of Chinese imports that would basically cast the tariff net on everything China sold in the American market, and he suggested he would more than double the tariff he'd already imposed.[7]

China, of course, wasn't just going to passively stand by and accept those tariffs without some form of retaliation. It responded by slapping its own tariffs on $110 billion worth of US exports. Moreover, China said it would take other "qualitative" measures against American products.[8] In a non-market economy like China, where the government wields enormous commercial power, qualitative measures can include banning Chinese consumers or businesses from buying specific products from certain countries. You can't sell what no one is willing to buy.

In terms of that level of response, even the hard-nosed Trump administration can't compete with Beijing. When Donald Trump tweeted that Americans needed to boycott Harley-Davidson after the iconic motorcycle manufacturer said it was moving production overseas to avoid European Union tariff retaliation, CNN responded by promoting the bikes.[9] But when President Xi uses the government-controlled internet to tell Chinese consumers and businesses not to purchase certain products—like US soybeans, for example—people do what they are told. American soybean farmers lost their biggest customer literally overnight.

With the clock ticking down to a Smoot-Hawley-type escalation of the tariff war, scheduled to go into effect in early 2019, the two presidents decided to huddle at a private dinner during the late-2018 G20 meetings in Argentina. There, they agreed to a temporary truce. For his part, Trump agreed to postpone the scheduled increase in US tariffs (to 25 percent), as well as the imposition of tariffs on a further $267 billion worth of China's exports. However, the prevailing 10 percent tariff on the originally targeted $200 billion worth of Chinese exports and the 25 percent tariff on another $50 billion worth of high-tech goods would remain in place until a new trade deal could be negotiated. In return, President Xi said that China would resume buying US soybeans and oil. In addition, he promised to cancel the additional 25 percent tariff China had imposed on US-made vehicles.[10]

Not everyone in corporate America is a fan of Trump's decision to engage in a trade war with China. For many companies, China is not only a low-cost source of components in their global supply chain but also an important end market for their products.

Soybean farmers in the US Midwest, for example, suddenly lost the world's largest soybean market—and soybean is the United States' most valuable agricultural export. Roughly a third of China's supply customarily comes from American farmers. In 2017, American soybean farmers sold more than $12 billion worth of their crop to China. But after being targeted by Beijing in retaliation for the imposition of new US tariffs, Chinese purchases of soybean fell to virtually zero in November 2018. As inventories of unsold soybean piled up, US prices took a nosedive, and with them the incomes of US farmers. (That shock has subsequently been lessened by the provision of up to $15 billion of federal aid to US soybean farmers—money Trump claims is being paid through the collection of newly imposed duties on imports from China.)

Nevertheless, President Trump continues to argue that the trade flows between China and the United States are so imbalanced that the United States can't possibly lose in this tariff war. In a big-picture sense, he is right. In 2018, Chinese exports to the United States ($506 billion) were four times greater than the value of US exports to China ($120.3 billion).[11] So if the two countries engage in a tit-for-tat war of matching tariffs, China will run out of US exports to punish well before the United States encounters the same limit against China's exports. And if the tariffs are set so high that they totally shut down bilateral trade between the two largest economies in the world, China's balance of payments would be more than $400 billion to the worse as a result. Moreover, the impact of shutting down exports would be a lot greater on the Chinese economy, where exports have almost twice the weight in the country's GDP as they hold in the United States.[12]

So far, its looks as if Trump is right in claiming that the United States is winning the trade war. Just compare how the two economies are doing since it started. The unemployment rate in the United States is at a half-century low, and the Federal Reserve Board, much to President Trump's chagrin, raised interest rates four times over the course of 2018 to apply a brake to economic growth before Trump literally ordered rate cuts in 2019. On the other side of the Pacific, Chinese economic growth in 2019 decelerated to its slowest pace in twenty-nine years, with weakness in the export sector the primary culprit. According to the country's National Bureau of Statistics, the Chinese economy will continue to face downward pressure on growth, with many now expecting it to grow below the politically mandated minimum annual rate of 6 percent.[13]

Slowing growth in the previous year is what led the People's Bank of China, the country's central bank, to cut the amount of cash that banks have to hold as reserves for the fifth time in a year, freeing up $116 billion for new lending in an effort to prop up flagging economic growth. Even with these measures, Chinese consumers have pulled back their spending. Vehicle sales in the world's largest market fell in 2018 for the first time in nearly two decades, as did cellphone sales. And as the US tariff measures took a bite out of trade, China's export volumes to the United States fell by 9.7 percent on a year-over-year basis in the first four months of 2019.[14]

Bloomberg Economics estimates that Chinese exports to the US from the thousands of categories of goods that have been hit by tariffs since July 2018 are down 26 percent year-over-year in the first quarter of 2019.[15] In many cases, Chinese imports have been replaced by imports from Taiwan, South Korea and Vietnam as more and more companies shift production out of China.

UPPING THE ANTE

A trade war between the two largest economies in the world isn't something global financial markets relish. Disrupting global supply chains potentially threatens the sales and profits of multinational firms all over the world. Even worse, the current slowdown in the Chinese economy has worrisome implications for world economic growth, considering that China single-handedly generated nearly a third of global GDP growth over the last decade.[16]

In early 2019, markets were hoping that a widely circulating rumour was true: China, it went, had offered to buy an additional $1.35 trillion worth of US goods over the next five years in exchange for the United States dropping its tariffs. If nothing else, this quid pro quo would have led to a huge improvement in the US's trade deficit with China, since the reported offer was roughly three times as much as China had imported from the United States over the previous five years. Beefed-up purchases of US oil, liquefied natural gas, agricultural goods and even cars were rumoured to be part of the new trade package.

But the expected deal fell apart in May 2019, with China

allegedly reneging on commitments it had made to Washington earlier in the negotiations. In response, President Trump wasted little time in escalating the trade war: in May 2019, he more than doubled the 10 percent tariff he had earlier imposed on some $200 billion worth of Chinese exports to a trade-stumping 25 percent.[17] In addition, he threatened to extend the tariff to another $300 billion worth of Chinese goods, which would effectively blanket all Chinese exports to the United States with the newly raised 25 percent tariff.

China was quick to retaliate, raising its tariff on some $60 billion worth of US imports to 25 percent as well. But it was running out of room to retaliate further, given that it had already imposed tariffs on $110 billion of the United States' $120 billion worth of exports to the country. The Trump administration, on the other hand, still had room to apply tariffs on close to another $300 billion worth of Chinese exports to the United States, which President Trump said he would do if a new trade deal was not signed.

In June 2019, President Trump again met privately with President Xi at the G20 meeting in Osaka, Japan. As they had done following the Argentina meetings, the two leaders announced a truce in the escalating trade war and a resumption of trade talks. President Trump temporarily lifted the ban on American companies like Google supplying Huawei, but maintained the ban that prevented the Chinese telecom giant from supplying 5G equipment to US carriers. And once again, China failed to deliver on any meaningful trade concessions.

In August 2019, with little progress to report on the renewed trade negotiations, Trump announced that by the end of 2019 he would be placing a tariff on the roughly $300 billion worth of remaining Chinese goods that are shipped to the United States, effectively rendering all of China's exports dutiable in the US market. In September, the Trump administration slapped a tariff of 15 percent on $125 billion worth of Chinese goods, including footwear, apparel and Apple Watches, with announced plans to impose the same tariff on a further $160 billion worth of products, including laptops and cellphones, in mid-December.

Aside from raising their own tariff on US agricultural products, Chinese authorities responded to the latest Trump salvo by deliberately allowing the yuan to depreciate past the psychologically important 7:1 ratio against the US dollar, hitting an eleven-year low against the greenback. A lower yuan exchange rate lowers the price of Chinese exports in the US market and thus partially mitigates the impact of Trump's latest tariff move.

But it does so at a cost to the Chinese economy. First, it's not just the American dollar that the yuan has fallen against—when China devalues the yuan against the dollar, it also devalues the yuan against the yen, pound, euro and most other currencies. That raises the price of all imports, which can't be good news for well-off Chinese consumers, who are renowned for their fondness for European luxury goods. For the manufacturers that currency devaluation is intended to help, the move is a mixed blessing, because it raises the price of the raw materials they typically import. It also can't help but encourage more illicit capital outflows, since wealthy Chinese people will want to park their money abroad instead of seeing its value at home fall steadily with a depreciating currency. Finally, a policy of depreciation undermines Beijing's carefully cultivated plans to make the yuan an international currency that can compete with the US dollar in world financial markets.

Shortly before the US was scheduled to hit Chinese-built smartphones , laptop computers, toys and clothes with a 25 percent tariff on December 15, 2019, the two countries announced a Phase One trade deal, which will bring at least a temporary ceasefire in the ever-escalating trade war between the two countries.[18] For its part, China agreed to boost imports from the US by no less than $200 billion over the next two years. Markets, particularly tech stocks, cheered the news, but there is still no timetable for the negotiation of a more comprehensive Phase Two agreement. Meanwhile, $250 billion of Chinese imports remain subject to a 25 percent American tariff, while another $120 billion of Chinese imports are subject to a reduced 7.5 percent tariff. And the actual trade balance between the two countries will no longer be left to market forces, but instead managed by this and future bilateral trade agreements that will sanction increasing Chinese purchases of American-made goods and services with little or no regard for WTO regulations. With an American election on the horizon in 2020, speculation is widespread that China is delaying a massive trade agreement with the United States in the hope that, in the not-too-distant future, it won't have to deal with Donald Trump anymore. You certainly couldn't blame Beijing for taking this approach. No other American president has come close to Trump in challenging China's commercial relationship with the United States.

But delaying is risky for a few reasons. The most obvious is that, like Bill Clinton, who also faced impeachment, Trump might get re-elected. But even if he doesn't, the tariff war he's set in motion has moved the goalposts significantly for his successor. After three years of escalating trade tensions with China, most Americans, even those who voted against Trump in 2016, have come around to the view that trade between the two countries is heavily skewed in China's favour and must become more balanced.

Even more important than the changing perception of American voters, at least as far as the global trading system is concerned, are rapidly changing corporate expectations. The longer the tariffs remain in place, the more they become the new normal in bilateral trade relations between the world's two largest economies. More and more companies with global supply chains are recognizing the need to adapt to a rapidly changing global trading environment. While most countries initially viewed the outbreak of the US-China trade war as a short-run aberration, fewer and fewer now expect a return to the pre-Trump era of liberalized trade under the auspices of the WTO. They are expecting today's tariffs—or possibly even higher ones in the future—to become the new normal. In response, they are shortening their supply chains and ensuring that they are located in regional trading blocks where they can be sheltered from rising tariff walls. And that means moving production out of China.

SHADES OF REAGAN'S STAR WARS

In many respects, President Trump's decision to engage in a full-fledged trade war with China is reminiscent of (and perhaps even inspired by) Ronald Reagan's decision to escalate the arms race with the Soviet Union back in the 1980s, when the Soviets were the Americans' chief rival.[19] Reagan's Strategic Defense Initiative, popularly dubbed Star Wars at the time, was as much an economic war against the Soviet Union as Trump's tariffs are against China.

The technology required for the Star Wars system to actually work did not exist in the 1980s (it still doesn't), but the programme exerted enormous pressure on the Soviet Union to keep up massive military spending in an already badly stagnating economy. Within half a decade, this contributed to economic collapse and the breakup of the Soviet Union.

President Xi is no Mikhail Gorbachev, whose ill-timed liberal reforms only exacerbated the economic crisis and led to the sudden and shocking downfall of the mighty Soviet empire. The sudden deregulation of the formerly state-controlled economy saw Russia lose nearly 30 percent of its GDP from 1991 to 1998, following the collapse of the Soviet Union.[20] In Russia today, Gorbachev has an approval rating well below that of Joe Stalin.[21] But I'm sure the parallel has crossed Xi's mind, not to mention the minds of others on the ruling politburo.

If the link between military spending and the economy seems far-fetched, it's worth considering the way things looked in 1952.

CHAPTER 9

TARIFF MAN

It wasn't all that long ago that American steel manufacturers, driven by a booming American manufacturing sector, dominated world markets. American mills produced nearly half of the world's steel in the 1950s. Europe and Asia were rebuilding after the Second World War, cities and highways were spreading out, and the economy was booming.

Also, North Korea invaded its southern neighbour, raising the spectre of international communist expansion and drawing the United States, along with Canada and Great Britain, into a war that would soon also involve China. Peace required a lot of steel, but mobilization for war required even more, and American mills ramped up production. But producing more steel was not as simple as the US government simply turning a knob on all the nation's blast furnaces. More spending on steel fuelled spiralling inflation, so the government moved to control the price of steel. Steel companies, which had been making record profits, balked at the price controls and production quotas introduced by the Truman government. And as more and more steel was diverted to military uses, less was left over for more profitable civilian manufacturing.

For their part, the powerful labour unions resisted inflation-fighting wage controls in their crucial industry, which their employers claimed would be necessary to keep the mills solvent if price controls were imposed on their products. The result was a three-way standoff between steelworkers, steel companies and the government that dragged on for months and brought the war effort and the economy to the brink of disaster.

By April 1952, supplies of ammunition were so low that Truman realized even a short strike could tip the balance of power in Korea, bring the economy to a standstill and even halt work on the atomic weapons programme. So when talks collapsed on April 3, and the union announced it would strike the next day, Truman wasted no time. He issued Executive Order 10340 and nationalized the entire steel industry on the grounds of national security.

Twenty-seven minutes later, industry lawyers filed for a restraining order. Faced with a choice between government ownership and striking workers, U.S. Steel and the other American steel companies took their chances with the United Steelworkers and challenged Truman's nationalization order in the courts. Full-page ads defending the steel companies appeared in newspapers across the country the next morning. Truman was compared to Hitler, and there were calls for his impeachment and bills introduced to make the seizure unworkable by denying him funding. But it was the courts that ended the possibility of nationalization. After several weeks of deliberations, the Supreme Court determined the president's constitutional powers did not allow him to seize the steel mills. The government handed back the mills the same day, and the steelworkers went on strike before sun-down. The owners had flexed their muscles. Now it was the unions' turn.

Layoffs in manufacturing industries began two days later, and steel shortages for consumer goods two days after that. Two weeks later, factories making tanks, trucks, rockets and shells were either shutting down or operating on part-time schedules. The auto industry shut down shortly after that. Some union members went back to work just to keep steel available for critical industries. Stockpiles had dwindled to nothing. Half a million workers had been laid off, freight trains were sitting idle, and farm produce was rotting because the steel normally used to can fruit and vegetables had been diverted to more urgent needs (tin cans are actually only between 1 and 2 percent tin).

To break the impasse, Truman prepared to nationalize the industry once again, this time using Section 18 of the Selective Services Act. Although he was on solid legal ground with this effort, the move was highly polarizing. The steel mills would belong to the government, and the steelworkers would be drafted into the US Army in order to keep the mills running. Having made his intentions clear, he put the negotiators for the steelmakers and the unions in a room in the White House and told them not to come out until they had a deal. Though the crisis had dragged on for more than a year, the deal was done within hours.

In the end, the unions got almost everything they had been fighting for. But the cost of the strike to the economy was huge. It was weeks before the furnaces were back up and running and the new steel had been shipped. By that time, unemploy-ment numbers had reached 1.5 million, and more than $4 bil-lion had been lost ($38 billion, in today's dollars). In the end, Truman was correct when he said the steel industry was of vital national importance.[1]

Hopefully the steelworkers savoured their victory—because they haven't had much to cheer about since. The American steel industry peaked in 1973 (around the time that real wages plateaued in the developed world). Since then, the ranks of the steelworkers have been decimated. In the 1950s there were around 650,000 of them. Today, according to the American Iron and Steel Institute, only 140,000 are left. Like most US manufacturing industries, the steel and aluminum industries have been steadily downsized as cheap imports have displaced domestic production, and once high-paying American blue-collar jobs along with it.[2]

If you're looking for the sector that best epitomizes the decline in American manufacturing, the steel industry is right at the top of the (lengthy) list. Once the largest steel producer in the world, the United States is now steel's largest importer, bringing in almost four times what it produces. Meanwhile, China's steel production grew from a fraction of the output of American mills in 1981 to catch up to US production in just over a decade. And since then, it has grown by 800 percent. China, now the world's largest producer by a country mile, accounts for half the world's total. It manufactures as much steel in a month as the US economy produces in a year.[3]

The US steel industry may have been shrinking for decades, but world steel production has certainly not missed its contribution. Global industry estimates put world production anywhere from 20 to 25 percent above demand. When world output is that much higher than what the global market will bear, major steel producers try to dump their product in foreign markets. China, where excess industry capacity is the greatest, has often been accused of this practice. "Dumping" is the commercial practice of selling product abroad at lower prices than at home. In some cases, export market prices aren't just lower than domestic prices but are actually lower than *costs*. Normally, that practice would put you out of business. But when you get state subsidies, as many Chinese steelmakers do, you can afford to sell below cost and just keep producing more steel.

The American aluminum industry hasn't fared any better than the American steel industry. A decade ago there were no less than twenty-three aluminum smelters operating in the country. Only about five are left. Domestic production is down about a third, while imports now account for 90 percent of the primary aluminum used in the US economy.[4] That has cut the ranks of American aluminum workers from forty thousand a decade ago to twenty-eight thousand today.

Not surprisingly, China is also far and away the world's largest aluminum producer, accounting for about half of world output, as it does for steel. Massive growth in the country's aluminum production, most of it state-subsidized, has led to a glut of the metal, depressing global prices. That has had a lethal effect on the non-subsidized American industry and its expendable workers, who have borne the brunt of depressed prices.

SECTION 232: TRUMP'S SECRET WEAPON

If you dust off a copy of the 1962 Trade Expansion Act so carefully crafted by early globalist C. Douglas Dillon, you will find buried within it Section 232—a relatively obscure and arcane provision that cites national security as a justification for tariffs or other forms of trade protection. Under Section 232, if import penetration in a particular sector reaches a level that is deemed by the administration to threaten national security, the president is granted discretion to levy whatever tariffs he deems appropriate. On March 18, 2018, President Trump signed two executive orders based on the presidential authority granted to him under Section 232, placing a 25 percent tariff on all steel imports and a 10 percent tariff on aluminum imports.[5]

Trump is not the first American president to impose tariffs or quotas on steel, and he probably won't be the last. In 1968, the US compelled Japanese and European steel producers to sign voluntary restraint agreements that limited their shipments to the American market for three years. President Nixon imposed tariffs back in the 1970s, as did President George W. Bush in 2002. In fact, President Obama, a committed free trader, was the only recent president not to offer the industry some form of trade protection. Much of the industry is in Pennsylvania, a swing state coveted by both Democrats and Republicans.

Trump is, however, the first US president to refer to himself as "Tariff Man." It's certainly not a label any past American president, at least in the postwar period, would have given himself. And it's a label few economists would endorse. That said, no one can question that he's earned it. Between October 2018 and March 2019, tariff revenue shot up more than 90 percent as a result of the inflow of nearly $24 billion worth of additional tariff revenue generated by the trade measures announced by the Trump administration.[6] And imports from China are by no means the only target. That became painfully apparent to the European Union and America's NAFTA partners Canada and Mexico when President Trump reached deep into his bag of tricks to find a secret weapon to protect American workers in the beleaguered steel and aluminum industries.

Since China is by far the biggest producer of both steel and aluminum, you might naturally think that China is the primary target of the 25 percent tariff on steel imports and 10 percent tariff on aluminum imports. Not so. While the White House often accuses China of dumping both metals and related products into the American market, China supplies only about 2 percent of US steel imports and 8 percent of its aluminum, according to 2017 data. The Trump administration claims China supplies much more through transshipments from other countries, but an investigation by the US Commerce Department was unable to quantify just how much Chinese steel and aluminum entered the American market that way. The fact is, most of those imports originate somewhere else entirely.

CANADA, NOT CHINA, HAD THE MOST TO LOSE

Trace the origin point for most of America's steel and, especially, aluminum, and an interesting fact emerges: the real target of all these tariffs is the United States' friendly neighbour to the north—and, to a lesser extent, its allies in the European Union. In other words, this is a trade war between friends and military allies, not between political adversaries and competing world powers, which makes the national security rationale behind the tariffs seem more than a little bizarre.

Although the American tariffs weren't specifically directed at Canada, Canadian exporters were the most severely affected, since Canada is the largest foreign supplier of both metals to the American marketplace. In 2017, Canada shipped $5.1 billion worth of steel to the United States, or one-sixth of total US steel imports. It was an even bigger player in the US aluminum market. In 2017, it shipped $7.4 billion worth of aluminum, accounting for more than a third of total US aluminum imports and more than 80 percent of total Canadian aluminum production. Provinces such as Quebec and British Columbia, both blessed with abundant and cheap hydro power, have built huge aluminum industries that supply the US market. Given their close proximity, and hence low freight costs, they had an important leg up on the rest of the world when it came to competing in the US market.

Brazil, South Korea, Mexico and Russia follow Canada as leading steel exporters to the United States. The European Union is also a major supplier, with large steel industries in Germany, France and Italy. The impact of the steel and aluminum tariffs on Mexico, America's other NAFTA partner, was significant, though it paled in comparison to the impact on Canada. Mexico exports about $2.5 billion worth of steel (half the Canadian level) to the American market, and about $500 million worth of aluminum (less than a tenth of the Canadian export level).

Initially, Canada and Mexico were granted a temporary exemption from the steel and aluminum tariffs, as they were in the midst of renegotiating NAFTA with the Trump administration. But when each country refused the settlement conditions demanded by Washington, tariffs were imposed on Canadian and Mexican exports as of June 1, 2018. That put the US steelworkers union in a tough spot.

Not only has Canada sent about half of its steel exports to the United States, but it also exported Leo Gerard, at that time the international head of the United Steelworkers of America union, whose membership spans both sides of the border. Given that Gerard represented both American and Canadian steelworkers, the tariffs put him in a difficult position. While Gerard applauded Trump's move to protect jobs in the US steel industry, he simultaneously sought a permanent Canadian exemption from the newly imposed American steel tariff, arguing that Canada was not the source of cheap steel being dumped into the US market, and that the Canadian and American steel industries were highly integrated and hence interdependent. His pleas, however, fell on deaf ears at the White House, which was looking for trade concessions in exchange for dropping the tariffs against any country. This was especially true when it came to Canada, which exported more steel and aluminum to the US market than any other country in the world.

Understandably, all of America's trading partners condemned the move as blatantly protectionist, but none was more outraged than Canada. Canada had the most to lose. Canadian trade officials argued that both aluminum and steel fell under NAFTA's provisions and hence should be exempt from tariffs. But chief US trade negotiator Robert Lighthizer, no doubt with the president's urging, insisted otherwise. He argued that the tariffs on aluminum and steel were separate issues, and that even if NAFTA were successfully renegotiated there would have to be stand-alone sectoral agreements covering them—in much the same way Washington and Ottawa had come to a separate agreement over softwood lumber. Then and only then would Washington lift the tariffs on Canadian steel and aluminum exports.

The Canadian government took particular offence over the national security grounds being used to justify the tariffs on Canadian steel and aluminum. Canada was America's trusted partner in NORAD (the joint North American Aerospace Defense Command), representatives argued, as well as a steadfast ally and close neighbour. It could hardly be perceived by the White House to be a security threat.

The Canadians had a point, but it was the wrong point. When President Truman acted to nationalize the steel industry in the 1950s, he had reason to believe that a lengthy US steel strike would pose a legitimate national security risk that could undermine the war effort at the height of the Korean conflict. This time around, however, neither Trump nor anyone in his administration really considered Canadian steel and aluminum—or, for that matter, imports of the same from the European Union—to pose a real national security threat. It wasn't national security that the Trump administration was trying to protect. It was the jobs of American steel and aluminum workers. And while the Canadian government feigned moral outrage and indignation, everyone on both sides of the negotiating table understood what was really going on.

What Lighthizer and the Trump administration were really angling for when they slapped tariffs on steel and aluminum imports was leverage to negotiate quota agreements on how much steel and aluminum its major suppliers could export to its market. It was turning back the clock on world trading rules, harkening back to a time when countries used to rely on absolute quotas instead of tariffs to limit the amount of imports they were going to allow into their markets.

For the last several decades, the WTO (and its predecessor GATT) has been working earnestly to rid the world of trade quotas that countries would often impose to limit import penetration of their markets. As an initial step, the world trade body sought the "tariffication" of quotas—that is, converting quotas that had defined an absolute ceiling for imports into a tariff equivalent where market forces were given more sway in determining actual import levels. Now, under the Trump administration, tariffs were being replaced by hard quotas limiting how much one country could export to another. If the original replacement of quotas with tariffs made it easier for imports to displace domestic jobs, the subsequent replacement of tariffs with quotas would help bring them back.

Faced with the newly imposed US tariffs, South Korea quickly agreed to a quota rumoured to be a third less than its current level of steel and aluminum exports to the United States. In exchange, South Korean producers were exempted from paying the Section 232 tariffs. Argentina, Australia and Brazil also agreed to quotas, and in return were granted exemptions from the US tariffs.

However, not every country capitulated. Initially, an out-raged Canada and Mexico stated that they could not sign a new trade deal with the United States while the American tariffs on steel and aluminum were still in effect. Both later reconsidered that stance and signed on to a new deal, although both claimed they could not ratify the agreement until the tariffs were dropped. Nor, for that matter, did the European Union agree to any quotas on their steel and aluminum exports to the United States.

Since all of the countries hit by American tariffs had large sectoral trade surpluses with the United States, they couldn't just respond by imposing reciprocal tariffs. There simply wasn't enough US steel or aluminum heading into their markets to offset the dollar impact that the American tariffs had on their own metal exports. So they had to impose tariffs on a whole range of other US exports to make their retaliatory tariffs cover the same value of goods that the American tariffs affected.

In the European Union's case, tariffs were slapped on a wide range of American goods, from bourbon to motorcycles to farm products, covering no less than $3.2 billion worth of US exports. Canada, for its part, not only imposed its own retaliatory tariffs on steel and aluminum imports, but also on seventy-one other categories of industrial and consumer goods, hitting some $16 billion worth of American exports. Mexico slapped tariffs on US agricultural products, among other American exports.

While both Canada and Mexico were reportedly prepared to accept quotas in principle in order to get exemptions from the US tariffs, they were willing to do so only if the quotas allowed for substantial export growth from current levels. In the end, their obstinacy paid off. After almost a year with tariffs in place, the stalemate with Washington ended when Trump, having just escalated the trade war with China, agreed to drop the tariffs against Canada and Mexico in May 2019.[7]

There was jubilation in Ottawa and Mexico City, with Canadian and Mexican government officials congratulating themselves on not giving in to Trump's demands for a quota. But the victory wasn't quite as decisive as their governments made it out to be. While there is no hard-ceiling quota like those the United States was able to secure from other countries, such as South Korea and Brazil, the new agreement stops well short of calling for the restoration of free and unmanaged trade flows of aluminum and steel products between the United States, Canada and Mexico.

The new agreement has a "trap door." Should there be any surge in exports from either Canada or Mexico, the United States reserves the right to reimpose the tariffs. And it is left to the capricious Trump administration to determine just what constitutes a surge. While Canada and Mexico are allowed to retaliate should the US reimpose the tariffs, the agreement specifies that, unlike in the past, they can retaliate only with tariffs against American steel or aluminum products, and not the wide range of goods they targeted before. The problem with that, as China has discovered, is that tit-for-tat tariff retaliation works only when both sides have the same value of goods to tariff.

THE US-EU BATTLEFRONT

With the dropping of the steel and aluminum tariffs against Canada and Mexico, all is quiet on the North American front of the trade wars, at least for the moment. But the transatlantic trade war is still escalating. Not only are tariffs on EU steel and aluminum imports still in effect, but Trump has threatened to impose tariffs as high as 100 percent on as much as $8 billion worth of imports from the EU—a figure the US claims matches the subsidies the EU has given its airplane manufacturer, Airbus.[8] In April 2019, US Trade Representative Lighthizer identified $7 billion worth of EU imports that could be tariffed and added another $4 billion to the list later in July.

Interestingly, this trade dispute long predates Trump. Washington and the EU have been locked in a dispute over subsidies to aircraft manufacturers for more than a decade and a half, with both sides claiming the other has violated trade rules by massively subsidizing its airplane manufacturers— Boeing and Airbus, the two largest in the world.

While tariffs have already been slapped on steel and aluminum, there is a bigger target lurking in the White House's gun sights. A US Department of Commerce study undertaken at the president's request found that auto imports have reached a level that poses a national security risk and could trigger Section 232 of the Trade Expansion Act. President Trump has threatened to impose a 25 percent duty on European and Asian car imports—ten times the current rate.[9] In May 2019, Trump decided to delay the promised move by up to 180 days in an attempt to clinch an effective trade deal with its partners. He is widely expected to further delay implementation of the tariff for another six months in exchange for greater investment by foreign car manufacturers in the United States.

WHO IS PAYING FOR THE TARIFFS AND WHO IS BENEFITING FROM THEM?

There is no question that tariffs have raised billions of dollars for the US Treasury. But the real question is, who is paying for them. Technically, tariffs are paid by US-registered firms to US customs for the goods those firms import into the United States. That much is clear. But the issue of who ultimately bears the real economic cost isn't as black and white.

Corporate America doesn't like Trump's tariffs because they threaten its profitable supply chains. Corporations have been publicly denouncing the tariffs, claiming that it's their customers—and not Chinese or other foreign exporters—who are being forced to pay for them through higher prices. For example, Nike and more than a hundred other shoe companies are warning that tariffs will cost Americans upward of $7 billion annually in higher shoe prices. Walmart, the nation's largest retailer, is similarly warning that its prices will have to rise. The aluminum tariff was even cited as reason why Americans would soon be paying more for their cans of beer. Heavy equipment manufacturer Caterpillar and tractor company John Deere both claim that tariffs have added $100 million a year to their costs, forcing them to hike prices to customers. Everyone from the pro–free trade Peterson Institute for International Economics[10] to the New York Federal Reserve Board has published studies estimating the billions of dollars that consumers have been forced to pay because of tariffs.

The one thing they are not telling you is the answer to this question: If everyone's prices are rising, why aren't those increases showing up in inflation? It's not that there hasn't been enough time for all those tariff-induced price hikes to show up in the inflation rate. The tariffs on China were imposed in 2018. Those on steel and aluminum lasted almost a year against Canada, America's largest supplier of both metal products, and are still in place against many other countries, including those in the EU. Yet in the third year of Tariff Man's administration, consumer price inflation is still well behaved, tracking for most of the time below the Federal Reserve Board's 2 percent target. So, if double-digit tariffs are indeed causing American consumers to pay billions more in higher prices, as industry claims, why aren't all those price hikes having an effect on the US consumer price inflation rate?

Maybe because it's not American consumers who are really paying for the tariffs. While that possibility gets little credence in the business press, it's the obvious explanation for why, despite pervasive tariffs, inflation remains subdued.

If you are an American corporation whose Chinese supply chain has been hit with a 25 percent tariff, you have three choices. First, you can pass the cost of the tariff on to the final price of whatever you are selling to your consumers, as industry widely claims it is being forced to do and as all those studies that estimate the cost to consumers routinely assume. But you can also do something else, which industry seldom mentions. Your second choice is to allow the tariff to eat into your margin, or force your Chinese suppliers to eat into theirs by discounting their selling price to compensate you for the tariff. That way, the price being charged to American consumers doesn't change, even though the tariff is being applied. And then there's the third option, which more and more companies are taking: move your supply chain somewhere else that isn't subject to tariffs like those being imposed on goods from China. When this option is chosen, countries like Vietnam and India are the big winners. China may not be paying for the American tariffs in the literal sense that President Trump claims, but the Chinese economy is nevertheless paying for them in other ways.

Companies from Apple to Google to Dell are shifting production out of their once-favoured country in response to US trade actions. Google has already moved assembly of its motherboards to Taiwan and is shifting production of Nest thermostats and server hardware out of China as well. Hewlett-Packard plans to relocate parts of its personal computer production to Southeast Asia. Foxconn, the giant Taiwanese assembler of Apple phones, is also considering moving production out of China, fearing that mounting trade tensions between China and the United States could jeopardize its shipments to the US market. Apple is rumoured to be considering shifting as much as 30 percent of its production from China to Southeast Asia, while Japan-based Nintendo has announced it will be moving the manufacturing of its video game consoles from China to Vietnam.

Similarly, Giant Manufacturing, the world's largest producer of bikes, has shifted some of its production out of China and now supplies its American market from factories in Taiwan to avoid paying Trump's tariffs.[11] Samsung Electronics is gradually shifting its supply chains out of China and into neighbouring Vietnam. The Korean electronics giant closed its Shenzhen production line in May 2018, followed by its Tianjin factory in December, and it plans to close its remaining iPhone production line in Huizhou as well.

In all of these cases, it's not American consumers who are paying for the tariffs. Instead, it's the Chinese economy that is losing investment, production and jobs.

Of course, you can argue that moving production from China to Vietnam or India doesn't create much-needed decent-paying middle-class jobs for American workers. But Vietnam and India aren't the only places seeing an uptick in manufacturing jobs.

Back in the final months of his administration, President Obama stated that manufacturing jobs were simply not going to be coming back.[12] Well, they certainly weren't with his administration kowtowing to the WTO's so-called rules-based trading system. But after the first two years of Tariff Man's administration, manufacturing employment has increased by almost half a million jobs. In 2018, the 264,000 new manufacturing jobs represented the highest number of new workers hired in the sector since 1988. As a percent of the total workforce, manufacturing rose for the first time since 1984.[13]

Tariffs are certainly helping the profitability of US steel companies, who are now sheltered from cutthroat import competition, if not outright dumping, by either the tariffs themselves or the quotas they have levered. Now sheltered from foreign competition, Nucor, the largest American steel producer, had record earnings in 2018, while competitor U.S.

Steel tripled its earnings. As a result, we are seeing new plants being built. Nucor is planning to open a new $240 million steel mill in central Florida, creating 250 jobs, while U.S. Steel is restarting production and rehiring five hundred laid-off employees in Granite City, Illinois.

Tariffs seem to be having the same effect on the once beleaguered US aluminum industry. Production, investment and employment in the industry are all up since the tariffs were imposed. In upstream production, Century Aluminum, Magnitude 7 Metals and Alcoa are either restarting plants or expanding production, adding more than a thousand jobs to industry payrolls. Double that number are being hired in the downstream industry (fabrication of aluminum products). For example, Braidy Industries recently announced it would spend $1.3 billion to build a new aluminum mill in Ashland, Kentucky, which will create 550 new manufacturing jobs earning an average annual salary of $65,000. Sure beats working in an Amazon warehouse or a Walmart store.[14]

Creating more middle-class jobs means creating opportunities for wage growth. While the recovery in wages has lagged well behind the recovery in manufacturing jobs, there are some hopeful signs. As of November 2019, average hourly earnings by the typical American worker had grown at or above 3 percent for sixteen consecutive months, the highest sustained rate of increase in a decade.[15] Moreover, juxtaposed against a still sub-2 percent inflation rate, it gave American workers something they haven't seen in a long time—a real-wage increase.

With the prospect of tariff protection remaining in place, the outlook for wages has not been this positive for a long time. American steelworkers are now in a position to bargain for wage increases. As the new trade rules swing the policy pendulum back in favour of domestic producers, it's only a matter of time before United Steelworkers' union members help themselves to a bigger slice of that suddenly growing industry pie. They may not be able to bring the economy to a shuddering halt, as they did in 1952, but for the first time in decades they no longer seem so expendable.

CHAPTER 10

MAYBE WHAT'S GOOD FOR
AMERICAN WORKERS ISN'T GOOD FOR GM

Oshawa, Ontario, may not get a lot of tourists, but those who make the trip tend to visit Parkwood Estate. Designed by the architectural firm of Darling and Pearson, who are better known for their elegant public buildings and the iconic tower of the Canadian Parliament, the sprawling Beaux-Arts mansion boasted extensive gardens and every luxury imaginable when built in 1915. Preserved as a point of civic pride, Parkwood today gives a glimpse of the wealth available to a carriage-maker who was building buggies and cutters when the automobile age arrived. (Movie fans may recognize it as the exterior of the Xavier School for Gifted Youngsters in the *X-Men* franchise.)

As it turned out, cars and globalization grew up together. In fact, if not for Canadian Samuel McLaughlin—the man who built Parkwood—there probably wouldn't be a global company called General Motors today.

McLaughlin's father, Robert, was one of the biggest carriage-makers in Canada. We tend to think of horse-drawn carriages as relics from a pre-industrial past, but that doesn't give the Robert McLaughlins of the world quite enough credit. He could churn out twenty-five thousand carriages a year in 1898; by 1915, he was building one every ten minutes.[1]

But there was a lot more going on in the early twentieth century than cutting-edge carriage-making. In 1908, Sam McLaughlin went into business with his friend, American carriage-maker William Durant. Like the McLaughlins, Durant had leveraged a carriage business to get into cars. The Canadians had launched the McLaughlin Motor Car Company with their wealth, and Durant had bought a struggling startup called Buick. When the McLaughlins had problems sourcing drivetrains, they signed a fifteen-year deal with Buick to supply them. McLaughlin now had the parts it needed, and Buick had the cash flow it required to survive. The two companies soon traded stock, and McLaughlin-Buick was formed. It would later become General Motors.

Car companies today love globalization, but Robert McLaughlin was staunchly against free trade with the United States, an idea floated by Wilfrid Laurier that outlasted his tenure as prime minister. Because Canada was part of the British Empire, McLaughlin could export carriages and cars tariff-free throughout the Commonwealth. And they did, shipping right-hand-drive versions of their cars to the United Kingdom, Australia, South Africa and India—markets that were protected from American imports. By 1923, Canada had the second-largest car industry in the world. McLaughlin had the best of both worlds—tariffs *and* global markets.

The writing was on the wall after the Second World War, however, when Canada joined the "Dollar Area." Great Britain was protecting its rebuilding auto industry with steep tariffs, and Sam McLaughlin suddenly faced the same tariffs in the Commonwealth as American car manufacturers did. The last

McLaughlin-Buick was built in 1942. After that, they were just Buicks.[2]

For his part, Durant had a tempestuous career. He built GM by adding Cadillac, Oldsmobile and the company that would later be known as Pontiac, along with several parts and paint suppliers. But he took on so much debt that he was ousted from the company in 1910. Undiscouraged, he partnered with a Swiss race-car driver named Louis Chevrolet to build a rival company—which soon merged with GM. By 1916, Durant had regained control of the company he'd founded alongside McLaughlin. It must have been a lively board. By 1920, Durant had been ousted again. He tried building a third company, Durant Motors, with a factory in Leaside, Ontario, now a neighbourhood in Toronto. But he couldn't pull off a third success to rival GM and Chevy. He was ruined by the Wall Street crash of 1929, and ended up bankrupt, living off a pension supplied by Sam McLaughlin.

McLaughlin Motors is long gone, and Parkwood Estate is a designated historic site. It turns out, even tycoons like Durant and his buddy McLaughlin were expendable. But the company they created, its executives claim, is not. Nearly one hundred years later, GM was deemed too big to fail, and the erstwhile advocates of competition and efficiency who ran the giant company went cap-in-hand to the Canadian and American governments, asking for billions in loans. Even as they take handouts from the countries that built them, the big car manufacturers have been steadily shutting down plants on both sides of the border. Oshawa and Detroit are hollowed-out shells of what they were when Durant and McLaughlin built what was for a long time the biggest car company in the world. As bad as it got for Durant by the end, it's gotten a lot worse for the people who used to work for GM.

The North American auto industry is a microcosm of everything that is either right or wrong with today's global trading system—depending on which end of the stick you happen to be holding. No industry better illustrates how globalization creates winners and losers.

THE CANADA-US AUTO PACT

Up until 1965, the North America car industry operated separately in the continent's three countries. Mexico's auto market, like those in many Latin American countries, was highly protected by tariffs, meaning that if you wanted to sell cars in Mexico, you had better produce them there. The Canadian market was also bounded by high tariffs, even though McLaughlin Motors had been gobbled up by General Motors long before. High tariffs meant minimal cross-border trade.

In order to provide Canadian customers with at least a semblance of choice when it came to shopping for a vehicle, American car manufacturers operating north of the border were forced to run very short production lines, given the small size of the Canadian market. That constraint prevented their Canadian branch plants from achieving the same economies of scale that American plants reaped serving their home market, which was ten times the size. Typically, the productivity of Canadian auto plants was only 60 to 65 percent of the levels of their larger-scale American counterparts.[3] The result was much higher production costs in Canada, and hence much higher vehicle prices for Canadian car buyers, as well as a much more limited selection of models.

That all changed when the United States and Canada signed the historic Auto Pact in 1965. In exchange for granting Canadian consumers duty-free access to American-produced vehicles, the Auto Pact guaranteed production in Canada by American car manufacturers at least equivalent to the size of their vehicle sales in the Canadian market. Equating production with sales was the essential quid pro quo that made the agreement work.

With tariffs no longer blocking the Canadian border, American car manufacturers were free to sell their US-produced cars in Canada without having to set up inefficient production facilities north of the border. In return, instead of trying to manufacture a whole range of different models in short and uneconomic production runs for the Canadian market, American auto manufacturers could instead use their Canadian plants to produce specific models in huge production runs to supply markets on both sides of the border. Canadian plants were suddenly re-engineered to achieve economies of scale they never could have attained in a small and highly fragmented domestic market.

That was a win-win for everyone concerned. Canadian car buyers suddenly got a better selection of vehicles at better prices than ever before. And GM, Ford and Chrysler got to transform their scale-inefficient Canadian plants into factories designed for the much broader continental marketplace. It was also a win for autoworkers—they had jobs.

As successful as the Auto Pact was for both countries, it was not a free trade agreement. It was instead a *managed* trade agreement based on the requirement that US firms had to produce as many cars in Canada as they sold in the country—a condition that they successfully met during the lifetime of the agreement. Canada was guaranteed never to see its industry downsized because of imports of cheaper-priced American-made cars.

In fact, there was nothing to stop US car manufacturers from moving even more of their production to Canada and producing in excess of their Canadian sales numbers. Some actually did. The Auto Pact safeguards were directed at guaranteeing a minimum level of Canadian production, not American production. But there was no real economic incentive for a massive shift of production to Canada, which is why the agreement worked so well for so long for autoworkers on both sides of the border.

Locating production in Canada did come with certain advantages. Public health care in Canada meant that companies like GM didn't have to shell out for the costly company health-care plans it had to fund for its American workforce. And a Canadian dollar that was often worth 20 percent less than the US dollar provided incentives for Canadian production. But these economic advantages were effectively offset by the Canadian Auto Workers union, which typically negotiated larger wage increases for its membership than their American counterpart—in effect capturing the economic advantages that public health care and a cheaper currency provided. All things considered, manufacturing costs were pretty well equalized across the border.

Industry production grew strongly in both countries, riding the coattails of ever-rising North American vehicle sales. In 1987, the Auto Pact was superseded by the Canada-US Free Trade Agreement. By that time, the Canadian and American industries had become pretty well integrated, with parts plants in one country often supplying assembly plants in the other. Under NAFTA, the expendables on both sides of the border would come to miss those days.

NAFTA: CHANGING THE PLAYING FIELD

Back in 1953, President Eisenhower tapped former GM CEO and president Charles Erwin Wilson for the job of secretary of defence. His nomination proved controversial, however, because of his links to his former company. Critics wondered whether he would be able to navigate ethically between what was good for GM, which had extensive defence contracts, and what was good for the country. During his confirmation hearing before the Senate Armed Services Committee, Wilson answered the criticism with the observation that "for years, I thought that what was good for our country was good for General Motors, and vice versa."[4]

It does make a certain sense that what is good for key industries is good for the country where those industries pay taxes and employ people. But Wilson didn't really speak for GM as a whole. He spoke as someone who had been on the board. More importantly, he spoke as someone who still held $2.5 million worth of stock in the company, or $19 million in today's money.[5] What was good for the country, and the company, might look very different to someone who counted on the automaker not for investment income but for wages.

NAFTA illustrates that divergence of interests perfectly. Before it came into effect, what was good for the automakers was good for both Canada and the United States. Afterward, the opposite was true. As soon as Mexico was included in the North American free trade zone, the idea that country and company could benefit from the same policy changed dramatically. The win-win was no more.

All of a sudden, a country whose wages were a fraction of those in either the United States or Canada was a member of a trade agreement that allowed for the duty-free movement of vehicles and parts. Mexico provided the auto industry with a convenient low-wage jurisdiction in which to relocate supply chains, one much cheaper than Canada and much closer to the US domestic market than the offshore labour markets in Asia. If you were an auto company executive, the temptations were irresistible.

In 1994, Mexico's auto industry was relatively small, producing 1.1 million vehicles a year—almost all for its own highly protected domestic market. Canada's production was over twice as much (2.3 million units), and US production, at 12.1 million units, was over ten times Mexico's output.[6]

After a little more than two decades under NAFTA, the auto industry is barely recognizable. Neither US nor Canadian production has grown for almost twenty years, despite huge gains in North American vehicle sales. But Mexican production has *quadrupled* to over 4 million units. The country's share of North American production has tripled from a meagre 7 percent to over 20 percent. During that time period the United States' share shrank from 78 percent to 67 percent, while Canada's share also declined, to around 13 percent.[7] Virtually all of the gains in North American vehicle production since 2000 have come from Mexico, as every year more and more of the industry's plants and equipment have moved across the Rio Grande.

As production shifted, so did industry trade flows. Mexico's trade surplus with the United States in autos and parts more than quadrupled under NAFTA. Autos and parts have so dominated US-Mexican trade that Mexico's industry trade surplus in vehicles and parts with the United States is greater than its entire trade surplus with the country (meaning that Mexico runs a small trade deficit in the rest of its trade with its northern neighbour, particularly in agricultural products). Similarly, Mexico's trade surplus in autos and parts with Canada has quadrupled.[8]

In contrast to the exploding trade deficits that the United States and Canada have both incurred with Mexico in industry trade, Canada's trade balance with the United States in autos and parts is basically at the same level that it was back when NAFTA first went into effect. What has kept the trade balance more or less in check is the way the industry was structured. While Canada enjoyed a trade surplus in assembled vehicles, it at the same time incurred a deficit in auto parts. The two trade flow patterns were largely interconnected and hence counteracting. The more vehicles Canada exported to the United States, the more parts it imported from south of the border to build those vehicles. So as Canada's surplus in vehicle trade with the United States grew, so too did its offsetting deficit in the trade in vehicle parts.

It isn't hard to figure out why both the United States and Canada were suddenly racking up huge trade deficits with Mexico in the vehicle and parts industry. Just follow the dotted line to where the industry was investing, and the trade flows between the countries suddenly come into focus. Virtually all of the industry's new investment had gone to Mexico. And all you had to do was compare wage rates between the three countries to know why all the new plants were being built there and not in Detroit or Oshawa. While wage costs were more or less the same on either side of the US-Canada border, Mexican wages in the industry were as little as an eighth of those paid to either American or Canadian autoworkers.

Mexico, as it turns out, not only offers much lower wage costs than in the United States or Canada, but also sports one of the lowest wages of any auto manufacturer in the world. The Mexican auto industry was able to avoid the industrial unrest that forced up wage rates in China's auto sector. Since 2009, Chinese wage rates in the sector have risen above Mexico's, and the wage gap has steadily widened in Mexico's favour, with hourly wages that are now half those paid in the Chinese industry.[9]

If you're wondering how wages could have remained so low in such a booming industry for so long, Mexican workers have their unions to thank.

MEXICO'S PROTECTION UNIONS

Virtually all workers employed in Mexico's auto industry are union members, as are almost 90 percent of Mexican workers employed in industrial enterprises with at least twenty-five employees. But belonging to a union in Mexico is a very different proposition from belonging to one in the United States or Canada. The vast majority of Mexican autoworkers belong to what are known as "ghost unions" or "protection unions." And it's not the membership that's being protected.

By ensuring that employers are protected from strikes and worker demands for better wages and benefits, protection unions safeguard the interests of the very companies they are supposedly engaged with on behalf of their workers. It's collective bargaining turned on its head. Not only are workers excluded from the arm's-length negotiating process, they are also never asked to ratify any agreement that their union makes. They are simply told, after the fact, what they will be paid—and they are expected to like it.

For their services, union leadership is paid handsomely by the companies through kickbacks. So much so that the workers, just like in American right-to-work states, don't have to pay union dues. That is just as well. For all intents and purposes, they don't belong to a union but to a corporate charade. Workers who attempt to organize independent unions are usually fired.

Once in a blue moon, workers rebel anyway. Back in 2010, workers at an auto parts company in Puebla owned by the US-based multinational Johnson Controls stood up to their company-controlled protection union and joined the Miners' and Metalworkers' Union—a real labour organization. They immediately won a huge 7 percent wage hike and a big increase in non-wage benefits, but the victory was Pyrrhic. The company has since closed the plant.

Little wonder. In Mexico, labour agreements are factory-specific, not companywide. So if workers in a particular plant finally break free of their protection unions, the company can just shut down the facility and open a new one.

Technically, NAFTA required that all three countries comply with International Labour Organization (ILO) standards. When Mexico was taken to task for its protection unions by the ILO, the government denied their existence. Nevertheless, former president Enrique Peña Nieto would often extol the country's seemingly miraculous record of labour peace when courting foreign investment. Of course, the labour peace wasn't so miraculous. It's part of the institutional fabric of the country.

Protection unions emerged from the very heart of Mexico's political system. The country's largest union, the Confederación de Trabajadores de México (CTM), was created as part of the ruling Institutional Revolutionary Party (PRI) back in the 1930s. Membership in the union automatically meant membership in the party. So, when elections came around, union bosses were able to deliver a captive blue-collar vote.

The arrangement has outlasted the PRI's decades-long rule of Mexico. The government (whatever its political stripe), corporations and their crony unions continue to work closely to hold down labour costs in the name of enhancing Mexico's global competitiveness. And as you can see from what's happened in the auto and parts industry, the model is working very well.

The wages paid to Mexican autoworkers may be a fraction of what American or Canadian workers get paid, but auto-manufacturing work is still considered a plum job in a country where the minimum wage is five dollars a day.[10] Some Mexican autoworkers actually live in gated communities, a popular choice with Mexico's middle class given the notorious corruption of local police and the security problems that creates. All the same, real wages for Mexican autoworkers haven't grown in decades, and continually trail behind productivity gains.

Getting a protection union agreement to hold down wage costs isn't just an option available to employers—it's an integral part of investing in a new car plant in Mexico. You don't invest there until you get yourself a union. When BMW decided to invest $1 billion to build a new assembly plant in San Luis Potosí that will soon employ fifteen hundred workers, the first thing it did was negotiate a wage contract with a protection union from the CTM. It was a sweet deal for BMW. The German multinational agreed to pay a starting wage of $1.10 per hour and a top wage of $2.53 in the plant.[11] For BMW, as is the case for other companies coming to Mexico to produce vehicles, it was important to have wage certainty before committing to become part of Mexico's industrial landscape. The wage contract was signed two years before BMW started building its plant.

Unlike his pro-business predecessor Nieto, newly elected president Andrés Manuel López Obrador comes from a labour background. As part of the 2019 trade agreement with the United States and Canada, he readily agreed to pass legislation that will give Mexican workers the right to organize real unions that engage in true collective bargaining with employers.[12] It will be interesting to see how exactly the López Obrador government, which came to power on an election pledge of raising wages and defending workers' rights, walks this narrow tightrope. Getting rid of crony unions and replacing them with real unions will certainly go a long way toward supporting chronically overdue wage growth for Mexican autoworkers. But if the promised labour reforms prove too successful, they will undermine the very basis for those auto jobs existing in Mexico in the first place.

Corporations like GM and auto-parts manufacturer Magna aren't in Mexico for the weather. They are down there in ever-greater scale precisely to take advantage of the cheap labour the country's workforce provides. And while there is an enormous wage gap to close with American and Canadian workers, the narrower that gap gets, the less attractive Mexico becomes as a destination for new plants and jobs.

MOVING UP THE VALUE-ADDED CHAIN

The moving of production to Mexico didn't happen overnight. That great sucking sound that Ross Perot warned Americans of back in the early 1990s was barely a whisper at the time. At first, only the most menial of jobs and the lowest-value-added components of the vehicle supply chain could be farmed out to Mexico's unskilled low-wage workers under NAFTA. Low wages didn't help the bottom line if they were accompanied by low productivity. But over time, Mexican workers steadily climbed the rungs of the value-added ladder. The large productivity gap between them and their American and Canadian counterparts closed rapidly. These days, even the most complex components—like engines or transmissions—can be built in Mexican plants. But with Mexico's auto wages continuing to lag well behind productivity gains in the sector, unit labour costs steadily fall, giving manufacturers larger and larger profit margins.

That's precisely what you're looking for if you are a shareholder in GM or Magna. As an investor, you want as much of your company's production to be moved to Mexico as possible. Why pay twenty or thirty dollars an hour for labour when you can get the same manufacturing quality for four dollars or less? Since NAFTA meant vehicle and parts companies no longer faced any steep tariff penalty for moving production from high-wage plants in the United States or Canada to low-wage plants in Mexico, the trade agreement made such calculations possible. NAFTA allowed auto and parts firms to do what the huge wage gap between Mexican and other North American workers compelled them to do. That was a game changer for the profitability of the North American auto industry—and an even greater game changer for the livelihood of its American and Canadian workforces.

Auto and parts companies have relocated to Mexico on a scale few (other than Ross Perot) expected when NAFTA was signed in 1992, leaving almost half a million workers without their once high-paying jobs in the United States and Canada. This departure was compounded by the mass movement of manufacturing jobs to China after China joined the WTO in 2001. So when someone like President Trump talks about a trade deficit, what he's really talking about is a *jobs* deficit.

The auto companies haven't done anything wrong, per se. On the contrary, according to their shareholders they are doing everything right. They were doing exactly what the trade rules under NAFTA and the wage differences between Mexico and its NAFTA partners were instructing them to do. After all, management's mandate is not to protect high-paying auto-manufacturing jobs in the United States or Canada. Management's mandate is ultimately to make money for shareholders, and they have done that in the way that best suited the circumstances of the day.

Employment in both the American and Canadian industries peaked two decades ago—when production peaked as well. Since then, the labour force in both countries has shrunk by more than a quarter, costing almost 400,000 auto jobs in the United States and another 50,000 in Canada. Meanwhile, employment in the Mexican industry has more than quadrupled to over 900,000, about seven times the entire auto-industry workforce remaining in Canada.[13]

But, curiously, if you ask auto-industry executives why all their jobs in the United States and Canada have vanished, they will tell you it has little to do with where they've moved their factories. Instead, they point to their machines.

BLAME THE ROBOTS

When it comes to an explanation for the job losses in the United States and Canada, the industry's default is to blame automation. The story is echoed by most of North America's business media and by defenders of globalization in general, who claim that the primary reason behind the loss of so many manufacturing jobs in G7 economies is labour-saving technological change in the form of pervasive digitization, robotics and, now, artificial intelligence. They argue that trade deals have had little to do with those job losses, because the manufacturing job losses would have happened even if domestic industries were better protected with tariffs. If you ignore the impact that trade deals have had on relocating production, you might be inclined to agree with them. But that would be like ignoring the impact that losing your job has had on the fact that you are now unemployed.

While it is certainly true than today's highly automated assembly plant doesn't have nearly the same employment footprint as a plant built two decades ago, any factory is still a major source of employment. Ford's assembly plant in Mexico, cancelled at Trump's urging,[14] was going to employ more than three thousand people, and a cluster of parts plants would have sprung up around it, hiring many thousands more workers.

The auto industry, like most manufacturing industries, is becoming more automated all the time, but that's not the primary reason so many jobs have left the United States and Canada. Technological change has significantly reduced the number of workers needed to produce a car, but it's the location where the car and its components are actually manufactured, and not the degree of automation, that is still far and away the biggest determinant of industry employment levels.

And if you want to know where that is, here's a clue: over the last decade, every single new North American assembly plant has been built in Mexico. Between 2010 and 2015, Mexico's vehicle and parts industry received a staggering $24 billion in new investment, including no less than eight new assembly plants. By comparison, the Canadian industry attracted one-fifth of that, and no new assembly plants. In 2014 alone, the Mexican industry attracted more investment than the Canadian industry saw over the entire six-year period.[15]

The new assembly plants being built in Mexico are just as automated as a new American or Canadian plant would be. After all, when Ford or GM builds a new plant in Mexico, they don't substitute cheap Mexican labour for robots. The only difference is that those highly automated factories are being operated by workers who make four dollars an hour or less, as opposed to American or Canadian workers who make between twenty and thirty dollars an hour.

That's obviously a good news story for the Mexican economy, just as it is for the profit margins of companies like GM that, if not for generous bailouts by both American and Canadian taxpayers in 2009, would not exist today.[16] What is less certain is whether Charles Wilson's claim that what is good for GM is good for his country still holds true.

What *is* clear, though, is that what's good for GM is also good for its competitors and suppliers. Volkswagen, Audi, Mercedes, Nissan, Toyota, Ford, Fiat Chrysler, Honda, BMW and Mazda all have or are in the process of building production facilities in Mexico. And what's good for the auto companies is also good for their parts suppliers, who have moved even more of their manufacturing to Mexico than the auto companies have.

Storm clouds began to darken that bright industry outlook in 2016, when presidential hopefuls Donald Trump and Bernie Sanders both took aim at NAFTA, and in particular the trade agreement's role in decimating jobs in the American auto industry. American car companies were suddenly taking an enormous amount of political heat for their profit-maximizing behaviour.

Just as suddenly, Japanese and German vehicle companies operating in Mexico woke up to the realization that if these two candidates won their respective party leadership campaigns, the United States could soon be slapping tariffs on the vehicles coming out of their sprawling Mexican plants.

Ford was the first company to feel the full blast of the heat wave sweeping across American politics. Its planned move of an assembly plant to San Luis Potosí, the centre of Mexico's burgeoning industry, became a lightning rod for the Trump campaign. Trump warned the car company that if he was elected and the automaker moved its plant to Mexico, he would slap a 25 percent tariff on the cars Ford exported to the US market. Discretion being the better part of valour, a chastened Ford Motor Company cancelled the $1.6 billion plant in Mexico and instead decided to invest $700 million in retooling an existing assembly plant in Michigan; in the process, it hired another seven hundred American autoworkers. In retrospect, it's not hard to figure out why American autoworkers voted en masse for Trump.

Once in office, President Trump didn't waste any time before announcing that he was terminating NAFTA, and inviting Canada and Mexico to negotiate the trade deal he had promised American autoworkers from the campaign trail. What Trump had in mind wasn't another free trade deal like NAFTA, which would encourage the continued migration of production to low-wage Mexico. Instead, he was picturing something more akin to the original Canada-US Auto Pact—a managed trade deal with production guarantees. Only this time the production guarantees would protect the United States, not Canada.

While the production guarantees afforded Canada under the Auto Pact were ultimately ruled illegal by the WTO in 2000,[17] long after the agreement was superseded by NAFTA, the Trump administration wasn't particularly concerned with what the global trade cop thought about its new trade policies. If new trade agreements were going to follow rules, they would abide by FART, not the WTO.

But US Trade Representative Robert Lighthizer's objectives in the auto negotiations—namely, to bring home more high-paying manufacturing jobs—ran directly counter to what the American vehicle and parts industry wanted. The American industry, as well as Canadian parts companies, argued that any attempt to force vehicle production back to the United States or Canada would result in higher costs and hence higher vehicle prices for North American consumers.

That was undoubtedly true. A big part of NAFTA's appeal was that it not only brought higher profits to American vehicle and parts manufacturers but also lower sticker prices to American consumers. However, that claim was hardly unique to the auto industry. The same could be said for the price of just about everything that used to be produced in America but was now imported from some global supply chain using cheap offshore labour.

In this case, however, the sticker price increases that would result from moving production out of low-wage Mexican plants and back to the United States (or Canada) wouldn't be nearly as big as for other goods. Why? Because the cost of actually producing a car isn't the only cost reflected in its final selling price. Not by a long shot.

When you see a commercial featuring a suave Matthew McConaughey getting behind the wheel of a swanky Lincoln, keep in mind that he isn't doing it for free. And the TV station airing it isn't doing so without handsome compensation. And the friendly salesperson who finally succeeds in selling you your car? She isn't providing that service for free either. Nor is the dealership that provides the glitzy showroom and the warranties that go with your purchase, or the financing division that's facilitating your lease. Add it all up and those advertising, sales, marketing and financing costs, along with dealership markups, comprise anywhere from 40 to 50 percent of the final sticker price of your vehicle.[18] Those are costs incurred in the country where the vehicle is sold, not produced, and as such wouldn't change if the factory relocated.

But what about the other 50 to 60 percent of the costs? One portion of the total that might well change if manufacturers relocated vehicle and parts production from Mexico back to the United States (or Canada) is their profit margin. Depending on how price-sensitive demand is for a particular vehicle, the car manufacturer always has a choice between passing on any additional costs to the consumer and eating some of those costs in its profit margin. In other words, sell fewer cars or make a smaller margin on the ones you sell. Not a choice any company wants to make if it can avoid it. Mexican factories allow them to avoid it.

Needless to say, car manufacturers and parts producers had no interest in reshoring jobs. In fact, they had a lot more offshoring planned. Nor were they enthusiastic about the changes Washington was proposing for auto trade with its

NAFTA partners, including an increase in the regional content that vehicles had to have before they could qualify for duty-free cross-border trade.

In the industry's eyes, NAFTA's 62.5 percent regional-content threshold was already too onerous, even though it excluded a lot of electronic components like touch screens (which didn't exist when NAFTA was signed, like many other electronic components now common in our cars). As a result, these components could be sourced from China or anywhere else in the world without jeopardizing the agreement's regional-content requirement. Auto unions and other industry critics argued that the omission of these categories from NAFTA's regional-content rules provided a convenient back door for Chinese and other Asian-made components to enter the US vehicle market duty-free by stealth.

The auto industry also wasn't crazy about the Trump administration's desire to include a provision against currency manipulation in the new trade agreement. If wages one-eighth of those in the rest of North America weren't enough of an incentive to move production to Mexico, consider how the Mexican peso has performed against the US dollar over the past two decades. Since 2000, the greenback has risen from an exchange rate of ten pesos to the dollar to almost twenty pesos today. In other words, the peso has lost almost half of its value against the dollar.[19]

While it would be a stretch to blame this on deliberate currency manipulation by the Mexican central bank (despite running big trade surpluses with the United States and Canada in vehicles and parts, Mexico has run a large trade deficit with the rest of the world), currency devaluation has nevertheless moved the needle even further in Mexico's favour. To illustrate just how much, consider that an equivalent percentage devaluation in the value of the Canadian dollar against the greenback since 2000 would peg the loonie at around thirty-five American cents.

If the Canadian dollar was trading at thirty-five cents against the greenback, I bet Sam McLaughlin's old company wouldn't be in such a rush to leave the country.

CHAPTER 11

FROM FREE TRADE TO MANAGED TRADE: THE US-MEXICO-CANADA TRADE AGREEMENT

The McLaughlin family had a lot of great ideas, but Tona-Cola was not one of them.

Sam McLaughlin had a brother, John. While Sam was building cars, John studied to become a pharmacist and ended up working in Brooklyn, New York. He noticed that customers were coming in not to buy medicine but to quench their thirst. The latest fashion was carbonated drinks, many of which claimed to confer health benefits. Customers couldn't get enough of what today we call soda pop. John saw that the real money was in fizzy drinks rather than pills, and in 1890 he returned to Toronto to set up his own soda dispensary.

Despite stiff competition, his business grew. By 1893 he had expanded into his third factory. By 1895, his products were distributed nationwide. He diversified into producing ornate soda fountains made of mahogany, onyx, marble, nickel, bronze and silver. But what customers really wanted was fizz, and McLaughlin had several products to make sure they never had to go thirsty: Hygeia, Hop-Tone and, of course, Tona-Cola—a rival to the newly introduced Coca-Cola.

In the world of global competition, Tona-Cola was destined to fail. People thought Coke just tasted better, and the brand soon disappeared. But McLaughlin did come up with something that would stand the test of time and conquer the world: his "Belfast-style ginger ale," better known today as Canada Dry. By 1910 there were Canada Dry plants across the country.

Though John McLaughlin died in 1914, and the family sold his company in 1920, his creation outlasted his brother's. The McLaughlin Motor Car Company has been all but forgotten, while Canada Dry is sold around the world and produced in the United States, Mexico, Colombia, Peru, Japan (where it is also available in a "wet" version) and several countries in the Middle East and Europe.

Of course, that means there is no America Dry. That's just the nature of globalization. For McLaughlin's drink to expand, someone else's had to make way. Back when John was a pharmacist in Brooklyn, the most popular sodas were Humdinger, Happy Hooligan, Gunther's Excelsior, Pugilists' Panacea and the Japanese Thirst Killer. I'm sure they all quenched your thirst, but there is room for only so many flavours of soda on the planet, and there's a reason you've heard of Canada Dry and none of its early competitors.

What is true of soft drinks is true of cars. In 2004, Oldsmobile went the way of the Japanese Thirst Killer and McLaughlin-Buick. It was the oldest American carmaker, and had produced more than 35 million cars over its nearly one-hundred-year history. But GM had given Oldsmobile the task of taking on the import market, and consumers in the early twenty-first century felt the same way about Olds as their late-nineteenth-century counterparts did about Tona-Cola. In

April 2004, the last Alero rolled off the production line, and a chapter in automotive history came to an end.

Still, it was unclear even then that worse was yet to come for North American automakers. Much, much worse. In fact, that year things looked particularly good in the Canadian industry. Ontario surpassed Michigan to become the largest vehicle-producing jurisdiction on the continent. GM's flagship plant in Oshawa was voted the company's most efficient. Canada ranked in the top five among global auto producers—no small feat given the limited size of its domestic market. The auto sector was the pride and joy of the Canadian economy.

A decade later, the outlook was very different. Canada had dropped from being the world's fourth-largest vehicle producer to its tenth. Mexico overtook it back in 2008, and it now produces almost twice as many vehicles a year as Canada does.[1]

That's the way it works: if there are going to be winners, there have to be losers. NAFTA was a mechanism for creating winners and losers, primarily when it came to investors in auto companies and the industry's American and Canadian workforces. So is the trade agreement that has replaced it. Only this time around, there may be some good news for the losers under the original NAFTA.

The US-Mexico-Canada Trade Agreement (USMCA)—or the Canada-US-Mexico Trade Agreement, or the Mexico-US-Canada Trade Agreement—is the result of the thirteen-month trade negotiations undertaken to replace NAFTA. There are two things you might have noticed about the deal when it was first announced: the first is that its name changes depending on where you live; the second is the absence of the word *free*.

The only people who continued to call the deal a free trade agreement were Prime Minister Trudeau and his chief trade negotiator, then–Foreign Affairs Minister Chrystia Freeland. Everyone else called it what it is: a managed trade agreement, much like the original Canada-US Auto Pact that the WTO eventually ruled to be illegal.

RELUCTANT PARTNERS

Neither Canada nor Mexico particularly wanted a new trade agreement. Neither country shared the Trump administration's urgent need to tear up NAFTA. The Obama administration had been content with the functioning of NAFTA, as were Ottawa and Mexico City. Had it been left up to the then–Mexican president, Enrique Peña Nieto of the Institutional Revolutionary Party (a conservative pro-business party despite its name), NAFTA would have been left alone. Canada's prime minister, Justin Trudeau, felt more or less the same way. Incoming US president Donald Trump had other plans.

Mexico had clearly been NAFTA's big winner. Its booming auto industry was now the seventh largest in the world, and the country was the fourth-largest vehicle exporter. Moreover, a whole manufacturing sector was developing around the auto industry. Of course, all those manufacturing jobs didn't come free; Mexico had paid a price to get them.

Under NAFTA, Mexico had been forced to open its farm sector to US agribusiness, no small political risk for the Mexican government when you consider that 13 percent of the country's labour force still works on a farm. (In the United

States and Canada, farm workers make up less than 2 percent of the labour force.) Over a million Mexican farm workers lost their jobs. Just as NAFTA had made American autoworkers expendable, Mexican farm workers were left on the outside looking in. But Mexico City didn't see itself as the avocado economy of the future—instead, it aspired to mimic the rapid industrial development that had occurred in China and elsewhere in Asia. And having duty-free access to the world's largest economy, even at the expense of its farming sector, seemed like a pretty good route by which to achieve that goal.

Canada's position should have been less clear than Mexico's, or at least more nuanced. In overall trade terms, NAFTA had worked well for Canada, as did its predecessor, the original Canada-US Free Trade Agreement. The United States was still Canada's most important trading partner, accounting for a remarkable three-quarters of Canada's total merchandise exports. And Canada was still the largest export market for American producers. While the total volume of trade between the two countries had slipped to second (behind the volume of US-China trade), that said more about the explosive growth of Chinese exports to the United States than it did about any flagging in trade between the United States and Canada.

Yet Canadian autoworkers had fared no better under NAFTA than their American counterparts. In fact, by some industry metrics, like investment, the Canadian auto industry had done even worse.[2] Much had changed in Ontario's auto industry, just as it had in the American Rust Belt. And none of it was for the good, at least if you were an autoworker.

WHAT EXACTLY DID CANADA AND MEXICO HAVE IN COMMON?

From the start of the USMCA trade negotiations, President Trump made it clear that Mexico, where all the auto jobs and investment had fled, was his primary concern. That's not to say that the United States didn't have trade issues with Canada—like, for example, dairy board protection or the long-running softwood lumber dispute. But Trump made a point of emphasizing that his issues with Canada were of a different order of magnitude ("tweaking" was the way he put it) than the trade problems the United States faced with Mexico.

Given the common experience of losing thousands of high-paying auto-industry jobs, it might seem as though the United States and Canada would be on the same page about any new trade agreement that dealt with the auto sector. If preventing high-paying auto jobs from moving to Mexico was going to be the key objective for Lighthizer and the rest of the Trump administration, Washington and Ottawa ought to have shared the same interests. And if Trump was beholden to his political supporters in manufacturing states like Ohio, Michigan, Indiana and Wisconsin, Prime Minister Trudeau should have been equally beholden to his supporters in Ontario, the home of the Canadian auto industry.

That's probably why the American negotiating team first reached out to Canada to sign a separate bilateral deal ahead of the negotiations with Mexico. To their surprise, Ottawa refused. Both Trudeau and Freeland characterized the American offer as a classic divide-and-conquer tactic, and claimed solidarity with Mexico.

As it turns out, Washington and Ottawa weren't on the

same page at all when it came to the all-important auto sec-tor. While Trudeau and Freeland both publicly championed workers' rights, even at one point insisting that American autoworkers be given greater safeguards to organize unions in right-to-work states, they didn't seem to have any problem with Canadian auto plants being shut down and the jobs moving to Mexico for a fraction of Canadian workers' wages. What Trudeau and Freeland really wanted to protect were the extensive industry supply chains that Canadian parts companies—including global giant Magna—had developed in Mexico.

Magna, the Canadian auto parts company founded by Frank Stronach, has become one of the largest privately owned employers in Mexico's manufacturing sector. It has no fewer than thirty-two manufacturing plants in the country. These days the company has been making news because its patriarch is suing his daughter, Belinda, who wrestled control of the com-pany away from him after claiming that the old man was pissing away the family fortune on frivolous investments like race-tracks. Meanwhile Frank's granddaughter Selena is suing her aunt Belinda for upkeep of her lavish globetrotting lifestyle.[3]

For Magna's Canadian workers, life poses a different set of challenges. If you are one of the 390 Magna workers who lost their jobs at the Grenville Castings unit in Perth, Ontario, you're not thinking about racetracks or monthly getaways to far-flung exotic locales. You're thinking about how you and your family are going to pay the bills.

The company has for some time claimed it has no plans to invest further in Canada.[4] Now that Magna is firmly established in Mexico, its Canadian workforce has become expendable. The company's sprawling Mexican operations employ far more staff than its head office in Aurora, Ontario, a community just north of Toronto. Of course, how many people are you going to be able to employ in Aurora at four dollars an hour or less? That's less than a third of the province's minimum wage.

But four dollars an hour is a good wage in Mexico, even for the skilled labourers who work in Magna's thirty-plus facilities there.[5] Those jobs exist only because, under NAFTA, Magna could ship the parts it produced at its Mexican plants duty-free to the United States or Canada. The last thing Magna wanted was to see US and Canadian tariffs slapped on those auto parts when they depart Mexico. Magna's CEO Don Walker warned that any attempt to impose high wage standards in Mexico would drive production out of North America.[6]

Other Canadian parts companies, like Linamar and Martinrea, were in the same boat: none of them wanted to see tariffs on what their vast supply chains in Mexico were producing either. Among them, Canadian auto parts companies have more than 120 plants in Mexico, employing over forty-three thousand workers.[7] So it turns out that NAFTA really is beneficial to some Canadians. They just happen to be the shareholders of auto parts companies, not the men and women who used to work in their Canadian plants.

Standing up to the blatantly protectionist and bullying tactics of the Trump administration seemed like a heroic position for the Canadian government to take. It was also a very investor-friendly one. If you were an investor in any one of those companies, you no doubt saw Canada's approach to protecting supply chains in Mexico as the right thing to do. In the end, it was *your* interests that Trudeau and Freeland were defending.

But if you were a worker in one those firms' remaining Canadian plants, you probably found yourself wondering when your government was going to get around to sticking up for *you*. You knew you were living on borrowed time, destined to become an expendable when your job was eventually snatched by the tentacles of your company's Mexican supply chain.

The dichotomy between the interests of Magna's investors and those of its workers demonstrates an intrinsic problem governments face in defining the national interest when negotiating trade agreements with other countries. You see, what is good for Magna's shareholders isn't necessarily what is good for Magna's Canadian workforce. In many respects, their interests are diametrically opposed. At the end of the day, then, governments have to decide whose interests to represent at the negotiating table. Unlike Trump, who was willing to trade industry profits for more American jobs, Trudeau and Freeland chose to defend Canadian parts companies' cross-border supply chains. *That* is why they had no interest in signing a bilateral deal that excluded Mexico, which would potentially put those supply chains at risk. In other words, they could stick up for Magna under the guise of sticking up for Mexico.

Unfortunately for Trudeau and Freeland, Mexico had its own ideas about how to proceed in the trade talks. Public solidarity with Canada might have sounded heartwarming, but it wasn't Canadian markets that Mexico was vitally interested in securing. What really mattered to Mexico's negotiating team was duty-free access to the US market. That's why the Trump administration, visibly pissed off by the rebuke from Canada (following a G7 meeting in Ottawa, Peter Navarro, Trump's trade advisor, claimed there would be a special place in hell for Prime Minister Trudeau),[8] offered Mexico its own bilateral deal. The Mexican government jumped at the opportunity.

Of course, outgoing Mexican president Nieto and incoming president-elect López Obrador both said they hoped Canada would later join the agreement. And I'm sure they were being sincere. But they were also both more than willing to sign on to a trade deal with the United States that didn't include Canada.

At that point, the Trudeau government had little choice but to sign on as well, accepting the terms that the Trump administration had already negotiated with Mexico. President Trump had gone as far as to threaten Canada with 20 to 25 percent American tariffs on its car exports to the United States if it didn't sign. As it turns out, the agreed-upon terms weren't so different from the deal all three countries had been negotiating when the talks were still trilateral. Canada held its line in the sand, requiring that the dispute-resolution mechanism in the old NAFTA agreement (chapter 11) be preserved in the new trade agreement.[9] Lighthizer had in earlier negotiations challenged the arrangement, claiming it superseded the authority of the US courts.

In exchange, Canada agreed to some modest loosening of its egregious protection of domestic dairy producers (primarily in Ontario and Quebec, through the workings of provincial dairy, egg and poultry marketing boards), and had to cede to a US demand for a modest increase in the length of patent protection for new drugs—a key demand from the US pharmaceutical industry. But in the seemingly all-important auto sector, Canada went along with the new provisions that the United States had negotiated with Mexico to safeguard future industry jobs in America.

THE NEW RULES TO SAVE AMERICAN AUTO JOBS

The USMCA contained three major changes in the rules for continuing duty-free trade in the motor vehicle industry. Auto companies weren't crazy about any of them. The first resulted from US insistence that the new agreement raise the regional-content requirement for duty-free movement of vehicles to 75 percent from NAFTA's 62.5 percent.[10] The new content threshold would leave less room for countries like China to gain back-door access to the US market by shipping cheap auto parts to Mexico, where they would be re-exported to assembly plants in the United States or Canada.

The second change—and the real kicker in the new trade deal—was its provision that high-value-added components like transmissions and engines could be shipped duty-free into the United States only if they were manufactured by workers earning at least US$16 an hour. More specifically, a minimum 40 percent of the value of any North American vehicle would have to be made by labour earning that wage in order to qualify for duty-free cross-border movement.[11] The setting of a minimum wage for labour was unprecedented in trade agreements, which until now had allowed firms to trade high-wage workers in one country for low-wage workers in another. In fact, the ability to arbitrage international differences in wage rates was one of the key attractions of such trade deals. In effect, trade agreements have been more about setting a global maximum for wages than a regional minimum.

The new minimum-wage requirement wasn't going to threaten any jobs in Canada. On the contrary, it had the potential to bring some jobs back to Canada, just as it might to the United States. But the stipulation was going to be a huge issue for Mexican auto plants, whose average wage was about a quarter of the new requirement. The Mexican government acknowledged that 30 percent of the industry's production in Mexico didn't meet the new regional-content and wage requirements on high-valued-added componentry.

The third change was the side agreements. They were kept out of the main body of the treaty, probably because what they contained was so blatantly in disregard of WTO regulations that including them would have risked embarrassing the governing body of global trade. One set limits on how many vehicles and vehicle parts either Mexico or Canada could export duty-free to the US market, in much the same way that the Auto Pact once guaranteed minimum production levels in Canada. (Remember, those provisions were ultimately ruled illegal by the WTO.)

Both Mexico and Canada had to agree to a 2.6-million-unit ceiling for vehicle exports to the United States, above which the US would be free to impose whatever tariffs it chooses to levy on imported vehicles.[12] The agreement also imposed a limit of $108 billion on imports of auto parts from Mexico and a $32.4 billion limit for Canada, anything above which would be assessed the prevailing US tariff.

While the export thresholds for both vehicles and parts were well above the pre-agreement levels (in sharp contrast to the quotas Washington negotiated for steel and aluminum), the USMCA nevertheless set an absolute limit on the growth of future import levels. In this critical respect, the USMCA was a managed trade agreement—not a free trade agreement that allowed the market to determine production and export levels.

Even so, Mexico's economy minister at the time, Guajardo Villarreal, noted in defence of the new agreement that the export quota still allowed for an almost 40 percent increase in Mexican vehicle shipments to the US market. Theoretically, it also offered a generous upside to Canadian vehicle exports. The only difference, as we would learn soon after the agreement was signed, was that the auto industry had little interest in maintaining, let alone growing, Canadian production, but it had a very keen interest in growing production in Mexico. So the limits placed on future vehicle and parts exports didn't really matter to Canada, because what's left of the Canadian auto industry is never going to come close to those export ceilings.

The ink had barely dried on the new agreement when General Motors dropped a bombshell. It was closing four of its US plants, including one of the largest, in Lordstown, Ohio—a state in which Trump had promised autoworkers more jobs and told them not to sell their homes. In Canada, GM was also shutting down the company's historic Oshawa plant, which had been operating since 1953. The closing of the Lordstown plant, where GM produces its compact Cruze, was particularly galling to the United Automobile Workers, who had agreed in mid-2017 to make $118 million a year in annual wage concessions to save the plant.[13]

In addition, GM was closing its Detroit-Hamtramck facility, its last remaining plant in what used to be called Motor City. In total, the company was shedding thirty-two hundred factory jobs in the United States and another twenty-six hundred workers in Canada.

GM rationalized the moves by claiming that the announced plant closures were necessary for the company to redeploy its resources toward developing autonomous self-driving and electric vehicles. While the stock market cheered the closing of the company's high-costs plants as well as other plans for shedding office jobs (GM's share price shot up 5 percent on the announcement), neither the UAW nor Unifor, the Canadian autoworkers union, was cheering. Nor was President Trump.

A shift to electric and autonomous cars sounds like a bold investment in a green-tech future, but critics of the company argued that the shift GM really had in mind was more backward-looking. Electric cars account for less than two percent of new vehicle sales in the United States. The real plan, it appeared, was to downsize passenger-car production, where sales had been badly flagging in recent years, and reallocate resources into building more gas-guzzling SUVs, whose sales are booming in response to lower pump prices. Ford had already announced that it would cease producing sedans—at least in any of its high-wage American or Canadian plants.

An outraged President Trump was quick to point out that the company hadn't closed any of its facilities in Mexico or China. While GM was technically right in claiming that the plants it was closing were producing models that weren't selling anymore, none of these plants had been given mandates to produce models that *were* selling. You can hardly blame welders in Oshawa for the fact that executives in Detroit were paying them to build cars no one wanted to drive.

In an effort to deflect growing criticism over its announced plant closures, the company had transferred about 1,305 affected employees to jobs at its other US plants. And it claims it will sell its closed Lordstown plant to Workhorse Electric, a small company that intends to produce electric-powered delivery vans.[14]

But a bigger question still hangs over the fate of the North American vehicle and parts industry: What will US tariffs on motor vehicles and parts look like in the near future? Will the US vehicle market be surrounded by a huge tariff wall—in which case, being inside it will become all the more valuable? A high tariff wall will affect the behaviour not only of those outside it, but of those inside as well. Manufacturers operating in Mexico will be highly motivated to actually comply with the new USMCA regulations instead of paying the current most-favoured-nation (MFN) tariff.

You see, there was always a loophole available to auto firms under NAFTA—and it remains, at least for the moment, under the new USMCA. Firms operating in Mexico who didn't meet NAFTA's 62.5 percent regional-content threshold could instead choose to pay the US's MFN tariff, which was only 2.5 percent for imports on vehicles (excluding light trucks and SUVs). That same option is available under the new agreement, and the fact that there are now more requirements to meet—notably the raised regional-content threshold and the new minimum-wage rate on high-value-added componentry—means that car manufacturers now have more incentive to ignore the rules and just pay the MFN tariff.

If you were Mary Barra (CEO of GM) or Donald Walker (CEO of Magna), what would you do? Give a fourfold wage increase to your Mexican labour force so as to comply with the new minimum-wage regulation, or keep wages as they are and pay a measly 2.5 percent tariff on shipments from your Mexican plants to the United States? The MFN tariff would look like a pretty sweet deal.

But will the United States' MFN tariff rate on vehicle imports remain at 2.5 percent? If you're the CEO of an auto manufacturer, you wouldn't want to bet the firm's bottom line on it—particularly if you're running a European or Asian car company targeted for tariff action. Following a Department of Commerce finding that import penetration in the American auto market endangered national security, President Trump threatened to use the same Section 232 of the Trade Expansion Act that he'd used to justify tariffs on steel and aluminum to impose tariffs on cars. Facing a showdown with China on trade, he gave European and Asian automakers a 180-day reprieve to negotiate better trade terms, possibly including quotas, before he would consider the imposition of a tariff as high as 25 percent on vehicle exports to the American market. The European Union's tariff on vehicle imports—primarily from Asia and North America—is 10 percent, or four times the United States' MFN most-favoured-nation rate.

The American market is far and away the largest export

market for European vehicle producers, accounting for almost 30 percent of their export earnings.[15] And Japan accounts for almost a quarter of total US vehicle imports.[16] Japan and Europe have a lot at stake, and for the moment President Trump has made it abundantly clear that he wants to see much more investment from their car makers in the US if they are to avoid paying a tenfold increase in vehicle tariffs.

UNCERTAINTY BRINGS ITS OWN REWARDS

They say uncertainty is the worst enemy of businesses—but it could be a friend to labour. And there is no shortage of uncertainty in the North American auto industry today.

There are those Section 232 tariffs the White House has threatened, not to mention the possibility that Trump, if provoked by any further movement of auto plants to Mexico, could simply ignore what has been agreed upon in the USMCA deal and unilaterally impose new tariffs on Mexico, as he had already threatened to do if Mexico didn't do more to halt the flow of migrants heading across the US border.

But for American autoworkers, the uncertainty caused by the Trump administration's threats seems to be pulling more investment and more jobs into the US auto industry. Toyota, for one, isn't waiting for clarity about future US tariffs; instead, the company has doubled down on the US auto industry. In March 2019, Toyota announced that it was upping its planned investment in the United States by another $3 billion, to $13 billion, between 2019 and 2022,[17] including a $1.6 billion assembly plant in Huntsville, Alabama, in partnership with Mazda.

Since Trump's election, auto manufacturing employment has risen by about forty-five thousand jobs, to just over 1 million. While a modest gain, it is nevertheless the highest level of industry employment in well over a decade.[18] Jim Lentz, Toyota's CEO of its North American operations, said, "I'd be disingenuous if I said we didn't have an eye on trade," when making the announcement of beefed-up investment in US plants.[19]

And Toyota won't be the only company boosting its investment in the US auto industry. So will GM. If America's largest auto manufacturer thought it was going to get a free ride to close down four major manufacturing plants in America, it had another thing coming. It wasn't just President Trump who was complaining. So was the UAW. And armed with the knowledge that there was a president sitting in the White House who had promised more auto jobs and was prepared to use tariffs to get them, autoworkers went on strike. The UAW closed down all of GM's US operations and even, due to supply chains, two of the company's plants in Mexico and one in Canada. The union wanted the company to commit to more investment and production in the United States, instead of continuing to expand its operations in Mexico.

Already having lost a reported $2 billion in a strike that lasted over forty days, GM offered $7.7 billion in new investment in US plants and another $1.3 billion in joint ventures, including the conversion of its Lordstone, Ohio, plant into an electric-vehicle facility. Of the $7.7 billion of promised investment, $3.5 billion would be at the Detroit-Hamtramck plant, which was one of the four American plants that GM originally said it would close. In exchange for closing three of the four plants, the company agreed to relatively generous wage increases for its 49,000 UAW members, including an $11,000 signing bonus and a 6 percent wage raise, bringing the hourly pay for veteran workers up to $32.32 per hour by the end of the contract.

The outlook for GM's workers in Canada, however, is decidedly less positive, particularly for its huge Oshawa workforce, which produced its Cadillac XTS and Chevrolet Impala. What was once one of the largest auto plants in the world, producing more than 730,000 vehicles a year and employing over twenty thousand workers, saw its production lines shuttered in December 2019. Only three hundred employees remain at the plant, which has transitioned into producing spare parts for discontinued models as well as housing a test track for autonomous vehicles.[20]

With no national champion like McLaughlin Motors left to support domestic production, and a federal government that, other than expressing disappointment, isn't prepared to do anything about fleeing auto jobs, it seems as if the Canadian industry will continue to be downsized even beyond the closure of the once industry-leading Oshawa plant. What was a century ago the world's second-largest auto industry now seems, for the most part, expendable.

CHAPTER 12

KEEPING CHINA AWAY FROM AMERICA'S BACK DOOR

Few hockey fans had heard of Huawei before 2017, when the telecom giant's logo showed up on Canada's most-watched television broadcast: *Hockey Night in Canada*. It was a bold advertising strategy by the Chinese company. What Huawei might not have realized, however, is that hockey isn't what it used to be in the country that invented the game. In the Greater Toronto Hockey League, for example, membership on a AAA team starts at $5000 a year and can go as high as $10,000. The legendary Gordie Howe may have learned to play on frozen ditches in hand-me-down skates, but today a kid without dry-land training, high-end nutrition and thousand-dollar skates is likely to be left behind. For most middle-income Canadians, whose real incomes haven't grown in decades, organized hockey has become a bridge too far. Nationally, enrollment in youth hockey has dropped about 10 percent in the past decade.

But it's not a love of the game that has brought China's telecom giant to the screens of millions of hockey fans. The National Hockey League's attempts to promote the game in China have met with a tepid response. Huawei's ads on *Hockey Night in Canada* are all about the company's sleek new smartphones—which are a lot cheaper than the ones Apple wants to sell you. But selling smartphones is not the only thing Huawei is after in Canada. In fact, it's not even the main reason the company bought some of the most expensive advertising on Canadian television.

What Huawei really wants are contracts to supply the country's telecom providers (like Rogers, Bell and Telus) with the switching equipment and other core hardware for the wireless 5G network that is about to revolutionize the speed at which telecommunications systems can operate around the world. And it's not averse to shelling out some bucks to achieve that objective. Aside from acquiring the lead sponsorship of *Hockey Night in Canada* broadcasts, the company spent $137 million in 2018 funding research into new 5G technology at ten Canadian universities. It's a sponsor of the Toronto International Film Festival. And the company supports a number of Canadian charities, such as the Jays Care Foundation (of Major League Baseball's Toronto Blue Jays). Huawei is turning on the charm with the Canadian public, hoping to create a bond between them and its brand. If it's going to secure those telecom contracts, it's going to need Canadians on its side.

In his "Made in China 2025" plan, President Xi has identified telecommunications as one of the key global technology industries he wants the country to dominate. As China's national telecom champion, Huawei is well on its way to delivering on President Xi's goal. Ren Zhengfei, a former engineer in the People's Liberation Army, founded the company in 1987. Since then it has surpassed Swedish rival Ericsson to become the world's largest provider of telecommunications equipment, and is second only to South Korean giant Samsung in the manufacture of smartphones.

So why is taking over a small market like Canada such a priority for a corporate behemoth like Huawei? Canada belongs to a group of Western democracies known as the Five Eyes—the United States, the United Kingdom, Australia and New Zealand complete its number. Along with common values (and the English language), the five countries also share highly classified intelligence. Three of the countries—the United States, Australia and New Zealand—have already banned Huawei from supplying the hardware for their 5G systems, citing cybersecurity concerns. Former Australian prime minister Malcolm Turnbull, whose government banned both Huawei and fellow Chinese company ZTE from supplying 5G equipment, defended the decision as a hedge against the potential for future Chinese aggression against his country.[1]

It is the company's close relationship with the Chinese government that has raised concerns. Western nations fear that its core equipment could provide a back door for China's massive and sophisticated state surveillance apparatus. They worry that China could not only eavesdrop but, even worse, gain control of vital operating systems if embedded into another country's core telecommunications system. Not surprisingly, Canada has received requests from its Five Eyes partners to join their ban on the use of Huawei equipment in its own 5G systems.

In addition to pleas from both Democratic and Republican lawmakers in the United States, three former Canadian security chiefs have publicly warned the Trudeau government that if it allows Huawei to build the new 5G telecommunications system, Canada's national security will be seriously compromised.[2] Following the lead of former prime minister Kim Campbell, who once remarked that a federal election "is not the time, I don't think, to get involved in a debate on very, very serious issues," Prime Minister Trudeau said a decision on the matter would not be made until sometime after the October 2019 federal election.

It didn't help sway Canadian public opinion when then–Chinese ambassador Lu Shaye publicly warned Ottawa that if Huawei was shut out from bidding on hardware contracts there would be "consequences for Canada."[3] Can you imagine the Swedish government issuing the same stern warning if Canada decided against buying Ericsson's telecommunications equipment, or the Finnish government warning Ottawa of grave consequences if Nokia didn't get a contract for telecommunications hardware? (Of course, you might wonder why you have to buy your telecom hardware from a Swedish or Finnish or Chinese company at all, and why you can't just buy it from a Canadian one—like Northern Telecom, which like so many other once world-class Canadian corporations ended up expendable in the global telecom market.) I'm sure Ambassador Lu's message went a long way in reassuring Canadians that Huawei and China's ruling Communist Party are unaffiliated, and that the company operates independently of government control.

Huawei counters that it is already operating in more than 170 countries without any incidents or complaints about compromised national security. Moreover, its executives argue that Huawei is no better positioned to use its equipment as a Trojan horse to eavesdrop on or override its customers' telecommunications systems than its competitors are. The firm also points out that regardless of who installs the hardware, it's the operating software that provides the portals for hackers, whether they're based in China or anywhere else around the world. Huawei is probably right. But who would you rather have designing and building your telecommunications network—a publicly traded Swedish electronics firm or a firm whose corporate mandate includes a commitment to aid the Chinese government whenever requested to do so?

As it turns out, Huawei faces much greater challenges in a market much more important to its mandate than Canada. In May 2019, following a breakdown in talks between China and the United States, President Trump upped the ante in the ongoing trade war by issuing an executive order that instructed the Department of Commerce to ban Huawei from any sales to US wireless carriers—and not just for their 5G networks.[4] Even more lethal to Huawei's business was the ban the White House imposed on American companies selling Huawei their technology or components. This affected not just the Chinese company's business in the United States, but its ability to be competitive anywhere.

Google, for example, announced that it would no longer provide Huawei with updates to its apps and services. Similarly, cellphone parts provider Lumentum Holdings stated that it would stop shipments to Huawei. Chip manufacturers Intel, Qualcomm, Xilinx and Broadcom announced that they, too, would stop supplying Huawei. While Trump's ban on selling to Huawei would have cost American suppliers an estimated

$11 billion a year, it could have had crippling effects on Huawei's ability to compete with the likes of Samsung in the highly competitive global smartphone market.

President Trump lifted that ban after the resumption of trade negotiations following his June 2019 meeting with President Xi in Osaka. But with the understanding that the reprieve could be temporary, a cloud still hovers over the Chinese telecom giant. Trump made it clear that American policy toward Huawei would be decided only after a trade deal was completed, and in the absence of such a deal, sanctions would be reapplied.

So, what does *Hockey Night in Canada*'s flagship advertiser have to do with the expendables?

More than you might think. The USMCA was a trade agreement between three countries, but it contained one clause targeting a fourth. Section 32 allows each of the countries to terminate the agreement if any one of them signs a free trade deal with a "non-market country."[5] The non-market country is, of course, China. Equipped with Section 32's escape hatch, the United States possesses the means to enlist (or coerce) the support of its USMCA partners in its trade war with China.

The provision wasn't aimed so much at Mexico as it was at Canada. The Trudeau government had been flirting with Beijing on the trade front, and at one point was reportedly even open to the idea of signing a free trade agreement with China. Ironically, the Canadian trade initiative was motivated by Ottawa's perceived need to diversify Canada's trade in the face of growing US protectionism. In any event, it signalled a sharp departure from the Cold War stance the previous Harper Conservative government had taken in its attitude toward and dealings with the authoritarian regime in Beijing.

For its part, China was intrigued by the concept of a free trade deal with America's northern neighbour and key trading partner. Canada would be a prize part of China's initiative of building trade routes and associated infrastructure throughout the world. While the Canadian market was not in itself large, access to it would nevertheless give China a strategic foothold right at America's back door. But if anyone in Canada thought the Americans wouldn't mind their global rival establishing a North American beachhead, they were dead wrong.

Hence, Section 32. It would force Canada to choose between the two superpowers. Canada's chief negotiator and then–foreign minister (now deputy prime minister) Chrystia Freeland claimed the provisions in the USMCA prohibiting free trade deals with non-market countries was not a big enough poison pill to scuttle any Canadian-Chinese trade negotiations. Trade experts, however, are divided on that assessment. But it appears that President Trump won't have to rely solely on Section 32 to shut the door on China making any trade deals with one of his USMCA partners. He has another ace up his sleeve.

BOOK HER, DANNO!

Changing planes to catch a connecting flight at Vancouver International Airport is for many travellers a routine affair.

But on a dreary December day in 2018, that was not the case for Meng Wanzhou, daughter of Huawei founder Ren Zhengfei and chief financial officer of the Chinese telecom giant. To her utter shock and horror, while changing planes en route to Mexico, she was arrested by Canadian authorities at the airport on an extradition request from Washington. And from that moment on, the Trump administration didn't have to worry about invoking Section 32 of the USMCA to keep China away from its back door.

Meng had prudently chosen to avoid travelling through American airports since 2017, when she'd learned she was the subject of a criminal investigation into Huawei's activities in the United States. As the firm's chief financial officer, she is accused of lying to US banking authorities about the company's dealings with a front company called Skycom Tech, which was involved in selling Iran embargoed goods and technology. If extradited to the United States, Meng could be staying for awhile. Bank fraud, the crime with which she is charged, carries a maximum sentence of thirty years in prison.

Meng obviously wasn't expecting Canadian authorities to arrest and hold her for extradition to the United States. But Canada has long had an extradition treaty with its southern neighbour—a legal arrangement Beijing had also been demanding from Canada in recent trade discussions. So when Washington called, the Trudeau government had to answer and act accordingly, nabbing Meng while she was on the ground in Vancouver and holding her in a detention centre until she was released on $10 million bail to a residence she owned in the city. There, she would await extradition or her release.

Faced with predictable Chinese outrage, Prime Minister Trudeau and then–Foreign Affairs Minister Freeland defended their country's actions by arguing that Canada is a country governed by the rule of law, and it therefore had no choice but to honour the extradition request. President Trump, in his own inimical way, jumped into the fray by publicly commenting that once Meng Wanzhou was extradited to the United States, he might just hold the imprisoned executive as a bargaining chip in his own trade negotiations with Beijing.[6] That didn't sound very much like the rule of law to the Chinese authorities. Nor did Trudeau's rule of law claim seem very credible, only months later, in light of headlines he was making at home. The prime minister had removed his attorney general, Jody Wilson-Raybould, from her cabinet post because she wouldn't drop prosecution proceedings against Quebec engineering giant SNC-Lavalin (accused of bribing officials to get contracts from the Qaddafi regime in Libya).[7] The firm's Montreal head office just happened to be in the prime minister's Papineau riding.

Beijing retaliated by imprisoning two unfortunate Canadians, one a former diplomat and the other a Canadian businessman, on trumped-up espionage charges. After being held in captivity for more than four months, the two were formally charged with espionage in May 2019. Another captive Canadian who was serving a fifteen-year sentence for drug smuggling suddenly had his sentence upgraded to execution. As news of China's reprisals dominated the Canadian media, there was naturally a sea change in the public attitude toward negotiating trade treaties with the Asian colossus. And the notion of Ottawa acquiescing to Beijing's earlier request for an extradition treaty now seemed completely out of the question.

If you were charged with a crime, which country would you want to be incarcerated in? Detained Canadians Michael Kovrig and Michal Spavor are reportedly kept in a cell where the lights are left on twenty-four hours a day, and they are interrogated four hours a day by Chinese security officials. Meng lives in her $5 million mansion in Vancouver and, other than wearing a GPS monitor, is free to come and go as she pleases in the Vancouver area.

That seemed hugely unfair to most Canadians. Meanwhile, Canada's ambassador to China, John McCallum, had publicly campaigned for Meng's release, suggesting that she had a very strong case to make against extradition to the United States (in case the judges hearing the case weren't able to come to that conclusion all by themselves). As it turns out, the final decision on any extradition decision in Canada rests not with the judiciary but with a cabinet minister assigned to the case. When an already censured Ambassador McCallum kept publicly repeating his message on behalf of Meng (and the Chinese government), Prime Minister Trudeau finally heeded widespread calls for the ambassador's resignation and fired him.

GRAVE CONSEQUENCES

At the end of the day, the extradition case against Meng turned out to be about trade. And on that front, President Trump, who was no doubt the real architect of this plan, can claim mission accomplished. While the full commercial fallout from the souring relations between Beijing and Ottawa has yet to be seen, it sure doesn't sound like Canada is about to lessen its trade dependence on the United States by increasing trade with America's Asian rival. And more importantly from Trump's perspective, it sure doesn't sound like China will be gaining a foothold at America's back door.

When Ottawa finally gave the green light to proceed with Meng's extradition hearing, China started throwing its commercial weight around. If you are the world's largest buyer of canola, as you are of soybean, you can have a huge impact on the livelihood of canola and soybean farmers all over the world. Canadian canola farmers got a taste of what had earlier stuck in the craw of their American soybean counterparts.

All of a sudden, Richardson International, Canada's largest exporter of canola, was dropped from the list of China's approved grain importers, allegedly on the basis of contaminated shipments. This just happened to be on the same day that the Canadian Ministry of Justice issued authority to proceed with Meng's extradition hearings. That suddenly brought Chinese orders for Canadian canola, valued at $2.5 billion a year, to a screeching halt.

In the wake of Richardson's ban, canola futures declined to their lowest level in more than two years, mimicking what had happened to American soybean prices after China effectively banned imports from the United States. The next thing you know, Viterra, another major Canadian canola exporter, had its licence revoked by Chinese authorities. Since then, all contracts with Canadian suppliers have been indefinitely suspended. Canadian farmers are expected to reduce their canola crop by at least 10 percent in 2020, as their principal export market has dried up.

Just prior to the Osaka G20 meetings in 2019, China ratcheted up its trade reprisals against Canada. It banned all exports of Canadian meat, claiming it had found trace amounts of the veterinarian drug ractopamine, legal in North America but not approved in China, as well as falsified health-inspection documents (China lifted the ban later that year following an outbreak of African swine flu). China is Canada's third most important export market for pork and its fifth for beef, with exports of the two meat products to China totalling some $374 million over the first four months of 2019. And with Canada exporting over $8 billion worth of agricultural products to China, there is certainly room for more trade reprisals, should China be so inclined.[8]

China is almost certain to do just that if Canadian authorities extradite Meng to the United States, or if Huawei is ultimately denied permission to build 5G networks in Canada. The country is certainly no stranger to suspending commercial relations to underscore a diplomatic point. After Australia banned the telecommunications supplier from its 5G network, Dalian, a major port in northern China, reportedly banned coal imports from Australia. Relations with New Zealand, with which China has a bilateral free trade agreement, also worsened after that country moved to ban Huawei from its 5G network.

Canadian-Chinese commercial links could unravel further on a number of fronts. Since Meng's arrest, tour bookings to Canada by Chinese government officials are reported to be down 95 percent.[9] Chinese tourism is estimated to be worth about $1.6 billion to the Canadian economy. And aside from having been a favourite destination for government-sponsored tours, Canada was a preferred spot for wealthy Chinese people to invest in real estate or send their kids to study.

Chinese real estate investors have already spurned the United States in response to mounting trade tensions. The National Association of Realtors reported that home purchases in America by Chinese buyers had declined by 56 percent in March 2019 from levels a year earlier. And it looks like they may be doing the same in Canada. That's not good news if you're selling a luxury property in Vancouver, but if you're a first-time home buyer looking for a place to call your own, you might want to thank the Chinese government for its retaliation to Meng's arrest.

Meng certainly isn't the only Chinese national to own upscale property in Vancouver. The city consistently ranks among the top six locations in the world for Chinese real estate investment. In 2015, the National Bank of Canada estimated that Chinese buyers had invested $13 billion into the city's real estate market, a third of the total that year.[10] Even local ski hill Grouse Mountain, an iconic spot for many Vancouver-area residents, is now owned by Chinese interests.

And real estate isn't the only asset China has been buying in Canada. China's national firms have been aggressive buyers of Canadian corporations, dating back to the China National Offshore Oil Corporation's huge, and ill-advised, acquisition of the Canadian oil sands producer Nexen. As recently as 2017, Chinese construction firm CCCC Holdings Ltd. offered $1.5 billion to salivating shareholders of the

Aecon Group, one of Canada's largest engineering and construction companies, before the takeover offer was thwarted by the Canadian government on national security grounds.

Meanwhile, in addition to the funding that Huawei provides many Canadian campuses for electronics research, Canadian universities benefit from the attendance of 150,000 Chinese students, all of whom are paying premium foreign-student tuition fees to do so.[11]

Given the state of Canadian-Chinese relations, President Trump won't need to use the poison pill provision in the USMCA with his northern trade partner; with the Canadian-Sino relationship at its lowest point since the two countries established diplomatic relations in 1970, chances are that after 2020, when Huawei's *Hockey Night in Canada* sponsorship agreement expires, the firm will want a new broadcast home on which to advertise its corporate banner.

If Meng is extradited to the United States, Ottawa knows it can forget about Beijing's cooperation on pretty well anything, including Canada's quest to be granted a seat at the UN Security Council. Trudeau, re-elected in October 2019, will be viewed as Donald Trump's stooge, an ironic perception given the thinly veiled contempt that Trump and his officials held for the Canadian leader during the tumultuous USMCA negotiations. At the same time, however, China will lose face in the world with the extradition and possible imprisonment of Meng in the United States—not a prospect it can afford while competing with the United States for world leadership and also losing economic ground in a gigantic trade war with its Western rival.

Completion of the on-again off-again negotiations for a massive new trade deal between the United States and China may yet result in a happy ending for Meng and the unfortunate Canadians being held hostage in China. The United States could well drop its extradition request as one of the many quid pro quos likely to surround a Phase Two comprehensive trade deal with China, in which case she and the Canadians will be released and free to go.

But a very unhappy ending to the US-China trade war could await Canadian exporters. China has already agreed to boost its imports of American goods by $200 billion over the next two years (a near doubling of current levels),[12] and much of those additional American exports could come at the expense of what China imports from other countries. In other words, compliance with US demands to buy more American-made goods will result in trade diversion, not trade expansion.

One of the countries most likely to be hurt is Canada. It exports to China many of the same goods that the United States does and could easily see its exports squeezed out to make room for more American goods. In 2018, Canada exported some $1.7 billion worth of soybeans and another $1.8 billion in meat and seafood to China. In addition, it exported $5.9 billion worth of forest products and another $2.9 billion in coal, oil, iron and copper.[13] Most of these quantities can be supplied by the United States. And increased American energy exports to China as mandated by the Phase One US–China trade agreement will likely mean that China will import liquefied natural gas from the US Gulf Coast instead of the terminal Canada is building in Kitimat, British Columbia. In other words, it's not so much Canada's new trade deal with the United States that is going to hurt Canadian exporters; it's China's deal with the United States that could take the heaviest toll.

There is undoubtedly no small irony in the fact that what started out as an initiative by the Trudeau government to open Chinese markets to Canadian exports and reduce the country's heavy trade reliance on the United States could end up closing those markets to Canadian exporters. The Trudeau government, one of the WTO's biggest supporters, is quickly learning what Canadian workers have been coming to grips with for decades: that in the new world trading order being shaped by international trade deals, it's easy to get left behind.

CHAPTER 13

MAKING CHINA GREAT AGAIN

I t's a great time to be an engineer in China. While much of the world stagnates and lets its infrastructure decay, you've probably got as much work as you can handle building a hyper-modern country pretty much from scratch, complete with skyscrapers, high-speed trains, next-generation military hardware and even quantum computers conducting experiments in orbit. Design a wide-body civilian aircraft to compete with Boeing and Airbus? No problem. Build the biggest concrete structure on the planet? Done it.

And there are considerable opportunities outside of China as well, as Chinese construction and scientific projects pop up in places as far-flung as Greenland and Antarctica. One place you might not want to be sent to, though, is Balochistan.

In 2016, operatives of the Balochistan Liberation Army (BLA) assassinated two Chinese engineers. In 2018, a suicide bomber from the group targeted a busload of Chinese engineers returning from a mining site. In November of that same year, three terrorists from the group attacked the Chinese consulate in Karachi in a failed suicide mission. The BLA is fighting for independence from Pakistan, not China. So why are they attacking Chinese engineers and diplomats?

The answer is that what some people call "globalization"—a complex supranational trading system that ignores or even tramples national interests—others may call "empire building." The Balochis have been at the crossroads of empires for millennia, and they have never been particularly accommodating. Alexander the Great lost at least twelve thousand soldiers retreating through the Gedrosian Desert of what is now Balochistan, near Gwadar. The British also found the limit of their power in the area. The internationally recognized border between Afghanistan and Pakistan is the Durand Line, which runs from Chitral in the north to Balochistan in the south. It was negotiated by Sir Mortimer Durand and the Amir of Afghanistan in 1893 and marked the edge of the British Empire. More than a century after its creation, the Durand Line remains one of the most dangerous borders in the world.

In 1948, the Balochis' territory was incorporated into the new state of Pakistan. While Balochistan accounts for almost half of Pakistan's area, its inhabitants earn less than 5 percent of the country's national income. While very poor and sparsely populated, the region is rich in natural resources. And it has something most countries do not: geopolitical value. It is where the Middle East, Central Asia, Southwest Asia and South Asia converge. Much of the developing world meets right where Alexander's army melted away (or half of it did, anyway; the other half sailed for Susa, which is now in western Iran).

But the area's history of rebuffing ambitious empires did not daunt the world's newest superpower. The stupendous trade surplus that China enjoys with the United States isn't a one-off. It's an annual event, and it adds up. Over the last ten years China has amassed a trade surplus with the United States in excess of $3 trillion. That has provided China with a huge cache of foreign reserves, and those trillions of dollars have been burning impressive holes in China's pockets.

So what does a developing economic giant do with all those acquired foreign reserves? Ironically, a good chunk of it gets recycled back to the United States through the purchase of American government bonds (Treasuries). China is far and away the largest foreign holder of US government debt, with approximately two-thirds of its foreign reserves held in US dollars.[1] The country's central bank, the People's Bank of China, has been buying US Treasuries for decades in order to keep down the value of its own currency, the yuan. (For a foreign central bank to buy US Treasuries, it first has to buy US dollars with its own currency. Hence, the more Treasuries China buys, the more it pushes up the value of the US dollar against the value of the yuan.) In turn, a cheaper yuan is vital for bolstering the competitiveness of the country's massive exports, which the Chinese economy has been so critically dependent upon. China is literally buying market share, and paying for it in American dollars.

But buying greenbacks is not the only thing that China does with its enormous cache of foreign reserves. Some are being recycled to finance President Xi's master plan.

ONE BELT ONE ROAD (AND ONE EMPIRE)

President Xi, or General Secretary Xi, as he is known to his comrades in the ruling Communist Party of China, is a big-picture thinker. After all, planning for the long run is supposed to be one of the great virtues of China's state-run economy. Many state-run enterprises don't have to worry about producing shareholder returns every quarter, a situation that frees them to make bold strategic plans that can take years, even decades, to come to fruition. In any event, state-run enterprises in China do what their political masters in Beijing instruct them to do. And right now, the instructions from Beijing are to make massive infrastructure investments around the world to support further growth in global trade—trade that, of course, will all flow through the Chinese economy.

President Xi's bold new vision of China's future harkens back to the fabled Silk Roads that shaped the country's imperial past. Not only was silk a highly prized luxury cloth, it once served as currency in global markets. And the centuries-old trade routes on which it was exchanged made China, for a time, the most powerful country on the planet. President Xi is hoping China's new routes will do the same.

This is, in other words, President Xi's plan to "Make China Great Again." It's funny how the same message can resonate so well on both sides of the Pacific. President Xi and President Trump seem to be on the same wavelength, which is probably why they appear to personally get along despite their countries' bitter trade war.

Xi first announced his brainchild, initially dubbed One Belt One Road, in the fall of 2013 on state visits to Kazakhstan and Indonesia. And like his American counterpart, Xi wasn't averse to the generous use of hype, boldly proclaiming his plan to be the project of the century. He envisioned building extensive infrastructure to support transit corridors stretching through more than sixty countries at an estimated cost of as much as $8 trillion dollars over the next two decades.

A sister programme, the Maritime Silk Road plan, was announced shortly after. What the former seeks to do for land transport, the latter attempts to do for sea travel. Since it was announced, China has started running twenty-nine ports in fifteen different countries through state-owned and -run global shipping giants such as China Merchants Group and COSCO.

With these initiatives, China has two objectives—the first defensive, the second offensive. All of the new roads, railways and ports are intended to provide China with a diversity of alternative supply and trading routes should the strategic Strait of Malacca—the primary sea passage between the Pacific and Indian Oceans—be blocked by some rival power (like the United States, for example).

China's potential vulnerability in the Strait of Malacca has been an obsession of Beijing's for quite some time. The waterway is particularly vital to the world's largest oil-importing country, dependent as it is on shipments of fuel from the Middle East. Nearly 80 percent of those shipments pass through the strait.[2] Block shipping there, and the wheels stop turning in the world's second-largest economy.

But the One Belt One Road mega-plan and its maritime sister plan are also designed to build a world-encompassing transport network, with China firmly ensconced at its hub. This network's land transport corridors would stretch across central Asia all the way to Europe, while its port infrastructure along maritime routes would connect the South China Sea with the Indian Ocean and beyond, all the way to the Mediterranean.

If you think China dominates today's global supply chains, just imagine how much more control the country would have in the future if it becomes the centre of a global transport network that links its economy to two-thirds of the world's population. And that population just happens to include the world's cheapest labour forces. Why not harness them to Chinese capital and technology? Look what its own cheap labour has already done for the country.

In principle, the One Belt One Road master plan uses the same model China first employed so successfully in Tibet. What Tibet taught the Chinese leadership was that if you want to integrate and assimilate a foreign people with a distinct culture living in a remote and isolated part of the country (although Tibet was no longer technically foreign, since the People's Liberation Army had "liberated" it in 1958), you need to build infrastructure to better connect them with the rest of China. Separation breeds rebellion and ultimately independence, whereas integration nurtures nation-building and, most of all, control.

Hence the construction of the nearly two-thousand-kilometre (1,243-mile) Qinghai–Tibet Railway linking the Chinese city of Xining, the largest city of the Tibetan plateau, with Lhasa, the centuries-old capital of Tibet. Reaching in parts an elevation of nearly five thousand metres (16,000 feet), it's the highest railway in the world—so high, in fact, that there are oxygen canisters in each of the specially designed train cars should passengers become short of breath. It's an engineering marvel, with much of it built on stilts over shifting permafrost.

Beijing claims that by breaking the transport bottlenecks that have long isolated Tibet from the rest of the world, it has brought economic progress to one of the country's poorest regions.[3] According to official Chinese economic statistics, Tibet has led the country in economic growth since the vital rail link was completed in 2006, averaging annual GDP growth of 10 percent.

But the railway has brought something else as well—trainloads of settlers from China. Officially, there are now some sixty thousand Han Chinese (China's ethnic majority) recently arrived and living in Tibet, and that doesn't include another forty thousand Chinese entrepreneurs who are considered temporary residents, or the anywhere from forty thousand to sixty-five thousand Chinese troops and militia permanently stationed in the supposedly semi-autonomous region.

Beijing reasoned that what worked so well in Tibet might work for China elsewhere too. Building infrastructure could not only better connect isolated western regions of China, like the Xinjiang region largely dominated by the Uyghur minority, with the country's heartland in the east, but it could also better connect China and its economy with countries all around the world, beginning with its Asian neighbours. And if infrastructure and trade corridors boosted economic growth in far-flung Tibet, why couldn't it do the same in other places that could be connected to China's burgeoning transit grid? Like neighbouring Pakistan, for example. To most of its neighbours, China's One Belt One Road master plan seemed to be a godsend.

What's not to like? Some benevolent country decides to invest billions of dollars, providing vitally needed infrastructure that your economy can't afford. Chinese companies build roads where there were once dirt tracks. They build power stations to give people who typically get electricity for only twelve hours a day the luxury of reliable and affordable power. They construct ports to allow your industries to export to world markets that were otherwise out of reach. And, most of all, they lend you the money to pay for all these marvellous development projects.

THE DEBT TRAP

But there's a catch—as there always is with things that look too good to be true.

China isn't just exporting technical expertise to build these projects all over the world. It's also exporting capital to finance them, and lots of it. The loans China offers to join its infrastructure spree are called "concessional loans," and that's because the countries receiving them will need to make concessions to China if they require debt relief. In most cases, if you can't pay back the money China has lent you to build all the wonderful new infrastructure, China seizes ownership of whatever they have built. That doesn't mean you don't get to use the infrastructure—you do, and hopefully that infrastructure, be it railways or ports or special economic zones, spurs your country's development. But it does mean that China will own it, and since your economy now depends vitally on this infrastructure, China has gained effective economic control.

Control is something Beijing values above anything else, including its own population. Admittedly, it can't be easy governing a country that has over a billion people in it. And no government around the world over the last two decades has done more to raise the standard of living of its citizens than the Chinese government (with a little help from the WTO). The ruling Communist Party of China today has as strong a claim to the Mandate of Heaven as any Chinese emperor ever had. So when Beijing feels that, in the national interest, it needs to crack down on dissidents in Hong Kong or send its restless Muslim Uyghur population into re-education camps reminiscent of those seen during Mao's Cultural Revolution, most Chinese citizens think they should cut their government a little slack. Similarly, when President Xi rewarded his own performance by amending the country's constitution to allow him to be leader for life[4]—following in the footsteps of the Great Helmsman Mao himself—most of his comrades nodded their approval.

But Beijing wants more than control over its own economy and people. It seeks control well beyond its own borders. The country is not unique in that respect. But instead of relying on its military muscle, as Russia or the United States often do to further their interests, China relies on economic muscle to achieve its strategic global objectives.

Nowhere is that being done on a grander scale than in neighbouring Pakistan, a long-time ally of China in conflicts with their mutual rival, India. A collection of infrastructure projects known as the China-Pakistan Economic Corridor (CPEC) is the crown jewel in the One Belt One Road master plan. It was announced as a $45 billion project by President Xi on his first visit to Pakistan in 2015. However, by 2017 the value of the project had grown to a staggering $62 billion investment in Pakistan's economy—more than all the foreign investment Pakistan has received in the past four decades.

While CPEC's initiatives cover all manner of infrastructure, the key developments are rail and road projects that will link Pakistan's economy to China's. They include a complete rebuild of the thirteen-hundred-kilometre (800-mile) Karakorum Highway that connects Pakistan to western China, from the ancient Silk Road city of Kashgar in the Xinjiang Uyghur Autonomous Region to Abbottabad in Pakistan's north. Pakistan's entire rail system is scheduled to be modernized and connected to China's Southern Xinjiang Railway, also connecting in Kashgar.

Aside from gaining an enormous amount of economic leverage in neighbouring Pakistan through CPEC, China also gains a trade outlet to the Indian Ocean, something it has coveted since the early 1950s, when it first began constructing the original Karakorum Highway. With that access, China can ship cargo from deep inside its industrial heartland across Pakistan by rail and truck, avoiding the longer, slower voyage by sea through other countries' waters. From its huge new port in Pakistan, it can ship to anywhere in the world.

However, that gleaming new port is Gwadar, in Balochistan, where Alexander the Great and Sir Mortimer Durand were taught lessons in humility, and where the BLA has continued a time-honoured tradition of making outsiders as unwelcome as possible.

And it's not only tribal militants who are questioning the benefits of President Xi's master plan. In 2018, Pakistan's newly elected government began to have some sober second thoughts about the flood of Chinese capital and technocrats pouring into the country. It has already hit the brakes on the seemingly never-ending number of infrastructure projects that China has offered to build in the country, including cancelling a major coal-fired power plant. What most worries the Pakistani government is whether the country will be able to service the massive amount of debt it is incurring to build and operate all these projects.

They have good reason to be concerned. All they have to do is look at what has already happened in Sri Lanka. China's financing of the port at Hambantota provides a cautionary tale. It's the second-largest port in the country and was originally owned by the Sri Lankan government and operated by the Sri Lanka Ports Authority. But when the Sri Lankan authorities couldn't generate enough revenue at the port to service the huge debt they had incurred when building it, China foreclosed on the project. In exchange for $1 billion of debt relief, the Sri Lankan government ceded control of the port and its operations to Beijing for the next ninety-nine years.[5]

It is widely rumoured that the same fate awaits the Chinese-financed port at Mombasa, Kenya, as freight volumes have failed to meet minimums needed to service the loan. Kenya is struggling under some $9.8 billion in concessional loans from China, which also financed the construction of a vital high-speed rail connection for both freight and passenger traffic between Mombasa and Nairobi.[6]

The Pakistani government might also have noticed what happened in Malaysia, another favourite destination for Chinese infrastructure investment. China had undertaken to finance and build a number of key infrastructure projects, most notably the $27 billion East Coast Rail Link connecting Port Klang on the Strait of Malacca to the northeast part of the country.[7] However, fearing that his country was about to fall into the same debt trap as Sri Lanka, newly elected president Mahathir bin Mohamad temporarily cancelled the project in 2018.[8] In fact, growing concern about Chinese dominance of the Malaysian economy was a major issue in the 2018 election that brought him to power.

Elsewhere, the island of Fiji owes China half a billion dollars, while island nation Tonga has run up a debt to China equal to a third of its GDP and has already acknowledged that it will need debt relief. A growing concern in the West is that the concessions demanded for debt relief will soon include the right to establish military bases on the debtor's territory, as has been widely rumoured in the case of Vanuatu, an island nation off the Australian coast.[9]

The inevitable debt relief that comes with Chinese concessional lending can also involve the actual transfer of territory. When Tajikistan encountered problems servicing its Chinese debt, it ceded disputed territory along its Chinese border, an area comparable in size to Albania.

While China's Asian neighbours are the main recipients of these loans and projects, China has even managed to recruit Italy to its sprawling trade programme. It's the first G7 country to join—although without question it is the basket case of the elite economic powers. Since the 2008 global financial crisis, the Italian economy has been mired in three separate recessions, which goes a long way to explaining why it is suddenly open to China's offer to help its badly limping economy. Saddled with huge levels of government debt, Italy hasn't exactly been flooded with foreign investment. However, China is interested in making major investments in port facilities in Palermo, Genoa, Trieste and Ravenna, much like it did when its COSCO group took ownership of Greece's main port, Piraeus.[10] And most of all, China now has an important ally deep within the ranks of the European Union, whose government in Brussels still considers the Asian colossus a "systemic rival."

China's infrastructure investment policy has been criticized as not only a debt trap but a new form of colonialism, a criticism Beijing vehemently rejects. Already, Djibouti, Kyrgyzstan, Laos, the Maldives, Mongolia, Montenegro, Pakistan, and Tajikistan have been identified as falling into that trap, with loans from China representing anywhere between 25 and 100 percent of their GDP.[11] Yet for many of those borrowers, China's investment is the only game in town. African leaders flocked to an investment conference in Beijing in April 2019 with caps in hand, requesting billions of dollars in more infrastructure funding. Many of the African nations attending noted that financial institutions in Europe and the United States were rarely interested in providing credit for development projects. President Xi announced that $64 billion of new infrastructure projects were signed at the conference.[12]

China claims that it is simply a developing country that is extending the hand of friendship to other developing countries so that they can follow in China's footsteps and lift their people out of poverty. In President Xi's words, the plan "promotes shared goals, common development and provides a win-win situation for everyone concerned." He even changed the name of his grand scheme from the original One Belt One Road to simply Belt and Road, as more and more countries began to figure out to whom exactly the "One" referred.

Whether China is still just another fellow developing country or a budding imperial power is, to say the least, a contentious point. Certainly, Robert Lighthizer, Peter Navarro, Larry Kudlow and Donald Trump wouldn't consider it just another developing economy. And you probably wouldn't either if you took a look at today's Beijing, Shanghai or Shenzhen.

TAKING OVER THE WORLD OR MAKING SOME REALLY LOUSY INVESTMENTS?

About forty-eight hundred kilometres (2,900 miles) down the road from Shenzhen is the Balochi town of Gadani. It's about a seven-hour drive along the Makran Coastal Highway from Gwadar, the former fishing village that figures in Beijing's plans as the terminus of its overland Belt. It's also where oil tankers and container ships go to die.

One day, these pack mules of the global economy are ferrying precious commodities and containers full of televisions and flip-flops to markets on the other side of the world; the next, they're being winched up onto the beach in Balochistan, where as many as two hundred workers, who are poor even by Pakistani standards, swarm over their unimaginably huge hulls, first salvaging all the wiring and electronics, and then slicing the ships up with liquid-oxygen cutting torches. Bit by bit, over the course of months, the ships' thousands of pounds of steel will be fed into seventeen-hundred-degree furnaces and melted down, emerging later as rebar and billets of steel. About a hundred ships a year end up in Gadani. That number used to be much higher, back when Gadani was the biggest shipbreaking yard on the planet, but competition from India and Bangladesh has eaten into its market.

Still, Gadani pumps out millions of tons of steel, most of it for domestic construction. That's a lot of rebar, and it should come as little surprise that the Pakistani concrete industry is based in Balochistan—there is a lot being poured there these days, with much more planned. Official plans call for the town of Gwadar to sprawl from a population of eighty thousand to over 2 million (including twenty thousand Chinese workers and supervisors). The ten coal-fired power plants of Gadani Energy Park will also require a lot of rebar and concrete by the time its sixty-six hundred megawatts of electricity is online (built with financial and technical assistance from, yes, China). Prime minister Imran Khan also broke ground in early 2019 on the New Gwadar International Airport, which at forty-three hundred acres will be the biggest in Pakistan. Unlike most other projects in the region, it is not financed through a concessional loan from China. The $246 million budget is instead being covered by a *grant* from China.[13]

The question is, will market forces be any more accommodating to China's grandiose plans for the region than the Balochistan Liberation Army has been? Will the remnants of all those forgotten ships live on as the infrastructure of a

Chinese transportation network that reaches all the way back to Shenzhen?

Whether China's massive investment in infrastructure in developing countries around the world will pay huge future trade and financial dividends remains to be seen. It's not exactly like Beijing has beaten Wall Street to the punch here. The countries that China is lending billions of dollars to are hardly the most credit-worthy of nations. The sovereign debt of twenty-seven of the nations with Belt and Road projects is rated as junk bonds by three international bond rating agencies, and another fourteen recipient countries have no credit rating whatsoever.[14] Not exactly the countries in which you would want to invest your retirement savings.

Nor, for that matter, would anyone else. In most cases, no other country or private lending institution would consider financing these massive infrastructure projects. That's why so little of the investment in Belt and Road projects has come from China's private sector. According to one estimate, 95 percent of the $208 billion invested in Belt and Road construction projects since 2014 has come from state-owned enterprises or the Chinese government directly.[15]

It could be that these investments were never expected to earn a sufficient commercial return and pay their own way. Maybe the real motivation behind them, as many in the West fear, is the expansion of China's political influence and its aspirations to become the most powerful country in the world. But how will China become the most powerful nation in the world if every country to which it has lent billons of dollars defaults on its loans? Doesn't the buck stop with the Chinese taxpayer, who will ultimately foot the bill?

I guess that depends on how you look at it. Certainly, China's taxpayers will have to make up any budgetary shortfall if Beijing never gets its money back. But the thing is, the money China is investing all over the world didn't come from its own economy. The market probably wouldn't have invested in those far-flung development projects, but thanks to the magic of globalization, *you* have.

Those trillions of dollars being used to pave dirt roads in Baluchistan and twist arms in Kenya and Sri Lanka once circulated in the United States, Canada and other advanced industrial economies. They used to be the wages of the men and women who made the things now made in China. They used to be the savings of the people now shopping at Walmart and dollar stores for the things they used to make. But these dollars have been gift-wrapped and delivered to China, where they've piled up so high that the Chinese can use them to triple down in ways that can only hurt the expendables. They inflate real estate prices in markets like Vancouver, which makes it that much harder for middle-class households to buy a home. They devalue the yuan, which makes North American products less competitive on the international market. And they finance Chinese infrastructure around the world, which increases Chinese influence and markets.

But how much longer will China be able to afford to gobble up the global Monopoly board? The strategy of recycling trillions of dollars of trade imbalance depends critically on maintaining those gravy-train trade flows with the United States.

If President Trump's tariffs get in the way of those huge trade surpluses, or a new managed trade deal with the United States does the same—not to mention the fiscal consequences of markedly slowing Chinese economic growth—the country may no longer have the financial wherewithal to underwrite all of those grandiose development projects.

Just as globalization begets further globalization, the reverse is also true. Chain reactions work both ways. If American tariffs threaten the exports that have made China the source of most of today's global supply chains, they may also threaten China's ability to finance the trade corridors that are intended to serve as the transport routes for tomorrow's supply chains.

If those trillions start flowing back where they came from, middle-class jobs will follow in their wake. That could be good news for wage earners. But demand is not the only factor determining the price of labour. The other is supply.

CHAPTER 14

ON THE MOVE

It's commonplace these days to hear the mainstream media and politicians refer to men and women who voted Donald Trump into the White House as "nativists." *The New Yorker*, among other media outlets, bemoaned Trump's transformation of the Republican party into a "nativist" party.[1] Canada's then–minister of trade, Chrystia Freeland, while testifying at a Senate hearing in late 2016, boldly asserted, "We're living in an era of nativism and protectionism, something I think is very dangerous for the world and for Canadians."[2] Prior to Trump's presidency, the last time you might have encountered the term was back in 2002, if you happened to catch Martin Scorsese's *Gangs of New York*.

In the film, Bill the Butcher (so brilliantly portrayed by Daniel Day-Lewis) objects to the surge of Irish immigrants during the mid-nineteenth century and welcomes them in his own inimical way. The charismatic, one-eyed Bill draws a strict line between "us natives, born right-wise, in this fine land" on one side, and "the foreign hordes defiling it" on the other. And he aims to cleanse New York of immigrants in an orgy of bloody violence. He's a compelling character, but the film doesn't exactly make the "nativist creed" an ideal to aspire to.

Not much has changed since. Any current references to nativists in editorials and political speeches make it clear that such people are not welcome in polite company.

Not that the swaggering demagogic Bill had much interest in being deemed polite. Neither, for that matter, do many today who share Bill's antipathy to "foreign hordes." Historically, surges in immigration have been met by the native population first with suspicion and then with violence. The question that makes this film (which was nominated for ten Oscars) resonate nearly two decades later—and far beyond the Five Points of nineteenth-century New York—is *why*?

THE POLISH PLUMBER

Some of the most resented outsiders in Europe aren't immigrants at all, strictly speaking. Throughout the European Union countries, they are known as "posted workers." More colloquially, especially by their detractors, they are known as "the Polish plumber." Some 1 million Poles, many of them tradesmen, have migrated to work in Western Europe since 2004, when Poland joined the European Union. A majority of them, 832,000 as of 2018, settled in the United Kingdom.[3]

There are nearly 17 million workers in the European Union who live and work in a country other than their own, double the number of only a decade ago. For the most part, they come from Eastern Europe and seek jobs in the more affluent West.[4] And a feature of their legal status gives them a huge advantage over the native labour force when it comes to finding employment: they are typically exempted from legislated local wage standards, and that provides an attractive commercial advantage to their employers. That is to say, Polish plumbers drive wages down for English plumbers.

Attempts by the European Union to enforce equal wage standards for domestic workers and posted workers have met with fierce opposition from the German Employers' Associations, who have no problem whatsoever with paying lower wages.[5] And many posted workers send generous remittances to families back home, an important source of income for many households in those countries. With foreign households and local employers both benefiting from the presence of posted workers, guess who loses out?

The fact is that new workers are almost never welcome in the labour force they are looking to join. As we saw in chapter 4, just as a capital-rich country has every incentive to pursue free trade with a capital-poor country, workers in labour-scarce countries should want to avoid free trade with a labour-rich country. You don't want to compete with the cheaper products they make, and you certainly don't want to be competing with them for wages at the factory or bidding against them for a local plumbing job down the street.

Not everyone's wages are threatened by competition from migrant workers. As usual, when the local economy is disrupted by global changes, there are winners and losers. In general, the more skilled you are, the less you have to worry about. It is unlikely that professionals, managers, business owners or skilled trades are going to be displaced by new immigrants. (Also, the highly skilled have always gone to great lengths to protect themselves from becoming expendable through competition—whether through highly secretive medieval guilds, which kept the supply of their trade's knowledge tight, or various colleges of physicians, which keep the supply of doctors tight.) But if your job can be done just as well by someone with little or no training, someone who is willing to work for less, then you have reason to be concerned—because your employer now has an incentive to replace you. One person's lower wage is someone else's higher profit.

Though resistance to immigration is often dismissed as racist or xenophobic, in fact the greatest beneficiaries of immigration enforcement in the United States are young men of colour, who often compete with immigrants for low-skilled jobs. According to a Cornell University study, "No racial or ethnic group has benefited less [from immigration] or been harmed more than the nation's African American community."[6] Not much in that regard has changed over the past century. The mass movement of emancipated slaves to the northern states following the Civil War didn't get going in earnest until after the First World War, when immigration levels were severely cut back.[7]

Of course, there is more to nativism than that. But the fact is, today's nativists likely aren't cold-hearted, conniving schemers like Bill, hungry for power and control—they are, for the most part, unemployed or underpaid, angry at having been deemed expendable.

The resentment the British expendables felt really had no avenue for expression, at least not within the traditional electoral landscape in the United Kingdom (not including Nigel Farage's Independence Party). But a referendum is a different matter, and the discussion of whether or not to remain part of the European Union suddenly provided a clear-cut avenue to express their anger. In June 2016, when Brits voted to leave the European Union during the Brexit referendum, they weren't voting so much to leave the free trade zone as they were voting against regulations that allow citizens of all EU member states to work and live anywhere they wish in the eurozone.

Though the "Leave" voters have since been accused of intolerance and racism, what they were objecting to was not simply the presence of foreigners in their communities, but the fact that many of them were accepting much lower wages than local labour was paid. For many British workers it was bad enough that local factories were relocating to low-wage countries in Eastern Europe. But to add insult to injury, workers from those very same countries were coming to Britain to compete for the remaining jobs—and getting them by accepting much lower wages. It turns out free trade doesn't just mean jobs chasing lower wages to poorer countries. It also means lower wages coming to your job.

Since the Brexit vote, the number of Polish migrant workers coming to the United Kingdom has dropped off dramatically.[8] Moreover, the number of Polish and other EU workers leaving the United Kingdom has soared to historic highs. Uncertainty over their legal status once Britain finally formalizes the terms of its divorce from the European Union has suddenly made the United Kingdom a much less attractive destination for them. At the same time, there has been a noticeable uptick in the migration of Polish workers to Germany.

For people like Nigel Farage, leader of Britain's anti-immigrant Independence Party, the diversion of Polish immigration from the United Kingdom to Germany validates the Brexit vote. But to like-minded politicians in the Alternative for Germany party, that spike in Polish migration has only added to the onslaught of newcomers already welcomed by the much more migrant-friendly government of Angela Merkel.

FROM RUSSIA WITH LOVE

Of course, not all migrant workers in Europe come from within the EU. Most, in fact, come from the Middle East or Africa. Some are legitimate political refugees, while others are of the economic variety. You can't really blame any of them; they are fleeing either poverty or war.

Migration to Europe surged in 2015, after Russia's President Putin answered the request for military assistance from Syria's desperate, crumbling Assad regime. Putin not only secured a strategic foothold for Russia in the Middle East—including the naval base at Tartus and the Khmeimim Air Base—but he also got a measure of revenge on NATO when an estimated 5 million Syrian refugees fled their country and its brutal regime. You can bet most weren't heading for Moscow. Instead, they were making their way toward NATO countries, the same NATO Putin felt was aggressively threatening Russia's western borders.

You see, back in 2004, Estonia, Latvia and Lithuania, all of which share a border with Russia, joined NATO. Four years later, Ukraine, also sharing a border with Russia, applied for NATO membership. To most people in North America and Western Europe, that seemed like a welcome and perfectly natural thing for those countries to do. The collapse of the Soviet Union provided a once in a lifetime opportunity for those countries to free themselves from the yoke of Russian domination and get under the mantle of a Western military alliance that pledged to come to the aid of any member country if attacked.[9] However, joining the NATO alliance seemed far less appealing to the large groups of Russian minorities who live in those countries. And the prospect of NATO forces and weapons along Russia's western border was even less appealing to the Kremlin, especially since NATO had explicitly promised Russia that it wouldn't do that.[10]

When you shove a stick up a polar bear's ass, you can't expect it to turn the other cheek.

The Syrian migrants might not have ended up in the Baltic countries or in Ukraine, where Putin no doubt would have loved to see them all go, but they nevertheless put huge stresses on the various NATO countries where they landed, and this has weakened the alliance.[11] As it turns out, the few migrants who made it up to the Baltic states didn't stay long. Of 349 asylum seekers taken in by Lithuania, 248 left as soon as they received official refugee status. Similarly, of the 136 who arrived in Estonia on the EU migrant relocation programme, 79 moved to greener pastures in Europe.[12]

Welfare provisions for newly arriving migrants in Estonia or Lithuania are a fraction of what is available in countries like Germany. That is why the quick exodus of migrants who made the trek all the way to the Baltic states worked out well for everyone concerned. Once granted asylum, refugees could travel freely within the European Union and settle wherever they chose, while the Baltic countries that accepted them just to watch most leave were deemed to have fulfilled their obligations under the EU migrant quota scheme.

But seen from the other side—from places like Italy, Greece, Germany and, more recently, Spain, where the vast majority of migrants did end up—things haven't worked out so well. The growing presence of migrants has led to a weakening in the political grip of many a NATO government, if not outright political upheaval and change. With President Trump at the same time openly questioning what America was getting in return for its leadership role in NATO, and in particular the burden its financing share places on American taxpayers, the alliance could be heading for shaky ground. If so, the balance of power in Europe could well shift to Russia's advantage.

Of course, not all of the migrants flooding into Europe are political refugees from the Middle East. Others who have made the sea crossing are simply economic migrants, similar to those coming from El Salvador, Guatemala and Honduras who want to cross the US-Mexico border. They come from everywhere from Afghanistan to sub-Saharan Africa, crossing a vast geographic crescent that stretches from Turkey to Morocco. Some places in that crescent, most notably Libya, are in a state of chaos, with no effective central government to police the shores against migrants heading across the Mediterranean toward the European coastline. When he was still around and ruled with an iron fist, Muammar Qaddafi would accept payments from southern European countries to keep migrants from launching their exodus from Libyan shores. But thanks to Western military intervention, the Qaddafi regime, like

Saddam Hussein's regime in Iraq, no longer exists. And between political and economic refugees, in the last four years almost 2 million migrants have come into Europe, with roughly half of them settling in Germany.[13]

Migrations of that size don't occur without consequences. This is all the more true when most of the refugees are visibly different from the majority of people who live in the countries where they end up. The migrants come from a different race; they speak a different language; they eat different types of food; and they practise a different religion. Assimilating them was never going to be a piece of cake. And not all of them wanted to be assimilated in the first place.

As more immigrants arrived in Europe, the backlash against them grew. The rise of right-wing populist parties is now a pan-European phenomenon that owes much of its support not only to the culture shock but to the potential economic stresses the migrants have triggered. The populist right's greatest appeal has been in the countries where the most migrants have set-tled. Parties such as Vox in Spain, the National Rally (formerly known as the National Front) in France, the Freedom Party in Austria, Alternative for Germany, the Dutch Freedom Party, or the Independence Party in the United Kingdom are all national manifestations of this movement.

A TICKET TO RIDE

It used to be, when motoring through Europe, you would have to stop at every border, get out your passport to show the border guards who you were, and tell them where you were going. Those days are long gone, of course, thanks to the Schengen Agreement. It opened the door for border-free motoring throughout most of Europe. But with the arrival of 2 million migrants since 2014, European borders may soon be back in style.

The agreement, implemented between five European Union countries back in 1985, eliminated national border stations and guards in favour of drive-through motoring. Membership in the Schengen Agreement has grown steadily and now encompasses most of Europe. Today, the Schengen area consists of Austria, Belgium, the Czech Republic, Denmark, Estonia, Finland, France, Germany, Greece, Hungary, Iceland, Italy, Latvia, Liechtenstein, Lithuania, Luxembourg, Malta, the Netherlands, Norway, Poland, Portugal, Slovakia, Slovenia, Spain, Sweden and Switzerland. With the exception of Norway and Switzerland, all countries that are part of the agreement are also member states of the European Union. In fact, only six European Union members do not belong to the area—Bulgaria, Croatia, Cyprus, Romania, the United Kingdom and Ireland.

Originally, the treaty that created the area was designed with the interests of its member states' populations in mind. Not only is the Schengen Agreement largely symbolic of a unified and seamless European Union, but it is also seen as an economic attribute for the free movement of millions of workers and billions of euros' worth of goods that cross these borders every day. It complemented the European Union's policy of allowing citizens of member states to work and live in all member countries. But the architects of the Schengen treaty didn't anticipate hundreds of thousands of refugees from the Middle

East and Africa crossing those unguarded borders. In the wake of those migrations, a number of countries felt the time had come to reconsider their policies.

Norway, Denmark, Germany, France and Austria all reimposed some form of border patrol in response to the flood of migrants crossing their borders, and to the rising number of terrorist attacks across Europe. Germany, a country that has taken in a million migrants, at one point temporarily closed its border with Austria in order to stem the inflow of migrants. In December 2015, the European Union threatened to boot Greece out of the Schengen Agreement if it didn't do a better job of preventing migrants from landing on its shores. Italian prime minister Giuseppe Conte has warned his EU partners that the migrant issue puts the Schengen Agreement in jeopardy. While the agreement remains in effect, the concept of open borders becomes highly problematic when you are facing a migrant crisis.

Not every country in Europe has opened its borders to African and Middle Eastern migrants. A few, belonging to what is known as the Visegrád Group, have gone to extreme lengths to keep them out. The group, consisting of Hungary, Poland, Slovakia and the Czech Republic, is known for comprising the bad boys of the European Union, at least in the eyes of its central government in Brussels. Together, these countries formed an anti-immigration alliance. Poland and Hungary have gone so far as to refuse to accept the EU-imposed quotas of migrants. Viktor Orbán, the colourful Hungarian prime minister who often speaks for the group, has challenged the European Union's open-arms welcome to the waves of migrants from Africa and the Middle East, calling for Brussels to take a much harder line on illegal immigration, as he has done in Hungary.

After some 200,000 migrants passed through Hungary on their way to Western Europe in 2015, Orbán walled off a 41-kilometre (25-mile) section of the Hungary-Croatia border with a 4-metre (13-foot) barbed wire fence[14] and threatened to do the same with the remaining 330 kilometres (205 miles) of border unless the onslaught of refugees stopped. A year later, Hungary completed a second fence running 155 kilometres (96 miles) that sealed off its border with Serbia, the other major crossing point for migrants. Orbán made it clear to neighbouring Slovenia and Romania that Hungary would construct similar barbed wire fences along their borders if those countries directed migrants toward Hungary.

While the construction of those two border fences was widely condemned by other countries in the European Union, they seem to have done their job. Since their construction, the flow of migrants coming into Hungary—principally from Syria, Iraq and Afghanistan—has slowed to a trickle. And like President Trump, who wants Mexico to pay for his wall, Orbán sent the European Union a bill to cover half the cost of erecting his border fences. Brussels, like Mexico City, refused to pay.

Orbán is frequently villainized in the European media, much like Trump is in the American press, but the fact of the matter is that every country in Europe was handing off refugees to their neighbours like so many hot potatoes. Serbia and Croatia were sending them to Hungary, which in turn was offloading them to Austria. And Austria was only too happy to send them along to Germany, where the vast majority remain. Of course, each country was pointing a finger at its neighbours for sending the refugees their way.

WE'RE FULL UP DOWN UNDER

Tensions are growing over migrant labour far beyond the European Union. Legislation aimed at limiting new migrants has become contagious, at least in many of the places that most migrants would like to move.

Take Australia, one of the preferred destinations for migrants, for example. Fraser Anning, formerly of the far-right One Nation party, used his maiden speech in the Australian Senate to call for a return to the White Australia policy, which restricted non-European immigration from 1901 until it began to be dismantled in the late 1960s. It was a page right out of Farage's playbook. While Anning's call for a plebiscite on the matter, which he provocatively labelled "the final solution,"[15] was widely condemned as being racist and xenophobic by mainstream Australian politicians, the fact remains that all of the parties have called for significant cuts to migration, some drastic in magnitude.

Those advocating deep cuts to immigration include Prime Minister Scott Morrison, whose Liberal Party won the 2019 election while pledging to cut current migrant numbers in half. Morrison made this promise even though, by the time he was elected, levels had already dropped to their lowest in a decade, to almost thirty thousand below the country's annual maximum. The bottom line of Australia's new population policy, regardless of party, is "Don't come here—we're full up."

It's essentially the same message you heard from New Zealand in 2017, when the new Labour government was elected and vowed to cut immigration by almost half. The announced cuts follow earlier moves by the New Zealand government to tighten regulations aimed at both foreign workers and foreign students under its Kiwi First policy.

Could even seemingly migrant-friendly Canada adopt a similar position? For obvious geographic reasons, Canada hasn't been a front-line country in the battle to stem the tide of illegal immigration. The migrants flowing across the Mediterranean into Europe would have to swim across an ocean or trek over the North Pole to get there. Canada has only one border, and the citizens on the other side are every bit as wealthy as Canada's own. Americans aren't exactly cramming onto boats to cross Lake Ontario in search of a better life for themselves and their children.

But other people are making a similar trek. Fearing imminent deportation under ever-tightening US immigration policies, tens of thousands of illegal migrants living in the United States have made a beeline for the Canadian border, betting that the Trudeau government would be far more tolerant of their presence than the Trump administration. So far, they've guessed right. Fifty thousand illegal immigrants from places ranging from Pakistan, Turkey, Yemen, Lebanon, Nigeria, Sri Lanka and Eritrea have crossed Roxhan Road from upper New York state to near Saint-Bernard-de-Lacolle, Quebec.[16] There haven't been that many people seeking political asylum in Canada from the United States since the draft dodgers made their way north during the Vietnam War.

That might be okay with the Trudeau government in Ottawa, which is always eager to show its political constituency how different it is from the current administration in Washington. But it doesn't sit too well with the provinces and cities where most illegal migrants ended up living—mainly Toronto and Montreal. The influx of thousands of illegal immigrants has put a huge strain on the limited public housing and other social services that are designated for the poor in those cities.

Facing an election in October 2019, the Trudeau government had some sober second thoughts on the issue. Technically, under its Safe Third Country Agreement with the United States, Canada can return migrants who cross its border. But that applies only to migrants entering at regular border crossings. Those entering unseen along the 8,891-kilometer (5,524-mile) border—as most of the migrants do—are not covered. Virtually all have been allowed to stay in Canada.

In the lead-up to the election, the Trudeau government made a sudden about-face on the migrant issue. It began negotiating with the United States to close that gaping loophole in the Safe Third Country Agreement, allowing Canada to return migrants to the United States no matter where they cross the border. And to cap off their newfound sensitivity to border security, the Trudeau government announced $382 million in additional funding for Canada Border Services agencies and $80 million for the Mounties to better patrol the border. They clearly understood that Canadians, while so far tolerant of immigration, have not had their tolerance tested to the same degree as Europeans. They aren't likely eager to welcome just anybody into the country, and if governments aren't on top of the issue as the migrant crisis continues, they could face the same hard swing to the right that is happening in Europe and Australia.

Meanwhile, the new right-of-centre Coalition Avenir Québec government passed its highly contentious Bill 21. The legislation—which is aimed at arriving migrants and bans the wearing of any religious symbols, including headscarves, by provincial government employees—resembles similar bills already in place in France, Belgium, Austria and the Netherlands. The Trudeau government has been highly critical of the province's hardline policy toward migrants. But at the same time, it was counting on ridings in Quebec in order to stay in power. Maybe that is why the federal government, for all its declarations about migrant rights and the openness of Canadian society, is building a new migrant detention centre in Laval, Quebec.

WALLS

Countries have always built walls, sometimes to protect the people living inside them and sometimes to keep people from getting out. Classical civilization might never have developed in Athens if the birthplace of democracy had not been surrounded by walls (their enemies, the Spartans, whose strong army and warrior society had no need for walls, enjoyed few of the Athenians' freedoms or luxuries, and lived off the labour of a vast underclass of slaves). The Great Wall of China, one of the seven wonders of the world, was built to keep the barbarians out of the Middle Kingdom. Hadrian's Wall was erected to keep the Picts from overrunning the western reaches of the Roman Empire. And the Berlin Wall was put up to keep the population of the Soviet Union's client states behind the Iron Curtain. Despite claims to the contrary, history strongly suggests that walls work.

Building walls is back in fashion. These days, they are erected to separate rich countries from much poorer ones, like the 245-kilometre (150-mile) wall that Israel built across the Sinai to keep African migrants from coming in. But none is more famous or contentious than the one President Trump is building along the 3,100-kilometre (2,000-mile) US-Mexico border. It was one of Trump's two campaign-defining promises—the other, of course, being to renegotiate America's flawed trade deals. The two initiatives are linked not only ideologically but financially. Trump originally promised his supporters that the tariff revenue he would soon start collecting from Mexico would finance the wall's construction. In the meantime, he wanted Congress to give him a $5.7 billion appropriation for the Department of Homeland Security so he could start building it.

The wall has become a "red meat" issue for many of Trump's supporters, and the subject of continual scorn and criticism from Democrats. In response to the growing resistance to immigration, many of the world's establishment papers, including *The New York Times*, the *Financial Times* of London, and *The Globe and Mail*, continue to earnestly remind us that, with our aging populations, what we really need is more immigration, not less; it is vital, we are told, to future economic growth.

(Curiously, the same papers warn that the much-hyped era of artificial intelligence will mean there won't be any jobs for these immigrants—and in fact, there won't be any jobs for anyone else either.)

In any event, extolling the benefits of legal immigration isn't really the issue today. The real issue is whether migration should be controlled by a process that begins with people applying at your embassies, or uncontrolled, with migrants instead paying smugglers to sneak them across the border into your country. The two routes are likely to attract very different types of people. Canada, for example, has a points system that assesses a potential migrant's skills to determine their suitability to work in the Canadian economy. But of course, that assessment wasn't conducted on the fifty thousand or so migrants who have crossed illegally into the country from the United States.

While the United States considers itself to be a country built by immigrants, it hasn't always welcomed them with open arms, particularly those who weren't European. Trump isn't the first, nor will he likely be the last, American president to make immigration a defining issue for their administration. Back in 1924, under President Calvin Coolidge, the US Congress passed the Immigration Act (or the Johnson-Reed Act). Immigration had spiked in the 1830s and plateaued at a high rate well through the early decades of the twentieth century, when it started to become obvious that the country couldn't safely absorb more. Income inequality was rampant, the nascent socialist movement was gathering steam and the "Red Summer" of 1919 saw 26 separate race riots, which claimed more than a thousand lives. At the time, immigrants constituted 12 percent of the population, only slightly less than today's near-record 14 percent.

The biggest supporters of immigration have always been capitalists, who saw the new arrivals as a source of cheap labour for their factories. That was as true back in 1886, when robber baron Andrew Carnegie called immigrants a "stream of gold,"[17] as it is today with the Koch brothers, among the most outspoken advocates of greater immigration.

Nor is Trump the first US president to authorize the construction of a physical barrier along the country's border with Mexico. While the very idea of walling themselves off from their Mexican neighbours runs contrary to the fundamental beliefs of many Americans, 1046 kilometers (650 miles) of border wall or physical barrier was already standing before Trump came to office. And it was built for a reason.

Illegal immigration across its southern border has been a huge and growing problem for the United States for decades. In 2000, it reached its apex when over 1.6 million people were apprehended trying to illegally cross into the United States from Mexico, prompting the initial wall construction under the George W. Bush administration. There are now some 11 million illegal migrants living in the United States with no path to American citizenship. Without proper documentation, they are often paid below statutory minimums.[18]

Trump frequently characterizes the people the wall is intended to keep out as rapists, drug dealers and generally bad hombres, like the *sicarios* you see in movies about Pablo Escobar. In reality, these hombres are simply poor, and many are actually women and children. For the most part, they are just economic migrants in search of a better life for themselves and their families. Many are not even Mexican. They come from Central American nations like Honduras or El Salvador or Guatemala, failed states where poverty and gang violence reign supreme.

Drugs and *sicarios* aside, illegal immigration across the US-Mexico border is really about basic economics. If you look at relative income levels, it's not hard to see why migrants want to live in the United States. Per capita GDP in Honduras in 2018 was $2,482; El Salvador, $4,058; Guatemala, $4,549; and Nicaragua, $2,028. In 2018, US per capita GDP was $62,641.[19] When there is a nearby country that is some twenty times richer than the one where you are living, chances are you want to move there any way you can.

Even Mexico, a country much wealthier than its Central American neighbours, has a per capita GDP ($9,698 in 2018[20]) less than a fifth of that of the United States. That in itself is going to make the policing of America's southern border a problem. What would you risk if the reward was five or twenty times your income? The poor in the region have a powerful and ever-present incentive to find a way over the US border.

The American migration issue was highlighted in the fall of 2018 when a caravan of some three thousand migrants from Central America entered Mexico en route to the US border just ahead of the mid-term elections. Their trek hit a roadblock at the US border, where machine-gun-armed US troops were waiting for them. Now it's incumbent on the Mexican border city of Tijuana to house and look after them.

Democrats were quick to claim that the spike in migrant attempts to cross the border speaks to the futility or even counterproductiveness of Trump's anti-migrant policies. But as far as President Trump was concerned, the surge in Central American migrants heading to the US border couldn't have come at a better time.

His earlier claims that the country was facing a national emergency and a humanitarian crisis on its southern border had been largely falling on the deaf ears of a skeptical American public. Not one to look a gift horse in the mouth, President Trump was quick to seize on the surge in border arrests to push his anti-migrant agenda further. He suspended all American aid to the so-called Northern Triangle (Honduras, El Salvador and Guatemala), from which the majority of migrants hail. Then he upped the ante by giving President López Obrador an ultimatum: stop the flow of migrants travelling to the American border or he would slap crippling tariffs on Mexico's exports to the United States, which would effectively negate all that had been negotiated under the USMCA.[21]

Trump wasn't kidding. When more than 144,000 migrants were encountered or arrested at the US-Mexico border in May 2019, a roughly 32 percent increase over the previous month and the highest monthly total in more than a decade, Trump pulled the trigger. Using his authority under the Emergency Powers Act, he threatened a 5 percent tariff on all Mexican imports, including cars, that would go into effect on June 10, and promised that he would raise it by 5 percent every month until it reached 25 percent unless Mexico City did something to clamp down on the migrant flows.[22]

Mexico agreed to deploy six thousand national guardsmen to its southern border to stop the caravans of migrants looking to pass through to the United States. Mexico claims there has been a more than 50 percent drop in migrants attempting to cross the US border.[23] Whether this has a lasting effect remains to be seen. But the message to the López Obrador government is clear enough: Mexico must deny migrants access to the US border, and doing so is the ongoing price Mexico will pay for access to its number-one trading partner, as guaranteed under the USMCA.

The wall has certainly become a symbol of the Trump presidency, but immigration hasn't been such a polarizing issue in the United States since the time when Bill the Butcher was rolling up his sleeves to fight the Irish. In fact, the wall was started back in 2006, with bipartisan support for the Secure Fence Act. And while Trump is regularly excoriated for his detentions and deportations of illegal migrants, Barack Obama actually enforced immigration laws more rigorously than Trump has, deporting more illegals per year than his successor.[24] As for turning back homeless women and children from Central America at the US border, here is what President Obama had to say in a 2014 interview with *ABC News*: "That is our direct message to the families in Central America: Do not send your children to the borders." That same year, he said that the US Border Patrol should "stem the flow of illegal crossings and speed the return of those who do cross over. . . . Undocumented workers broke our immigration laws, and I believe that they must be held accountable."[25] Bernie Sanders, in many ways Trump's opposite, came to the same conclusion on immigration, although he sees the issue from a very different angle: "What right-wing people in this country would love is an open-border policy. Bring in all kinds of people, work for two or three dollars an hour. That would be great for them. I don't believe in that."[26] There is nothing new about Donald Trump's position on immigration, other than the fact that it's being espoused by an avowed plutocrat.

What *is* new is the sense that more is at stake. The scale of international migration is bigger than ever. Nearly 70 million migrants were on the move in 2017. Every year more and more join their ranks. According to the United Nations, no fewer than 272 million people around the world have moved and are now living in another country.[27]

That is just the tip of the iceberg. According to a Gallup poll published in December 2018, more than 750 million adults (their children were not counted) around the world wanted to move.[28] Most of them live in countries that President Trump once candidly referred to as "shitholes," with per capita incomes a small fraction of those found in places like the United States, Canada or Australia. For example, the World Bank estimated that Americans were nine times richer than Latin Americans, seventy-two times richer than sub-Saharan Africans and an astounding eighty times richer than South Asians. With disparities like that, it is hardly a surprise that people want to move. Let's keep in mind that, for the most part, globalization has made those disparities worse, not better.

Almost two-thirds of those who have already left live in high-income countries.[29] Although migrants aren't exactly getting a warm welcome in the United States these days, over a fifth of aspiring migrants, or some 158 million, as cited in the Gallup poll, still want to immigrate there. Another 46 million chose Canada as their preferred destination (Canada's population is only 37 million), while 36 million others chose Australia (whose population is 25 million). The numbers give a sense of what is at stake for the destination countries—not just wage competition, but a seismic disruption of their labour force.

If you think about how the global economy operates, the free movement of goods is in large measure a substitute for the free movement of people. If people were free to move wherever they wanted, there wouldn't be the huge income and wage disparities that drive the direction of trade from countries with cheap labour markets to countries with high-cost ones. Migration flows would level the wage field.

For example, if the 158 million adults who wanted to move to the United States were suddenly free to do so, the US labour force would suddenly increase by 75 percent. And if the number of people wanting to move to Canada and Australia were allowed to do so, the labour forces in those countries would more than double. That surge in labour supply would inevitably take its toll on wages.

But a movement of labour at that scale would also quickly change the dynamics of global trade. If wages and incomes fell in migrant-engorged economies in North America, Western Europe and Australia, it would no longer be necessary to move factories out of those countries. The huge wage incentives that drove companies to close down their factories in the rich countries of the world and move them to the cheap labour markets of much poorer ones would soon disappear, or at a minimum be sharply reduced. Why move your factory to China when you have plenty of people at home willing to work for same wages as someone in China?

As we saw in chapter 4, the argument for globalization relies heavily on David Ricardo's theory of comparative advantage. The idea, which most economists buy into, is that individual countries are better off if each focuses on what it does best and trades for what it does less well. In Ricardo's famous example, he points out that England could produce both cloth and wine if it really wanted to, but it would be more profitable to produce only cloth (England was a pioneer in industrial textile manufacture back when Ricardo was writing), sell it in global markets and import wine from a country like Portugal, which could produce wine more efficiently.

The thing is, while most economists accept Ricardo's argument that the free movement of goods yields efficiencies that leave everyone better off, the same goes for the free movement of labour—at least insofar as net global welfare is concerned. Development economists have long argued that migration is one of the most effective ways of eradicating poverty around the world. But *global* welfare gains are a different type of animal from *national* welfare gains.

Instead of having to redistribute income *within* a country to compensate those who lose as a result of free trade deals—which, as we've seen, is hard enough—the global welfare gained by suddenly unchaining the world's labour force would involve redistributing income *between* countries. What it comes down to is this: for everyone in the world to be better off on average, everyone in the G7 countries would have to be worse off. And there is certainly no global consensus for that, especially not in the wealthy countries where most of the world's population would like to move. On the contrary, opposition to migration in those countries is probably fiercer than it has been during the entire postwar era.

While the free movement of people across the world would be the ultimate expression of globalization, that degree of mobility has seldom been proposed by globalization's adherents, and certainly not by the WTO. The only place where it's been attempted is within the European Union, where the free movement of people among member countries is a fundamental, if highly contentious, right. But the European Union is an agreement between countries with more or less the same standard of living. Even the income gap between its poorer Eastern members and their Western counterparts is a fraction of the gap that separates the developed world from Africa, the Middle East, South Asia or Central America. And even under these more ideal conditions, freedom of movement is causing enormous strain, as highlighted by Britain's decision to leave the European Union.

That is why the WTO doesn't campaign for open borders the way it does for free trade. Nor, for that matter, does the United Nations. Its Universal Declaration of Human Rights guarantees the right of movement within countries, but offers no such right to move between them. As Bernie Sanders says, the idea of open borders is tantamount to doing away with the idea of the nation-state. And no government is going to sign on for that.

Bill the Butcher certainly wouldn't sign on for it either. Would we really expect him to? Scorsese depicts him as a psychopath, but Bill wasn't wrong. Surplus labour *was* keeping wages flat in the United States, even as GDP was soaring. Measures of well-being, including life expectancy, average height and age of marriage, were dropping as the surplus increased. Measures of political polarization and economic inequality closely matched immigration rates. Racial tension was sparking into violence as different groups competed for scarce resources. That was the reality of Bill's New York.

When we look back at history, today's backlash shouldn't surprise us. We can condemn it as xenophobic but, knowing what we know, is ever-greater ethnic polarization in our society something we really want to *pursue*?[30]

Economics, like politics, relies on the assumption that we can pursue our own rational self-interest. Of course, we don't have to do *only* that. It is not hard to make a case for the redistribution of wealth on ethical grounds, and most people would consider a more just world to be a more sustainable and livable world. But it is difficult to make the case for making oneself and one's family much poorer, especially if it means abolishing the very things that defined what used to be one's country.

If that is what is at stake, it's not hard to see why opinions on immigration everywhere are hardening. If the free movement of populations is the logical endgame of globalization, then it's perhaps not surprising that expendables like Bill would want less of it.

CHAPTER 15

DÉJÀ VU

*T*he *Economist* was first published in 1843. Today, it remains the preferred source of glossy financial news and opinion for the global MBA and executive class. It is dogmatically free trade and has always been so. In fact, it began as a free trade pamphlet, and just kept going in that direction.

The issue consuming Britain in the first half of the nineteenth century was the question of what to do about the Corn Laws. Corn meant "grain" back then, not maize, and the government had imposed huge tariffs on wheat, barley and rye coming into the country during the Napoleonic Wars. The effect, of course, was not only to deny French farmers access to British markets during a time of conflict between the two countries, but more fundamentally to greatly enrich British landowners, since they could charge whatever they liked for the grain produced on their land without fear of lower-priced foreign competition. And since Parliament was full of landowners, the laws remained on the books long after Napoleon had ceased to be a threat. Indeed, the Corn Laws proved tougher to defeat than the French emperor. The Duke of Wellington prevailed decisively at Waterloo, but when he became prime minister, he found he could not prevail over large British landowners and repeal the Corn Laws.

Labourers hated the laws; the legislation drove the price of bread so high that merely feeding their families consumed most of their wages. Merchants and manufacturers hated them just as much; the landowners were skimming off so much wealth that households couldn't afford any other goods. But of course, few of those who opposed the laws had the right to vote. In those days, the expendables had to content themselves with rioting when their stomachs were empty.

It was only a series of bad harvests that brought things to a head. When British farms couldn't produce enough food to feed everyone, people began to go hungry (and in Ireland, where the Great Famine was raging, they starved or emigrated). On June 25, 1846, the House of Lords passed the Importation Act, which not only repealed the Corn Laws, but changed the way pretty much the whole world did business.

Those who had campaigned for decades against the Corn Laws had argued that free trade was not just preferable to protectionism but morally superior, as it promised to increase the wages and standard of living of the working class at the expense of the landowners—pretty much the same promise we heard from the pundits and columnists dismissing the protesters' concerns in Seattle. James Wilson, the founder of *The Economist*, made the case for repeal based on the ideas of Adam Smith and the principles of freedom, and the magazine makes the same case today with regard to the repeal of all trade barriers.

It is worth noting, however, that Wilson was not entirely a disinterested party. He was a businessman, not a theorist or politician. And it was business, not the starving masses, that really benefited from free trade when it finally arrived. Victorian London and Liverpool were never short of starving masses, but the financiers made out just fine. Indeed, Karl Marx derided *The Economist* as the mouthpiece of the "aristocracy of finance"—he saw that it was capital, not labour, that benefited from free trade.[1] In any case, the repeal of the Corn Laws marked a decisive victory for the investor class over the landowning class.

The result was globalization's first rodeo. The period from 1870 to 1914 marked rapid growth in the movement of goods, capital, people and ideas around the world, anticipating in many ways the world we live in today. Dramatic increases in trade, in part spurred by equally dramatic declines in the cost of transportation with the advent of steam-powered ships and railways, led to an unprecedented degree of global economic integration. In fact, some consider this global capitalism's true golden age.

Once Britain opened its market to imported grain, it followed suit with other products. The result was a tripling of foreign trade over the forty-year span between 1870 and 1910. British companies owned about half of the world's shipping, and built about 80 percent of the world's ships.[2] That meant cheap access to new markets. Between 1840 and 1880, British exports to markets outside Europe rose nearly 400 percent. Not surprisingly, for a capital-rich country with a policy of free trade, imports rose by almost 700 percent.[3]

During that period, world growth soared. Intra-European trade quickly eclipsed the old colonial trading relationships.

Spectacular rates of economic growth in emerging economic powerhouses like the United States at the turn of the twentieth century foreshadowed the growth performance posted by the Chinese economy a century later. And it wasn't just the American economy that was booming. New World countries like Canada and Argentina saw the size of their economies triple in the space of two decades, furnishing per capita incomes well in excess of those of established European powers like Germany and France.[4]

Then as now, globalization encouraged economic specialization. Countries doubled down on what they did best, following Ricardo's dictum of comparative advantage, just as the opponents of the Corn Laws had predicted. The huge expansion in global trade also allowed countries to stop producing what they *didn't* do best and instead import those items from countries that did it better. Nowhere was that shift more in evidence than in agriculture. Land-rich countries like Canada, Australia and Argentina quickly rose to dominate agricultural trade. Whereas just before the turn of the century these countries produced less than 20 percent of the wheat cultivated in Western Europe, by the outbreak of the First World War their production was exceeding that of all of Western Europe.[5]

Needless to say, this was devastating to British farmers and landowners. But, as Ricardo and *The Economist* would argue, the United Kingdom would be foolish to compete with the countries of the New World in agriculture when they had an immense advantage in technology and industrial output. The United Kingdom figured it was better leaving the farming to countries blessed with far more agrarian land.

Eventually, globalization eroded even that comparative advantage as other countries, chiefly Germany and the United States, began to catch up with British industry. But by then Britain could afford to cede market share. Its head start had given it an immense advantage in another field: finance. As imports poured into England, capital poured out. Britain was easily the world's chief banking power, exporting over half of its capital. In fact, by the end of the nineteenth century, half of the investment capital in the world originated in London.[6]

Though the British trade deficit seemed to widen every year, as the country imported more and exported less, the increasing return on foreign investment more than made up for the trade imbalance. Despite producing less, the economy earned more. Cheaper imports, particularly for food, drove down prices and wages, but capital was earning typically 50 to 75 percent more on its foreign investments, like railways, than it would on domestic investment in manufacturing or agriculture. As is the case today with China's Belt and Road investments, most of the capital Britain exported to places like the United States, Canada and Australia was for infrastructure like ports, railways or power plants. While some British industrialists objected to the loss of tariff protection, their concerns were drowned out by London's all-powerful financial sector. The same community, for the same reasons, gave its unequivocal support to free trade, as it does today, arguing that if the countries to which it had lent so much money were free to export their goods back to Britain, those countries could continue to service their loans.

Of course, repayment of those loans required strict rules. If you lend money to a company in a foreign country, how can you be sure that the loan is repaid with currency of the same value that was lent? The solution was to tie currencies to the value of gold. The gold standard, as it was called, did for global capital flows what the reduction in tariffs did for global trade. Tying currencies to the value of gold ensured that lenders (principally Britain) could be confident of being profitably repaid.

It was a golden era for global capital, but not everybody was a fan of globalization. At the time when John McLaughlin was launching his soft drink empire, it wasn't just European farmers who couldn't compete with land-rich wheat farmers on the Canadian prairies or Argentine pampas. (Though back when agriculture made up the bulk of the workforce in any country, farm workers were a hugely important constituency.) Italian factory workers, who were equipped with less than half the capital that American workers were and consequently had less than half their productivity, discovered that they had a choice between poverty and emigration. Traditional societies and their largely self-sufficient economies were torn asunder, and many of their inhabitants suddenly became economically obsolete as trade allowed for the importation of all kinds of goods from countries that, for whatever reason, were better suited to manufacture them.

And if falling trade barriers weren't enough of an adjustment to the global marketplace, the rigors of maintaining the gold standard made it all the more difficult for those on the wrong side of the comparative-advantage equation. Gold imposed a brutal discipline on borrowing countries that were dependent on international capital flows to spur their rapid development. When trends in global markets turned against their economic strengths, they couldn't shield their farmers or workers by devaluing their currency (which would make imports more expensive and exports cheaper—acting as de facto tariffs and subsidies to protect jobs). Nor could governments use monetary policy to bring relief to their economies when they fell into recessions, since any reduction in interest rates would jeopardize the currency's fixed peg against the value of gold.

Even the United States felt the pain. Though the country did not adopt free trade policies, as the world's biggest borrower it had no choice but to adopt the gold standard. When world grain prices fell in 1893, and global financial markets were spooked by political upheaval in Argentina, the American economy sickened and American farmers were particularly hard hit. Opposition to the gold standard provided momentum to the campaign of Democratic-Populist presidential candidate William Jennings Bryan, whose call to not "crucify mankind upon a cross of gold" resonated with much of the American electorate, particularly in the agricultural parts of the country. Ultimately, the power and influence of America's financial sector prevailed. Despite winning the Democratic nomination three times, Bryan never did become president, and the electorate deemed it more important to keep bankers happy than farmers, just as today it's more important to keep investors happy than industrial workers.

The brutal discipline of the gold standard meant that when workers lost their jobs, the only route to recovering them was to lower their wage demands. The same terms held for farmers.

If global markets turned against the price of whatever they were growing, they had no choice but to accept lower incomes. The gold standard provided lenders a degree of certainty against foreign governments devaluing their currencies—but the cost was increased uncertainty for the expendables. Under the yoke of the gold standard, farmers and workers were increasingly held hostage to the cyclical gyrations that so often rock global markets.

That meant globalization had profound distributional effects, creating not just winners but many losers. For those who lost, emigration offered the opportunity for gain. So many people were uprooted by the sea change of globalization that the effect was perhaps the greatest migration in history.

During the latter half of the nineteenth century and first two decades of the twentieth century, migration exploded, principally from Europe to the United States, Canada, Australia and Argentina. (Not much has changed in that regard over the past century. As noted earlier, the United States, Canada and Australia are still the three most-preferred destinations for migrants.) During the Age of Mass Migration (1850–1914) more than 30 million Europeans migrated to the United States, attracted by the prospect of higher wages as well as the ease and reduced cost of getting there, thanks to new steam-powered ships.[7]

The scale of migrant flows just prior to the First World War dwarfs current flows, even counting the recent surge in Middle Eastern and African migrants to Europe, or Central American migrants to the United States.

In the United States, one in five workers was an immigrant. Between 1870 and 1910, immigration had increased Argentina's labour force by 75 percent, while in Canada and Australia immigration boosted the size of the labour force by over a third of what it would have been otherwise.[8]

Not surprisingly, migration was a flash point for discontent. While the governments of North America and Australia were openly encouraging immigration, their native labour forces were becoming less than enthusiastic. The new arrivals were looking for higher wages than they had left behind, and they were generally not disappointed. At the turn of the century, wages in the United States and Canada were about three times as high as in southern Europe, providing a powerful magnet for Italian and other Mediterranean-area workers.

But what was a raise for the new arrivals was often a pay cut for the workers who already had jobs. The onslaught of new migrants, most of them unskilled, inevitably drove down wages. Pay is estimated to have been a quarter to a third less in Canada and Australia than it would otherwise have been, and almost 20 percent lower in the United States.[9]

A study of migrant flows between 1890 and 1924 found that every one percentage point increase in the foreign-born share of the American population reduced wages by 1 to 1.5 percent, with larger reductions, up to 3 percent, occurring in industries with large migrant labour forces, such as men's clothing.[10] When Americans didn't want to compete with new arrivals for low-wage work, they were often forced to relocate to less desirable locations in the country's interior. In other words, they were displaced, particularly from coastal cities where migrants typically first settled.[11] At the same time, mass migration was powering impressive gains in American GDP and GDP per capita. Europe's export of labour to America was just as vital to this growth as the capital Europe was investing in this emerging economic giant. But just as now, Bill the Butcher and his fellow expendables weren't always sharing in the newfound economic prosperity.

Human behaviour is complex and nuanced. There are no immutable laws of sociology. But no one should be surprised by the fact that workers around the world weren't happy about losing between a fifth and a third of their income, or about being forced to relocate to avoid competing for jobs with a sudden influx of immigrants. They eventually applied enough political pressure to do something to stem that flow. Where labour had political strength, as in Australia, it acted to severely restrict immigration. While the resulting White Australia policy was openly racist and targeted Asian migrants, it was also motivated by an economic recognition that these migrants would be far more willing to work for lower wages than migrants coming from Europe and would hence generate more downward pressure on wages paid to the native Australian labour force.

The same process was unfolding in the United States. Concern by American labour that the massive movement of some 30 million migrants since 1850 was pushing down the wages for American-born labourers led to the Dillingham Commission, which advocated much tighter immigration policies. The first step was legislation in 1917 that imposed a literacy test on all migrant applicants, which was estimated at the time to reduce immigration by between 25 and 40 percent. But more far-reaching and draconian legislation was soon to follow. The Emergency Quota Act of 1921, later amended by the

Immigration Act of 1924, slashed immigration levels that were running as high as 1,000,000 migrants a year to 150,000.[12] Once imposed, those restrictions on migrant numbers lasted for decades. The immigration quota wasn't raised until 1965. In the interim, the percentage of the US population that was born outside the United States plummeted, from 14 to 5 percent.[13] It has since approached its previous peak.

But immigration wasn't the only casualty as the globalizing sweep of history came to an abrupt end with the First World War. Globalization had a number of consequences that neither the winners nor the losers had foreseen. The first was that war had become just as global as finance and trade. When global rivals Germany and Great Britain went to war in 1914, neither expected that they would *both* lose. Four years later, Germany had signed a punitive peace treaty, and the British economy had been permanently wrecked by the staggering expense of war. The British war effort relied on global trade—nearly all its oil, more than two-thirds of its grain and more than half of its shell casings were imported. Even aircraft engines had to be bought from foreign suppliers. That meant foreign debt. It was the United States that won the war—not by fighting it but by lending to the combatants. Though strictly speaking neutral for most of the conflict, the United States placed a $2 billion bet on the United Kingdom and France (or about $35 billion in today's money). By 1918, not only did it have the world's dominant industrial capacity (by far), but it was also the world's largest hoarder of gold (again by a wide margin). It had gone from being the global economy's biggest borrower to its biggest lender.

However, the United States hadn't figured out globalization the way Great Britain had. The result was the second unforeseen consequence—it turned out that economic crises were also now just as global as growth. Germany was forced to borrow from the United States to pay reparations to France and England, and England and France needed those payments to service their loans to the United States. The result was a cycle of obligations that proved highly profitable to the financial sector, but that could never be sustained. When the whole arrangement blew up, the result was the Great Depression—which also marked the end of the first great experiment in globalization, and which is perhaps best symbolized by the Smoot-Hawley Tariff we discussed back in chapter 2.

The major economies of the world became much more autarkic. Soviet Russia and Nazi Germany achieved staggering economic growth by turning inward rather than trading according to the model of comparative advantage theorized by Ricardo and advocated by *The Economist*. While the First World War's victors stagnated in depression, their ideological rivals were growing by leaps and bounds. Meanwhile, international trade was the biggest loser—crushed by rising tariffs and even more by the Depression and the ensuing contraction in global GDP. As a share of global GDP, exports and imports (the so-called trade openness index, which many economists follow), which had risen from around 6 percent in 1870 to 30 percent by the outbreak of the Great War, had been almost entirely reversed.[14] In many ways, it was as though globalization had never happened.

And yet, between the repeal of the Corn Laws and the passing of Smoot-Hawley, the world had been changed nearly beyond recognition. On the one hand, unimaginable wealth had been created; competition had wrung undreamt-of techno-logical innovation out of the planet's scientists and entrepre-neurs; and interconnectedness had brought incredible benefits to humankind.

On the other hand, global capital had extended its reach into every corner of the globe, opening up the undeveloped world to exploitation. Inequality within and between nations was growing dizzyingly. Millions had been uprooted from their homelands and livelihoods. And the planet stood on the preci-pice of the most destructive war in history.

Could globalization's second act follow a similar trajectory?

SHADES OF THE PAST

If you squint through the veil of history, you can see the Battle of Seattle as a reprise of the Corn Law riots—a struggle between local interests and global capital, with the expendables caught in the middle. And just as the first round of globalization lasted about sixty years—if you count from the Cobden-Chevalier Treaty of 1860, which established free trade between England and France, to the beginning of the First World War—it's now been about sixty years since the Dillon Round of the GATT negotiations. Though these parallels are hardly scientific, you can't help but wonder whether globalization is itself cyclical.

If it *is* cyclical, what drives its dynamics? Is it ultimately self-limiting? That is, does globalization contain the seeds of its own destruction? And could that lead to a collapse today of the kind that unfolded about a hundred years ago?

Just as the Great Depression had a devastating impact on globalization and world trade, so too has the more recent Great Recession and world financial crisis. World trade plunged by 12 percent in 2009, the largest decline since the 1930s and more than five times the decline in global GDP during the recession.[15] Global supply chains were ripped asunder and have yet to be fully restored to their pre-recession levels. Even before the Trump administration came to power, there was already a marked increase in protectionist measures, particularly among G20 countries, which collectively account for about 85 percent of world GDP and about three-quarters of all world trade. And now, with the trade war that Trump has initiated against China, US tariff action is on a scale not seen since Smoot-Hawley.

According to the World Bank, the ratio of trade (exports plus imports) to global GDP peaked in 2008 at just below 61 percent, the triumphant apex of a globalizing trend in the world economy that had risen steadily for decades.[16] Not only did it fall sharply during the Great Recession, but almost a decade later it has yet to get back to its pre-recession peak. And with all the US-led hikes in tariffs being imposed around the world, the ratio is starting to head the other way. Through 2018 and 2019, growth in global trade trailed GDP growth.[17]

Similarly, the volume of global trade, while still growing, is doing so at about half the pace it had grown prior to the Great Recession and ensuing financial crisis. Ominously, the growth of world trade has closely tracked the growth of Chinese industrial production over the last two decades, as the country has become, for all intents and purposes, the factory of the world economy.[18] I say "ominously" because since the trade war with the United States began, China's industrial production has seen its slowest growth in decades.

Many today would argue that the foundations for globalization are built on much firmer ground than they were a century ago. They might point to the existence of the World Trade Organization, for example, as a check on the rampant protectionism that swept the world after the First World War.

But the global trade watchdog and ultimate arbitrator of trade disputes is hobbling around on life support. The institution's key dispute resolution mechanism is on the verge of collapse as a result of the Trump administration's deliberate attempt to undermine the body by refusing to appoint appellate justices.[19] While countries still routinely register complaints with the WTO, they are appealing to a void, with no WTO appellate court judges to hear their cases. Instead, countries are responding to their trade grievances by taking unilateral action, with little regard for WTO rules and regulations.

And when the two largest economies in the world are engaged in a raging trade war with tariffs the likes of which we have not seen since the Depression, it's hard for other countries not to follow suit and get swept up in growing global trade tensions.

For example, Japan and South Korea, two Asian economic powerhouses, are providing an engaging sideshow to the main event between China and the United States. An old grievance stemming from Japan's wartime use of forced Korean labour during the Second World War has been the catalyst for an ongoing high-tech trade war. When Japan responded to Korean demands for compensation by reminding Seoul that it had already paid $500 million in compensation back in 1965, it added an exclamation point by restricting the export of three key chemicals needed to produce smartphones. Korea responded by saying it would restrict exports to Japan of OLED screens, used in high-end TVs made by Japanese companies such as Sony and Sharp.[20]

Of course, the degree of globalization today is much greater than it was after its first wave. Despite the recent decline in the ratio of exports and imports to GDP, exports and imports are still almost 60 percent of global GDP, double their share of the world economy on the eve of the First World War. But as we have seen before, what can go up can just as quickly go down.

TWO-FACED DEMOCRACY

Liberal democracy is two-faced. Its political face is the one it likes to show. Ever since the Athenians came up with the idea of making decisions collectively, free elections are the way most people want to be governed. We have shown again and again that we are willing to die for the right to vote. Of course, the fact that liberal democracy has a good reputation for making people rich hasn't hurt its cause either. The freedom to vote and the freedom of capital—the other face of liberal democracy—have always gone together.

But they are not the same. Capital moves to the pull of profits, as reliably as gravity draws water downhill. Political decision-making is much more nuanced. It takes into account criteria like justice, or a sense of community. It must accommodate tradition and the needs of future generations. Capital doesn't concern itself with these things, nor should it. That's not its job.

The two faces of liberal democracy are often stamped on the same coin. Take, for example, George Soros, renowned philanthropist and investor. Soros has spent hundreds of millions of his own dollars funding institutions that promote the virtues of democracy and an open society. He has even founded a university in his native Hungary to further those values. His Open Society Foundations championed the struggle for democratic rights everywhere from Eastern Europe to Haiti.

But the other side of Soros's coin isn't quite so altruistic. Just ask the people of Malaysia, who back in 1997 learned what the freedom of capital really feels like. Even though the country was doing everything the International Monetary Fund and global investors felt developing countries should do to attract capital and investment, it apparently wasn't doing enough to satisfy Soros and his hedge fund during the Asian currency crisis of the late 1990s. Soros bet billions of dollars against Malaysia's currency, the ringgit, and made a handsome profit for himself and his investors by engineering its collapse.

However, it wasn't just Malaysia's currency that collapsed. So did the country's economy, destroying the livelihoods of the more than eighty thousand workers who lost their jobs. When the outraged Malaysian prime minister Mahathir bin Mohamad accused Soros and his fellow speculators of causing untold misery in his country, Soros responded by invoking

Ricardo's dictum of comparative advantage, arguing that the free movement of capital through foreign exchange markets facilitated trade, which in turn brought the world tremendous benefits.

What Soros failed to mention was that while foreign exchange markets once served trade, they now had a new master: speculators. In the early 1970s, the volume of foreign exchange transactions on a typical day was six times that of trade flows; by the time of the Malaysian currency crisis, foreign exchange transactions had mushroomed to fifty times trade volumes.[21] All around the world, trading floors were filled with speculators looking for opportunities to exploit. The jobs of those eighty thousand expendable Malaysians were sacrificed not to invest in a more productive economy but to wring profit out of a trading opportunity. That's what capital does. I'm sure Soros's hedge fund clients weren't complaining. Nor should they have been.

If you think that's something that happens only to workers in the developing world, think again. As we've seen, a lot more than eighty thousand jobs have disappeared from OECD countries as global capital has migrated to low-wage countries. But there are many other ways the expendables can be squeezed by capital. A study by the National Bureau of Economic Research found that more than half of the $23 trillion rise in the value of American non-financial corporations since 1987 has come not as a result of economic growth but rather as the transfer of income from wages to profits—that is, from workers to investors, or from the middle class to the wealthy.[22] So not only are American workers excluded from sharing in the market's gains, but to a large extent those gains have come *at their expense.*

And what are companies doing with those record profits? They're doing what shareholders want them to do. They're buying back their own stock or raising dividend payouts, which raises share prices, which in turn triggers bigger bonuses for management. That was certainly the case when corporate America received one of the largest tax cuts in history from President Trump's Tax Cuts and Jobs Act in December 2017.

Companies are also free to expense the generous stock options they grant to their executives as cash expenses to be applied against earnings—a favourite practice of many tech giants. In other words, the more the company rewards its executives with share options, the less corporate income tax it has to pay. Not hard to figure out which direction management will lean.

Amazon, for example, was able to reduce its taxes by more than $1 billion in 2018 by expensing such options. For a second year in a row, the company will avoid paying any federal corporate income tax at all, despite its profits more than doubling to $11.2 billion in 2018. In fact, Amazon claimed a federal income tax *rebate* of $129 million. Netflix also paid no income tax in 2018, despite posting an $845 million profit. The Institute on Taxation and Economic Policy found that the net effect of the Trump tax reform package was to double the number of Fortune 500 companies that paid no tax at all in 2018 to sixty.[23] In fact, some of America's largest companies actually received a tax refund through tax credits even though they hadn't actually paid any corporate tax that year.

There exists a select club of multibillion-dollar companies that includes some of the country's largest corporations. Let's call them the Fortunate 60. In addition to Amazon and Netflix, it counts oil giant Chevron, power mogul Duke Energy, pharmaceutical giant Eli Lilly, General Motors, Delta Airlines, pipeline company Kinder Morgan, computer manufacturers IBM and Honeywell, and brewery giant Molson Coors among its distinguished list of corporate elite. The criterion for club membership is that these corporate behemoths pay no tax. Instead of paying some $16.5 billion in corporate income tax on the combined $79 billion of profits they earned in 2018, the Fortunate 60 received a net corporate tax rebate of $4.3 billion. That may make sense to corporate CFOs and to shareholders, but it's hard for the expendables to get their heads around it.

Will the seeds of globalization's self-destructive tendencies germinate again? The failure to better redistribute the gains from trade led to the collapse of the global trading system at the dawn of the twentieth century. Once again, the system seems under siege.

IS LIBERAL DEMOCRACY OBSOLETE?

They say a picture is worth a thousand words. The photograph taken of world leaders at the 2019 Osaka G20 summit certainly is. In the front row, flanking their Japanese host, Premier Shinzō Abe, were President Xi and President Putin on one side, and Donald Trump and Mohammad Bin Salman of Saudi Arabia (which assumes the presidency of the G20 in 2020) on the other. Not exactly a roundup of the apostles of liberal democracy. Stalwart liberals like Germany's Angela Merkel were shoved to the very end of the row, almost out of view, while others like Justin Trudeau were lined up in the back row.

Shortly before the group assembled to grin for the camera, President Putin had pronounced in an interview that liberal democracy was obsolete. He may have jumped the gun, but his obituary was not too wide of the mark. Nor could many take issue with his observation that the ideas of liberal democracy are today in conflict with the interest of the majority of the population in countries where the ideology still holds sway.

And it's not just the angry old men who have lost their once high-paying industrial jobs who are beginning to see things Vladimir Putin's way. Discontent cuts across the entire demographic spectrum. In fact, nowhere is the rejection of liberal democracy greater than among young millennial voters in many OECD countries. They are pessimistic about their own futures and equally so regarding the future of the world they live in. While they listen to their governments and media endlessly extolling the virtues of strong GDP growth, low unemployment and ever-rising stock markets, they are aware that none of these conditions have trickled down to them. Instead, they face unprecedented economic precarity at their workplaces. It's not surprising that they are wide open to the notion of radical change, even if that change puts these seemingly important achievements at risk. Unlike their baby boom parents, millennials don't have an unquestioning commitment to liberal democracy or globalism. Instead, they are flocking to populist or authoritarian figures who openly challenge those tenets, including even the concept of democracy itself.

Globalization may have brought hundreds of millions of people out of poverty in China and India, but in OECD countries it has made people less sure of their own economic future, and even more unsure about their children's. Today only 37 percent of Americans believe their children will be better off financially than they themselves are. Only 24 percent in Canada or Australia feel the same. And in France, that figure dips to only 9 percent.[24]

These men and women have good reason to be pessimistic. The fading dream of the middle class is written in the steadily shrinking percentage of Americans who have climbed up the economic ladder and earned more than the generation before them. Outearning your parents used to be the expectation of every generation of Americans. Those who didn't were the exception, not the rule. In the early years of the postwar era, 90 percent of Americans went on to surpass their parents' earnings. Today, it's less than 50 percent. And that fading middle-class dream isn't just an American phenomenon. It is in evidence throughout the OECD countries.

Changing economic conditions lever changing political attitudes, just as they did at the tail end of the last cycle of globalization. When nine out of ten Americans can expect a better life than their parents had, as the baby boomers could, their support for a democratic form of government is all but assured. When those odds are the same as on a coin flip, that support can no longer be taken for granted. Today, less than half of Americans believe democracy is essential to their lives.[25] It's the mirror image of the declining percentage of Americans who have surpassed their parents in earnings. A World Values

Survey showed that only 30 percent of American millennials thought democracy was essential to their well-being. Similar percentages of millennials felt the same way in Australia, New Zealand, Sweden and the United Kingdom.[26]

Though columnists and politicians fret openly about the resurgence of nationalism in Europe, they tend to explain the trend as a legacy of racism rather than the outgrowth of young people's economic frustration. But the troubling facts are in plain sight. For example, more than 40 percent of Austrian voters under the age of thirty voted for Sebastian Kurz, a far-right candidate for chancellor who ran on a largely anti-migrant, anti-globalization theme. In neighbouring Germany, Alternative for Germany was the first far-right party to grab seats in parliament since the Second World War, enjoying broad support from millennial voters. And in France, both the Marxist candidate Jean-Luc Mélenchon and the far-right candidate Marine Le Pen enjoyed greater support among millennial voters than did the eventual winner, establishment candidate Emmanuel Macron. It is impossible to say definitively what any individual voter has in mind while casting a ballot, but it seems fair to speculate that these young people are justifiably worried about the future rather than haunted by ghosts of the past.

Waning support for the status quo reflects the growing economic precarity this generation is experiencing. Unlike their boomer parents, who lived, for the most part, comfortable middle-class lives, millennials have had to contend with wage stagnation and, for many, a declining standard of living. Moreover, youth unemployment in many countries is a multiple of the jobless rate for the rest of the labour force. The economic conditions they find themselves in have had a huge impact on how that generation views traditional values like the need for democracy or neoliberal economic policies that promote global integration.

Historically, the middle class has been the staunchest defender of our democratic institutions. Income stagnation has led to a discernible shift in political views toward new forms of nationalism and populism driven by a growing mistrust and suspicion of global governance. The authority of multilateral institutions—whether the United Nations, the World Trade Organization or even the European Union—is being challenged like never before.

LEFT-WING OR RIGHT-WING, POPULISM IS NOT GOING AWAY

Steve Bannon, the one-time campaign strategist for President Trump and noted guru of the American alt-right, argues that the future is populist. Not necessarily the populism of the right, however. The left is every bit as militant, and has populist candidates within the rosters of legacy political parties, as well as vocal, often violent cadres of demonstrators ready to take to the streets. If the Democrats are going to beat Trump, they are more likely to do so with a left-wing Trump than another establishment candidate like Hillary Clinton.

Already there are loud and angry calls from the left for redistributive justice, just as there were in the wake of the last global crash. A twenty-one-country survey conducted in 2019 by the OECD found that the vast majority of respondents wanted their governments to raise taxes on the rich to pay for greater social security benefits for those increasingly being left behind.[27] But today there are powerful obstacles to redistributing the gains from trade, even more than there were during the first great era of globalization. The unprecedented mobility of investment and production precludes the payment of any major compensation to the losers, even when governments are so inclined. While national governments remain sovereign in name, their sovereignty is limited by global trade regulations that rule out measures that would impede the free flow of capital and goods around the world. In short, their sovereignty is subordinate to the imperatives of the global trading system.

At least it was. Then, all of a sudden, the world's largest economy was headed by a president who rejected the global trading system and asserted American independence in the face of its many rules.

Was Donald Trump's election and the subsequent rise of American protectionism really the black swan event that it is so conveniently characterized as in the mainstream media and by advocates of the status quo? Or was the stage already set for his triumphant entrance? Trump's election can be considered a random occurrence only if there was no rationale for it to occur—if it were somehow the result of a freakish combination of transient, unpredictable events. But the media that first dismissed Trump's chances and then ridiculed his victory is the same media that largely ignored the plight of all those people who voted for him or, for that matter, for Bernie Sanders—another rogue politician in the media's eyes.

Or did Trump intuitively feel the changing nature of the times? It wasn't Trump who had left the middle class and the American worker behind. You can thank the policies of every president from Bill Clinton to Barack Obama for that. Rather, it was Trump who first recognized their plight and made political gain from it. He won't be the last.

At its core, populism—right or left—is a grassroots rejection of globalization, whether it refers to the unfettered flow of goods, capital or migrants. In Europe it is largely of the right-wing variety, but in France, especially, the populist left also polls strongly. Having seen globalization flame out once before, we should know there is nothing intrinsically right-wing about populism. In fact, it was the left that was first out of the gate after the First World War. In Italy, the Biennio Rosso (or "Red Two Years") kicked off in 1919 with over sixteen hundred industrial strikes by over 1 million workers. In Spain, the socialist Popular Front formed a government in 1936. In France, the left fielded four mainstream communist and social-ist parties, and in 1936 they formed the government. Édouard Daladier, a Radical-Socialist, was the prime minister of France when the Second World War broke out. In Germany, commu-nists led an armed revolt in January 1919 in Berlin known as the Spartacist uprising. Similar movements kicked off across the country, demanding higher wages, better working condi-tions and the regulation of capital. And, of course, there was Russia, which had lit the powder keg of class warfare in 1917.

Continental Europe wasn't alone in tilting violently to the left. In 1926 a general strike in the United Kingdom led to the first Labour government (which back then was made up of militant union organizers). In the United States, various socialist, communist and union organizations were transforming the political landscape. In 1921 miners in West Virginia fighting for better working conditions engaged in pitched combat with the rifles and machine guns of the coal companies, which were backed by the police and army. The Battle of Blair Mountain, as the fight was called, killed more than one hundred people, and more than a million rounds were fired. In Canada, two strikers were killed and dozens more wounded during the Winnipeg General Strike of 1919. And in Cape Breton, a strike roiled on between 1922 and 1925, pitting coal miners against the British Empire Steel Corporation. It ended only when a miner was killed and the company store and other buildings were looted and burned to the ground. Labour made huge progress during the interwar years, gaining concessions like minimum wage and reduced working hours. But they had to fight every step of the way. And their bosses fought back.

The Biennio Rosso set the stage for Mussolini's Blackshirts. The response to the Spanish Popular Front was the Spanish Civil War and the brutal Franco dictatorship that followed. And in Germany, it was Hitler's Brownshirts who promised to take back the streets. The result was a tide of right-wing regimes across the continent during the 1920s and early 1930s. Democracies in Hungary, Spain, Italy and Albania were replaced by right-wing dictatorships. Poland, Portugal and Lithuania followed suit. Then, with the advent of the Great Depression, a new round of right-wing dictatorships arose in Yugoslavia, Romania, Austria, Latvia, Estonia, Bulgaria, Greece and, most importantly, Germany.[28] Indeed, by the mid-1930s, right-wing dictatorships were the norm in Europe, not the exception.

These new dictatorships were marriages of convenience, brokered by fascist regimes between the lower middle class and domestic capitalists who enjoyed state-granted monopolies. It was the very real threat of left-wing populism that made the right so appealing to the bourgeoisie. Though we associate capitalism with democracy, it isn't always as choosy as you might think. Capital will work with any political system, although as history has shown, if forced to choose, it prefers fascism to communism.

Some see the current rise of right-wing populism in Europe as an ominous parallel with the past, raising the spectre of military dictatorships. Yet there have been no recent coups d'etat in Europe, and the right-wing populist governments that have been elected in countries such as Italy, Poland and Hungary do so as a result of democratic elections. Those regimes seem to be getting more popular by the day, as evidenced by the May 2019 EU elections. Right-wing populist parties were the clear winner in the elections, which saw the largest voter turnout in more than twenty years. It was the first time in over four decades that the centrist parties that have always dominated the EU government failed to win a majority. In many respects, the 2019 vote was a referendum on the future of the European Union itself, pitting the establishment vision of the Merkel-Macron axis of a United States of Europe against the Euroskeptic notion of a Europe of independent nations, as envisioned by the likes of Marine Le Pen or Matteo Salvini.

And as has been the case in many a recent European election, immigration continues to be a bread-and-butter issue for populist right-wing parties across Europe. In France, Marine Le Pen's National Rally won with 23.31 percent of the vote, beating French president Emmanuel Macron's La République En Marche alliance, which garnered only 22.41 percent. Similarly, in Italy, the ruling anti-EU Lega party led by Salvini won, capturing over a third of the vote. In Hungary, Victor Orbán's right-wing Fidesz party scored a huge victory, capturing over 50 percent of the vote. In Greece, the right-wing opposition party New Democracy won with more than 33 percent.[29]

In the 2019 UK election Boris Johnson and his Conservative party won an overwhelming majority on a "get Brexit done" platform that sets the way for the country to act on its earlier referendum result and leave the EU. The Conservatives cemented their victory, the largest majority since Margaret Thatcher was elected in 1987, by sweeping a slew of working class seats across the industrial north of England that have traditionally voted Labour. In the language of a true populist, Johnson declared his government will be "a people's government."

But the new right's policies aren't the only ones vying for the support of today's discontented middle class. Voices from the left can also be heard. Redistributing wealth through more progressive taxation, cracking down on global tax shelters for large corporations and the super-rich, protecting jobs from offshoring through resurrecting tariffs, raising the minimum wage—these are alternative responses to the immiseration in which the middle class finds itself. While in North America and Europe left-wing populism has yet to enjoy the electoral success that its right-wing variant has, that could easily turn around.

Whichever way the political tide turns, one thing is becoming increasingly clear: globalization's status quo is no longer acceptable to a growing majority of people in the developed countries of the world. It has taken a few decades, but the expendables have finally woken up to the fact that they have been subsidizing a banquet of global growth the likes of which history has never seen—and from which they have been almost entirely excluded. One way or another, things are going to have to change.

In the 1990s, at the time of the so-called Washington Consensus,[30] American political philosopher Francis Fukuyama famously wrote that the triumph of liberal democracy over all competing ideologies marked the end of history.[31] Countries that were guided by the tenets of liberal democracy were more stable. And economies guided by the liberal democratic principles of free trade and self-regulating markets unshackled from government intervention were the most prosperous.

It looks like history is about to make a comeback.

WILL THE PANDEMIC BURY GLOBALIZATION?

Globalization, as we have seen, means many things. It means companies can go shopping for low wages around the world. It means long international supply chains that end in big-box stores on the edge of town. It means razor-thin margins and just-in-time delivery. It means structural unemployment. Add it all up, and it means a raw deal for the expendables.

It also means that something as unremarkable as a cup of coffee requires twenty-nine different companies doing business across eighteen different national borders. And if that's what it takes to brew a coffee, imagine what it takes to build a ventilator.

As it turned out, when COVID-19 began to ravage the world's most advanced economies, the global market couldn't provide ventilators at any price. Not to rich Milanese, not to rich Americans. Just-in-time was just too late.

There *were* ventilators out there, though. Chinese factories were pumping them out. Russia, drawing on its Soviet-era legacy of excess capacity, had planeloads of the things to send to hard-hit Italy and Serbia. And Switzerland also had stockpiles set aside, just in case.

Just in case is pretty much the opposite of *just in time*. Another word for it is *hedging*. Although Switzerland was hit hard by COVID-19 (it borders Italy's Lombardy region), it was well prepared for a long shutdown. The Swiss had 63,000 tonnes of sugar, 160,000 tonnes of flour, 33,700 tonnes of cooking oil, and about 400,000 tonnes of feed for dairy cows. They also had 15,000 tonnes of coffee beans. In November 2019, the government had decided to stop stockpiling coffee, since it has zero nutritional value. But democracy is robust and swift in Switzerland, and a public outcry kept the coffee-hedge safe. I'm sure the Swiss weathered the pandemic more contentedly, knowing they would not run out of *kaffee crème*.

In other words, the Swiss weren't counting on global markets to save them "just in time." They bought their coffee, and their ventilators, *before* the market failed. While other countries were doing the equivalent of scouring crowded supermarkets with bare shelves, the Swiss were ready.

By the way, California once had a similar contingency plan under Governor Arnold Schwarzenegger. He invested millions in a mobile version of the insta-hospital the Chinese built in Wuhan: three two-hundred-bed mobile hospitals, each the size of a football field, with surgery rooms, an intensive care unit and X-ray equipment. Their stores would include 50 million N95 respirator masks, and, yes, twenty-four hundred ventilators. The strategic reserves would allow for an additional twenty-one thousand beds for emergency care. That was back in 2006, when the avian flu looked like a real threat. But the mobile hospitals cost about $5.8 million a year to maintain, so they were defunded. The moment they became necessary, they were all but impossible to replace.

So if globalists think a Democratic victory in the 2020 elections will mean a return to the open and free markets they cherish, they are sadly mistaken. Because today's global supply chains must now contend with a far more lethal opponent than the most protectionist president in postwar history.

There are plenty of lessons to learn from COVID-19. But while many were arguing over who was to blame, and which country had the right response, and whether it makes sense to eat wild animals, one thing was clear from the very beginning: if you think global markets will solve your problems, you are destined for disappointment—or worse. Real problems require more robust solutions than markets are likely to provide. As the caseload became critical, and stockpiles of supplies ran low, American Hospital Association CEO Rick Pollack went to the press: "We urge that the Defense Production Act be fully employed."

In other words, when the real trouble starts, don't count on the efficiency of the markets. Call the government instead. After all, it worked in the past. During the Second World War, Ford was ordered to produce bombers under the Defense Production Act. During the COVID-19 battle, the White House once again used the act to issue a command. This time, the auto manufacturer, along with its competitor General Motors, was to produce thousands of ventilators for American hospitals. The same legislation used to protect American jobs was breathing new life into an idle factory in Michigan.

All of a sudden, globalists were worried about a whole new kind of protectionism. Ever since GATT and the WTO, corporations have been sacrificing labour (and governments their citizens) for the sake of access to foreign markets. Protecting jobs and domestic industries by reducing imports was considered backward. But now it's not import bans we're worried about. As national governments squirrel away precious resources, it's *export* bans that threaten global supply chains.

In late March 2020, India, which along with China supplies the bulk of ingredients for the world's generic pharmaceuticals, banned the export of hydroxychloroquine when it began to look as though the drug could be effective in fighting COVID-19. American officials also worried about shortages of sedatives for patients on ventilators, and albuterol, a drug that increases airflow in the lungs.

Similarly, China choked off exports of the very things the market desperately wanted to buy. With one new regulation, Beijing disqualified 81 of the 102 companies previously licensed to export test kits, face masks, protective clothing, ventilators, and infrared thermometers to the EU from doing so. And the United States did the same thing, banning exports of face masks to Canada.

After all, why would you ship your scarce medical supplies off to another country when you don't have enough yourself? The trouble is, in a complex global network—where even a cup of coffee requires the work of twenty-nine different companies—an export ban on medical components ends up hurting everyone. It's not as though we live in David Ricardo's world, where one country makes N95 masks and another makes ventilators, and the two can trade. Export bans may make it impossible to make *anything in a world where virtually everything is made through an elaborate link of global supply chains.* As German ventilator-maker Stefan Dräger put it in *Der Spiegel*, "The parts come from all over the world, including from Turkey. I very much hope that the supply chains remain intact despite the protectionism. If someone decides to disrupt them, there will no longer be any ventilators, for anyone."

But this argument works both ways. You can argue against protectionism on the grounds that it disrupts global supply chains. Or you can take a look at global supply chains, see how vulnerable they are to disruption, and decide you're better off sourcing things locally. And that is exactly what is going to happen more and more now.

A TARNISHED MODEL

It's no small irony that the COVID 19 pandemic—or Wuhan virus, as it was first dubbed—that shuttered factories and stores all around the world originated in China. As we've seen, China is the industrial epicentre of the global supply chains that serve markets around the world. Globalization begins there, and it may well end there.

It wasn't all that long ago that even musing aloud about the costs and risks of global supply chains was enough to make you sound naively nostalgic. But as the virus shutters economies all around the world, triggering a global recession of possibly unprecedented proportions, the appeal of an interconnected and interdependent world economy suddenly seems to belong to some distant, bygone age.

In the space of only a couple of months, the pandemic brought the greatest quarterly contractions in GDP since the Depression, some of the sharpest declines in stock markets since the 1929 crash, and gave every sign it would create one of the biggest spikes in unemployment in history. Global oil demand collapsed, with the International Energy Agency reporting that in March 2020, demand fell by a record 10.8 million barrels a day.

As the virus migrated from continent to continent, so did its economic impact. It's not only 1.25 billion people who were locked down around the world but the industries they worked in. With economic activity at a standstill, economic barometers dropped at a pace seldom if ever seen before. Economic activity plunged in a locked down China during the first three months of 2020, which saw the Chinese economy shrink by 6.8 percent, the first quarterly contraction in GDP since the end of the Cultural Revolution in 1976. Chinese industrial production—for all intents and purposes the world's factory—fell an unprecedented 8.4 percent over the first quarter, the first time in three decades that it had fallen.

As quarantined factories sever global supply chains with surgical precision, the economic impacts cascade across the world. Hyundai closed its assembly plants in South Korea because key components from China were no longer being delivered. Nissan cut production in its assembly plants in Japan because it too was dependent on Chinese auto parts. German auto manufacturers that rely on suddenly quarantined manufacturing hubs in northern Italy for parts found themselves in the same boat. Similarly, Nintendo found itself unable to meet US demand for its Switch gaming console because its factory in Vietnam required critical electronic inputs from China.

And just as those factories were gradually restarting, once China finally contained its contagion, the stores halfway around the world that they typically supply started to close. As the pandemic's epicentre shifted from China to the United States, so too did its devastating economic impact.

After enjoying spectacular gains in recent years, investors were about to discover what stock markets look like when booming economies are suddenly placed under effective quarantine. It wasn't pretty. The S&P 500 declined more than 20 percent during the first quarter, beginning the year with the worst start in its history. The downturn in the once even hotter NASDAQ wasn't far behind. Some of the daily losses on the Dow rival those posted during the 1929 crash and the ensuing depression. The initial sell-off in stock markets around the world had at one point vaporized as much as $20 trillion from equity market valuations. If globalization had made investors rich, it was suddenly making them a lot poorer. US GDP contracted by almost 5 percent in the first quarter, owing to the shutdown in March and the second quarter contraction in GDP is expected to be a multiple of that of the first quarter.

While the markets and the economy will rebound, the economic and financial carnage from the pandemic will be hard to forget. The result looks more and more like the tipping point for globalization, exposing the fragility of a system that only yesterday was not only seen as desirable but inevitable.

THE BIG BAILOUT

Extreme conditions call for extreme responses. Governments in the United States, Canada and elsewhere have promised massive financial support to those whose jobs the virus stole and to companies that health regulations prevented from operating. Central banks, like the US Federal Reserve Board, were quick to come to the rescue by slashing interest rates to near zero. And just as the financial crisis of 2008 forced the Fed and other central banks to open up their balance sheets to distressed subprime mortgage-backed assets, the coronavirus has forced them to open them again. Only this time, they are holding all manner of distressed corporate debt, including high-yield or junk bonds as they are better known. The amount of credit that the Fed may end up taking on its balance sheet this time could be double or more what it took on during the financial crisis back in 2008–09.

Socializing the losses from corporate bankruptcies and defaults seems laudable in a time of crisis, but it doesn't obviate the fact that those losses have occurred. In the end, someone will have to pay for them. Last time central banks massively engaged in what has become known as quantitative easing, it was the taxpayer who ultimately picked up the tab for the bailout of Wall Street and all its toxic subprime mortgage-backed assets. Will this time around be any different?

The fiscal levers have been pulled just as hard as the monetary ones. The US Treasury has enacted the largest fiscal stimulus package in history—a $2 trillion-plus bundle including income replacement cheques for most of the Americans who have lost their jobs. Other countries are unveiling similar fiscal support to laid-off workers and shuttered businesses. Prime Minister Trudeau announced a similar income-replacement program for Canadians whose jobs have been sidelined by the virus. Collectively, the G20 countries have pledged over $5 trillion worth of stimulus to combat the pandemic's economic fallout.

That, of course, will soon mean exploding budgetary deficits, which as a percentage of GDP are likely to reach postwar highs. When they do, rest assured that today's massive stimulus will quickly morph into tomorrow's punishing restraint.

BORDERS WILL THICKEN

Globalization didn't just entail the mass movement of goods around the world; it moved people too. There's no doubt the pandemic has disrupted trade, but it's immobilized international travel in a manner seldom if ever seen before. The United States not only sealed its southern border with Mexico, a move President Trump repeatedly threatened as a way to halt the flow of migrants from Central America, but sealed the northern border with Canada as well.

Similarly, the EU closed its borders to foreign travellers, while member countries also sealed themselves off from their EU neighbours. The borderless EU sanctioned by the Schengen Agreement is no more. How willing will EU countries be to restore the agreement when the pandemic subsides? Will there even be an EU in the aftermath? Or will the union itself become another failed experiment in globalization? Indeed, the pandemic's fiscal and economic impacts may create a chasm between the EU's northern and southern members that is too wide to bridge.

If you're a migrant, you suddenly lost whatever vestiges of political protection you might still have enjoyed. On April 22, 2020, President Trump used the pandemic as justification for signing an executive order temporarily halting immigration into the United States for at least sixty days. Even migrant-tolerant Canada announced it would take the unprecedented step of immediately returning all migrants who cross its border back to the United States. Most of the more than fifty-seven thousand migrants who crossed the border since 2017 remained in Canada under a legal loophole in the Safe Third Country Agreement with the United States. In the face of a pandemic, that loophole, like the Schengen Agreement, no longer applied.

The virus won't quarantine countries forever, and ultimately borders will once again reopen, at least to travellers coming from countries where the contagion has been successfully contained. But when they are reopened, they are likely to be far thicker than they were before.

An argument you often hear in times of crisis is that individual freedoms must be curtailed for the greater public good. Around the world, liberals and progressives who, until the arrival of the virus, were committed to an ever-growing list of individual rights were soon demanding draconian measures to halt the spread of the contagion. That meant the police cracking down on kids playing in the park, or families walking their dogs or people being fined for walking too close to each other. And it meant that tighter border control became a bipartisan issue. Like the argument for greater economic self-sufficiency, the call for much tighter border control is about to become mainstream.

A SILVER LINING FOR THE EXPENDABLES

It's not just GDP that has been crushed. When factories and stores are shut down, suddenly people aren't working anymore. The devastating impact on employment is unprecedented. It's one thing for companies to gradually prune their labour force in the face of slackening demand, as happens in any recession. But it's an entirely new order of magnitude when, literally overnight, companies slash virtually their entire work force and shut down their operations in compliance with emergency health regulations of uncertain duration. The job losses that would normally accrue over the course of several quarters of economic contraction are suddenly left at the doorstep of governments.

Most OECD countries went from a state of near full employment to a record number of unemployment insurance claims. In the United States, 33 million workers applied for unemployment insurance over a seven-week period. In Canada, over 3 million workers lost their jobs during the first two months of the economic shutdown caused by the pandemic, a decline unprecedented during any past economic downturn. The jobless rate in April 2020 soared to 13 percent, the second highest level in the country's history. Meanwhile, the EU declared that the current recession in the region will be the deepest in the organization's history, while the International Labour Organization warned that as many as 12 million European workers were in danger of losing their full-time jobs.

It's a terrible thing for the pandemic to pull your job out from under you—a devastating blow that many of us have felt.

But this one may actually have a silver lining.

The coronavirus pandemic will eventually pass, like the Spanish flu and all other pandemics that have come before it. But the fear the virus has unleashed will linger on well after its contagion passes. There are other zoonotic viruses, some potentially far more lethal than the coronavirus, patiently waiting for their animal hosts to be eaten so they too can jump the species barrier and infect a human. Immunizing our economy from their spread will be every bit as important as finding a vaccine. And that will require a major economic restructuring: a return to local sourcing no matter the wage cost.

That's the good news for the millions of expendables who have been victimized by global supply chains that either reduced their wages or stole their jobs. They may take some solace from the one historical constant that pandemics from the Black Plague to the Spanish flu have left in their wake: they all boosted wages in the decades that followed.

In the past, it was the decimation of the population that suddenly made the supply of labour scarce, and hence its price dear. While the death toll from the coronavirus will likely prove to be modest compared to the deadly carnage unleashed by past pandemics, its impact on global supply chains could be just as lethal.

When your life may depend on something, the question of comparative advantage no longer seems quite so relevant as it did only yesterday. The advantages of economic specialization and the international division of labour that global trade provide may sound great in theory, but when the factory on the other side of the world—the one you're relying on to supply vitally needed medical equipment—has been closed or some government official decides where the goods made at that factory can be shipped, local sourcing all of a sudden sounds like a very good idea. In what seems like the blink of an eye, the call for economic self-sufficiency has leapt from the populist agenda to mainstream thinking.

After all, how comfortable will businesses around the world be with remaining dependent on Chinese factories to produce their goods when those factories at a moment's notice can be either quarantined or commandeered? Soon it won't be just a protectionist president but shareholders themselves who will be calling for their companies to immunize themselves against those kinds of global disruptions in the future.

What is likely to emerge from the pandemic is the polar opposite of globalization. Local sourcing means local production by local workers paid at local wage rates. And that means that many of us won't be quite as expendable anymore.

Toronto, Canada
May 2020

ACKNOWLEDGEMENTS

I would like to thank Nick Garrison for his invaluable help in not only editing the manuscript but developing the entire narrative of the book, and in particular the historical perspective. This marks the first time that Nick and I have had a chance to work together since he was the editor of my first book, *Why Your World Is About to Get A Whole Lot Smaller*. I would also like to acknowledge the very valuable contribution made by Craig Pyette, who not only helped with the editing but shepherded the book through the various stages of publication. Linda Pruessen, the editor of my third book, *The Carbon Bubble*, did her usual diligent job in copy editing the manuscript. Matthew Sibiga, imprint sales director of Random House Canada, made a number of valuable comments and read the manuscript through its creation. Sharon Klein, as usual, did a great job generating publicity for the book. And of course I would like to thank Anne Collins, my publisher, for giving me another at-bat and providing the project with considerable editorial resources. Last but not least, I would like to thank my old friend and fishing buddy Harvey Bradley, who helped me navigate through the US Bureau of Labor Statistics and Statistics Canada data.

NOTES

INTRODUCTION

1   US Bureau of Labor Statistics. Employment, Earnings and Hours, Database Series Id # CES300.

2   Statistics Canada, "Cansim Table 282-0008: Labour Force Characteristics by Industry, Annual (x 1,000)," last modified, November 11, 2019, https://www150.statcan.gc.ca/t1/tbl1/en /tv.action?pid=1410002301.

3   John Vidal and David Adam, "China Overtakes US as World's Biggest CO_2 Emitter," *The Guardian*, June 19, 2007, https://www.theguardian.com /environment/2007/jun/19/china.usnews.

4   "Each Country's Share of CO_2 Emissions," Union of Concerned Scientists, July 16, 2008, last modified October 10, 2019, https://www.ucsusa.org/resources/each-countrys-share-co2-emissions.

5   Organisation for Economic Co-operation and Development (OECD), *Under Pressure: The Squeezed Middle Class* (Paris: OECD Publishing, 2019), https://www.oecd.org/social/under-pressure-the-squeezed -middle-class-689afed1-en.htm.

CHAPTER 1: THE NEW POPULISM

1   Julian Zelizer, "How Ross Perot Shaped Our World," CNN, July 09, 2019, https://www.cnn.com/2019/07/09/opinions/how-ross-perot -shaped-our-world-zelizer/index.html.

2   Jacob Schlesinger, "Trump Forged His Ideas on Trade in the 1980s," *Wall Street Journal*, November 15, 2018, https://www.wsj.com /articles/trump-forged-his-ideas-on-trade-in-the-1980sand-never -deviated-1542304508.

3   According to official Apple documents, the vast majority of their top two hundred suppliers, based on spend, are in China (Apple Supplier

Responsibility 2019, Supplier List, https://www.apple.com/supplier
-responsibility/pdf/Apple-Supplier-List.pdf).

4 OECD, *Under Pressure*, 12.

5 Wilson Andrews, Kitty Bennett and Alicia Parlapiano, "2016
Delegate Count and Primary Results," *New York Times*, July 5, 2016,
https://www.nytimes.com/interactive/2016/us/elections/primary
-calendar-and-results.html.

6 "Brexit vote was a revolt against the rich," Socialist Worker, June 28,
2016, https://socialistworker.co.uk/art/42982/Brexit+vote+was+a
+revolt+against+the+rich.

7 "The Battle of Amiens: Macron Jeered by Whirlpool Workers after
Le Pen's Publicity Stunt," The Local, April 26, 2017, https://www
.thelocal.fr/20170426/le-pen-leaves-macron-in-a-spin-after-surprise
-visit-to-whirlpool-factory.

8 "In Numbers: How the French Voted," The Local, May 8, 2017,
https://www.thelocal.fr/20170508/in-numbers-how-the-french-voted
-and-how-they-didnt; Eshe Nelson, "A Record Number of French
Voters Were So Disgusted They Cast a Blank Vote for Nobody,"
Quartz, May 7, 2017, https://qz.com/977925/french-presidential
-election-emmanuel-macron-won-despite-a-record-number-of
-french-voters-so-disgusted-they-cast-a-blank-vote-for-nobody/.

CHAPTER 2: CHANGING THE RULES

1 William D. Popkin, "Less Developed Countries and the Revenue
Act of 1962," *Indiana Law Journal* 40, no. 1 (Fall 1964): Article 1,
https://www.repository.law.indiana.edu/cgi/viewcontent.
cgi?referer=https://www.google.com/&httpsredir=1&article
=3543&context=ilj.

2 Bojen Pancevski, "Stung by Trump Criticism of Russian Gas Deal
Germany Makes Its Own Threats," *Wall Street Journal*, April 29,
2019, https://www.wsj.com/articles/stung-by-trumps-criticisms
-of-russian-gas-deal-germany-makes-its-own-threats-11556623921.

3 Ryan Browne, "NATO Report Says Only 7 Members Are Meeting
Defense Spending Targets," CNN, March 14, 2019, https://www.cnn
.com/2019/03/14/politics/nato-defense-spending-target/index.html.

4 The infant industry argument provides a rationale for protection by
noting that nascent domestic industries typically lack the economies
of scale that their established international competitors have
achieved and thus need a temporary period of protection from

imports before they can capture equivalent economies of scale.

5 Jeffry Frieden, *Global Capitalism: It's Fall and Rise During the Twentieth Century* (New York: Penguin, 2006), 65; and "Economic Growth: The Last 100 Years," National Institute Economic Review, July 1, 1961, https://doi.org/10.1177/002795016101600105.

6 "Smoot-Hawley Tariff Act," Wikipedia, last modified November 3, 2019, https://en.wikipedia.org/wiki/Smoot–Hawley_Tariff_Act.

7 "Politicians Cannot Bring Back Old Fashioned Factory Jobs," *The Economist*, January 14, 2017, https://www.economist.com /briefing/2017/01/14/politicians-cannot-bring-back-old-fashioned -factory-jobs.

8 See H.R. 764—United States Reciprocal Trade Act 2019, https://www.congress.gov/bill/116th-congress/house-bill/764/text.

9 In response to mounting international pressure to open up its vehicle market, the largest in the world, China reduced its tariff on imported cars from 25 percent to 15 percent. But it subsequently raised that tariff by 25 percentage points, to 40 percent, against US vehicle imports in retaliation to President Trump's tariffs on Chinese imports. The additional tariff levied against US vehicles has been lifted during the current negotiating ceasefire in the ongoing US-China trade war (Staff, "China Tariffs Will Add 25 Per Cent to Cars Imported from U.S.," Driving, August 23, 2019, https://driving.ca/auto-news/news /china-tariffs-will-add-25-per-cent-to-cars-imported-from-u-s).

10 Simon Kennedy, "China Will Overtake the U.S. in Less Than 15 Years, HSBC Says," Bloomberg, September 25, 2018, https://www.bloomberg .com/news/articles/2018-09-25/hsbc-sees-china-economy-set-to-pass -u-s-as-number-one-by-2030.

11 Economic Policy Institute, "Nominal Wage Tracker," https://www.epi .org/nominal-wage-tracker/.

12 Simon Lester, "The WTO Still Considers China a Developing Nation," CNBC, April 25, 2018, https://www.cnbc.com/2018/04/25/what-trump -gets-right-about-china-and-trade.html.

13 NAFTA's Legacy: Lost Jobs, Lower Wages, Increased Inequality," Public Citizen, October 2019, https://www.citizen.org/wp-content /uploads/NAFTA-Factsheet_Deficit-Jobs-Wages_Oct-2019-1.pdf.

14 Alexia Fernández Campbell, "One Reason the Rust Belt Turned Red," *The Atlantic*, November 14, 2016, https://www.theatlantic.com /business/archive/2016/11/one-reason-the-rust-belt-turned-red /507611/.

CHAPTER 3: TODAY'S WORKER: I AIN'T NO FORTUNATE ONE

1 Julie Bort, "Amazon Now Employs One Half a Million People, and It Plans to Hire Thousands More," *Inc.*, October 27, 2017, https://www.inc.com/business-insider/jeff-bezos-amazon-employees-hiring-spree-second-largest-company-behind-walmart.html.

2 Seattle City Council voted unanimously to impose a 2.25 percent tax on total income above $250,000 for individuals and above $500,000 for married couples, which would raise $140 million a year for housing, education and public transit in the city. When a lower court ruled the tax unconstitutional (Washington is one of seven states that does not levy a personal income tax), the city took the issue to the state Supreme Court, which has sent it back to the Court of Appeals. The Appeals Court ruled in the city's favour during the summer of 2019 (Nick Bowman, "Court Rules Seattle Can Impose an Income Tax in Stunning Decision," MyNorthwest, July 15, 2019, https://mynorthwest.com/1451150/seattle-income-tax-lawsuit-appeals-court-decision).

3 The tax will charge $275 per employee to build or preserve nearly nine hundred units of affordable housing and provide wraparound services for the homeless. With forty-five thousand workers at its downtown Seattle campus, Amazon, the city's largest employer, is expected to account for about a third of the $47 million that will be collected annually for the next five years (Gregory Scuggs, "Seattle Unanimously Passes an 'Amazon Tax' to Fund Affordable Housing," CityLab, May 15, 2018, https://www.citylab.com/equity/2018/05/seattle-unanimously-passes-its-amazon-tax/560411/).

4 Abigail Hess, "Alexandria Ocasio-Cortez: Amazon Cancelling its Plans for a New York Headquarters Proves Anything Is Possible," CNBC, February 14, 2019, https://www.cnbc.com/2019/02/14/ocasio-cortez-amazon-cancelling-nyc-hq-proves-anything-is-possible.html.

5 Amie Tsang, "Amazon HQ2: How New York and Virginia Won the Beauty Contest," *New York Times*, November 14, 2018, https://www.nytimes.com/2018/11/14/technology/amazon-hq2-newyork-virginia-recap.html.

6 Karen Weise, "Amazon Muscles In on Seattle Election," *New York Times*, October 18, 2019, https://www.nytimes.com/2019/10/18/technology/amazon-seattle-council-election.html.

7 The legislation's full name is the Stop Bad Employers by Zeroing Out Subsidies Act, although the BEZOS acronym provided Sanders with a

handy dig at one of his main targets (Abha Bhattari, "Bernie Sanders Introduces 'Stop BEZOS Act' in the Senate," *Washington Post*, September 5, 2018, https://www.washingtonpost.com/business /2018/09/05/bernie-sanders-introduces-stop-bezos-act-senate/).

8 Sarah Salinas, "Amazon Raises Minimum Wage to $15 for All US Employees," CNBC, October 2, 2018, https://www.cnbc.com/2018/10 /02/amazon-raises-minimum-wage-to-15-for-all-us-employees.html.

9 United States Department of Labor, Bureau of Labor Statistics, "Table B-3. Average Hourly and Weekly Earning of All Employees on Private Nonfarm Payrolls by Industry Sector, Seasonally Adjusted," last modified, November 1, 2019, https://www.bls.gov/news.release /empsit.t19.htm.

10 Louise Auerhahn, Chris Benner, Jeffrey Buchanan, Bob Brownstein and Garbriela Giusta, "Innovation Inequality: How Tech's Business Models Concentrate Wealth while Shortchanging Workers," Working Partnerships USA, October 8, 2019, https://www.wpusa .org/research/innovating-inequality/.

11 Tamsin McMahon, "Silicon Valley's Motor City: As Big Tech Adds Fuel to a Housing Crisis, Poorer Residents Live in RVs," *Globe and Mail*, September 12, 2019, https://www.theglobeandmail.com/world /article-silicon-valleys-motor-city-as-big-tech-adds-fuel-to-a-housing -crisis/.

12 Carl Frey and Ebrahim Rahbari, "Technology at Work: How the Digital Revolution Is Reshaping the Global Labor Force," VOX CEPR Policy Portal, March 25, 2016, https://voxeu.org/article/how-digital -revolution-reshaping-global-workforce.

13 Leonid Bershidsky, "Germany's Economy Runs on Low Wages," BNN Bloomberg, April 9, 2019, https://www.bnnbloomberg.ca/germany -s-economy-runs-on-low-wages-1.1241460.

14 Julia Kollewe, "IFS: UK Wages Have Not Recovered to Pre-Crisis Levels," *The Guardian*, September 13, 2018, https://www.theguardian. com/business/2018/sep/12/uk-wages-have-not-yet-recovered-to -pre-crisis-levels-says-ifs.

15 "Nominal Wage Tracker (chart 1)," Economic Policy Institute, n.d., https://www.epi.org/nominal-wage-tracker/#chart1.

16 United States Department of Labor, Bureau of Labor Statistics, "Employment by Major Industry Sector, Table 2.1," last modified September 4, 2019, https://www.bls.gov/emp/tables/employment -by-major-industry-sector.htm.

17 Statistics Canada, "Cansim Table 282-0008."

18 Ibid.

19 For a comparison of hourly commendation rates between jobs in the goods sector and those in service industries see Statistics Canada, "Cansim Table 282-0008."

20 Alexis Keenan, "Uber and Lyft Face 2 Big Threats to Their Business Model after New California Law," Yahoo Finance, September 12, 2019, https://ca.finance.yahoo.com/news/uber-lyft-lawsuit-contractors -employees-law-174002068.html.

21 Kate Conver and Noam Scheiber, "Californnia Bill Makes App-Based Companies Treat Workers as Employees," *New York Times*, September 11, 2019, https://www.nytimes.com/2019/09/11/technology/california -gig-economy-bill.html.

22 Maya Kosoff, "Travis Kalanick Is Officially a Billionaire," *Vanity Fair*, January 18, 2018, https://www.vanityfair.com/news/2018/01 /travis-kalanick-is-officially-a-billionaire-uber-softbank.

23 "How Much Do Uber Drivers Actually Get Paid?" Economic Policy Institute Facebook page, May 15, 2018, https://www.facebook.com /EconomicPolicy/photos/a.10151281228111668/10156289074556668 /?type=3&theater.

24 Niall McCarthy, "The State of Global Trade Union Membership," *Forbes*, May 6, 2019, https://www.forbes.com/sites/niallmccarthy /2019/05/06/the-state-of-global-trade-union-membership-infographic /#594addb92b6e.

25 Branko Milanovic, *Global Inequality: A New Approach for the Age of Globalization* (Cambridge, MA: Belknap Press, 2016), 105.

26 One study estimated that for non-union private-sector male workers, weekly wages in 2013 would have been an estimated 5 percent higher—or over $2,000 a year—if union membership had stayed at the same share of the workforce as it was in 1979. The effects of union decline on the wages of non-union female workers are not as substantial, since women were not as unionized as men were in 1979. Even so, weekly wages for non-union female workers would be approximately 2 to 3 percent higher if union density had remained at its 1979 levels (Jake Rosenfeld, Patrick Denice and Jennifer Laird, "Union Decline Lowers Wages of Nonunion Workers," Economic Policy Institute, August 30, 2016, https://www.epi.org/publication /union-decline-lowers-wages-of-nonunion-workers-the-overlooked -reason-why-wages-are-stuck-and-inequality-is-growing/).

CHAPTER 4: LEFT BEHIND

1 OECD, *Under Pressure*.

2 Ibid., 8.

3 Ibid., 18.

4 "Nearly a third of UK households too poor to make ends meet, research shows," Centre for Research in Social Policy, Loughborough University, cited in *Weekly Welfare*, November 17, 2017, https://welfareweekly.com/nearly-a-third-of-uk-households-too-poor-to-make-ends-meet-research-shows/.

5 OECD, *Under Pressure*, 19. Baby boomers are defined as those born between 1943 and 1964; Generation X, 1965–82; Millennials, 1983–2002; and Generation Z, since 2003.

6 Jeff Rubin, "Has Global Trade Liberalization Left Canadian Workers Behind," Centre for International Governance Innovation (CIGI) Paper No. 163, February 2018, https://www.cigionline.org/sites/default/files/documents/Paper%20no.163web_0.pdf.

7 The full leaders' debate is available at "1988 Canadian Federal Election Debate" (YouTube video, 2:56:23, posted by Canuck Politics, July 23, 2105, https://www.youtube.com/watch?v=Oiq3-OWDR6Y). To see Brian Mulroney's warning, go to the eight-minute mark.

8 David Ricardo, *The Principals of Political Economy and Taxation* (London: Dover, 2004).

9 The delineation of winners and losers was first postulated as the Stolper–Samuelson theorem, which in turn was based on the earlier Heckscher-Ohlin theorem that postulated that a country's comparative advantage was determined by its factor endowments.

10 Frieden, *Global Capitalism*, 297.

11 Ibid., 366.

12 "Margaret Thatcher: A Life in Quotes," *The Guardian*, April 8, 2013, https://www.theguardian.com/politics/2013/apr/08/margaret-thatcher-quotes.

13 Some economists use a scale between zero and one hundred, with one hundred representing extreme inequality, as does one in the more conventional measure of the Gini coefficient.

14 Milanovic, *Global Inequality*, 107.

15 Rubin, "Global Trade Liberalization."

16 Marshall Steinbaum, "Effective Progressive Tax Rates in the 1950s," Roosevelt Institute, August 8, 2017, https://rooseveltinstitute.org/effective-progressive-tax-rates-1950s/.

17 "Income Tax in the United States," Wikipedia, last modified October 21, 2019, https://en.wikipedia.org/wiki/Income_tax_in_the_United _States#cite_note-congress.gov-26.

18 "List of People Named in the Panama Papers," Wikipedia, last modified October 29, 2019, https://en.wikipedia.org/wiki/List_of _people_named_in_the_Panama_Papers.

19 Annette Alstadsaeter, Niels Johannesen and Gabriel Zucman, "Who Owns the Wealth in Tax Havens? Macro Evidence and Implications for Global Inequality," National Bureau of Economic Research (NBER) Working Paper No. 23805, September 2017, www.nber.org /papers/w23805.

20 David Scharfenberg, "Trillions of Dollars Have Sloshed into Offshore Tax Havens. Here's How to Get It Back," *Boston Globe*, January 20, 2018, https://www.bostonglobe.com/ideas/2018/01/20/trillions -dollars-have-sloshed-into-offshore-tax-havens-here-how-get-back /2wQAzH5DGRwomFH0YPqKZJ/story.html.

21 Zach Dubinsky, "Wealthy Canadians Hiding up to $240B abroad, CRA says," CBC News, June 28, 2018, https://www.cbc.ca/news/business /cra-tax-gap-foreign-holdings-1.4726983.

22 Jeremy Kahn, "Google's 'Dutch Sandwich' Shielded 16 Billion Euros from Tax," Bloomberg, January 2, 2018, https://www.bloomberg.com /news/articles/2018-01-02/google-s-dutch-sandwich-shielded-16 -billion-euros-from-tax.

23 The practice typically involves a company's foreign subsidiaries paying licensing fees for the use of company trademarks and other intangible assets. The licensing fees can dramatically shift earnings from subsidiary operating companies to a company that holds the licences, which is typically in a low-tax or no-tax jurisdiction like Ireland or Bermuda, for example.

CHAPTER 5: GREATER GLOBAL EQUITY (FOR THE RICH)

1 Justin Lin and David Rosenblatt, "Shifting Patterns of Economic Growth and Rethinking Development," *Journal of Economic Policy Reform*, July 2012, 6, https://www.tandfonline.com/doi/full /10.1080/17487870.2012.700565.

2 Measured in US dollars, US GDP per capita was forty times that of China's in 1980. Today it is barely six times greater (International Monetary Fund, *World Economic Outlook Reports: Challenges to Steady Growth*, October 2018).

3   Edward Moyer, "A Tale of Apple, the iPhone, and Overseas manufac-
    turing" CNET, January 12, 2012, https://www.cnet.com/news/a-tale
    -of-apple-the-iphone-and-overseas-manufacturing/.

4   *The Future of Work: OECD Employment Outlook 2019*, 7.

5   Oya Celasun and Bertrand Gruss, "The Declining Share of
    Manufacturing Jobs," VOX CEPR Policy Portal, May 25, 2018,
    https://voxeu.org/article/declining-share-manufacturing-jobs.

6   Sonali Jain-Chandra, "Chart of the Week: Inequality in China,"
    IMFBlog, September 20, 2018, https://blogs.imf.org/2018/09/20
    /chart-of-the-week-inequality-in-china/.

7   Milanovic, *Global Inequality*, 25.

8   Branko Milanovic, "There Are Two Sides to Today's Global Income
    Inequality," *Globe and Mail*, January 22, 2018, https://www.theglobe-
    andmail.com/report-on-business/rob-commentary/the-two-sides
    -of-todays-global-income-inequality/article37676680/.

9   Staff, "Billionaires: The Richest People in the World," *Forbes*, March 5,
    2019, https://www.forbes.com/billionaires/#c488a87251c7.

10 Frieden, *Global Capitalism*, 297.

11 Michael W.L. Elsby, Bart Hobjin and Aysegul Sahin, "The Decline of
    the U.S. Labor Share," Brookings, Fall 2013, https://www.brookings
    .edu/bpea-articles/the-decline-of-the-u-s-labor-share/.

12 Ibid.

13 Heidi Chung, "The Richest 1% own 50% of Stocks Held by American
    Households," Yahoo Finance, January 17, 2019, https://finance.yahoo
    .com/.../the-richest-1-own-50-of-stocks-held-by-american-house.

14 Edward N. Wolff, "Household Wealth Trends in the United States,
    1962 to 2016: Has Middle Class Wealth Recovered?" NBER Working
    Paper No. 24085, November 2017, www.nber.org/papers/w24085.

15 Nikil Saval, "Globalisation: The Rise and Fall of an Idea That Swept
    the World," *The Guardian*, July 14, 2017, https://www.theguardian
    .com/world/2017/jul/14/globalisation-the-rise-and-fall-of-an-idea
    -that-swept-the-world.

16 David H. Autor, David Dorn and Gordon H. Hanson, "The China
    Shock: Learning from Labor Market Adjustment to Large Changes
    in Trade," NBER Working Paper No. 21906, January 2016, www.nber
    .org/papers/w21906.

17 See, for example, Kevin Carty, "Tech Giants Are the Robber Barons
    of Our Times," *New York Post*, February 3, 2018, https://nypost.com
    /2018/02/03/big-techs-monopolistic-rule-is-hiding-in-plain-sight/.

18 Adjusted for inflation, Rockefeller's net worth would be about
    $30 billion in today's dollars. By comparison, Jeff Bezos's wealth
    comes in at an estimated $150 billion.

CHAPTER 6: THE NEW ECONOMY: NON-INCLUSIVE GROWTH

1   Randy Alfred, "March 25, 1954: RCA TVs Get the Color for Money,"
    Wired, March 25, 2008, https://www.wired.com/2008/03/dayintech
    -0325/; Brent Cox, "How Much More Do Televisions Cost Today,"
    The Awl, November 18, 2011, https://www.theawl.com/2011/11
    /how-much-more-do-televisions-cost-today/.

2   Federal Reserve Bank of St. Louis, "Economic Data: Personal Savings
    Rate," last modified September 27, 2019, https://fred.stlouisfed.org
    /series/PSAVERT.

3   Matt Lundy, "Less savings, more debt: Inside a multi-decade shift in
    Canadians' finances," *Globe and Mail*, November 17, 2019 (updated
    November 18, 2019), https://www.theglobeandmail.com/business
    /economy/economic-insight/article-why-canadians-arent-saving
    -like-they-once-did/.

4   OECD Data, "Household Spending," 2018 or latest available,
    https://data.oecd.org/hha/household-spending.htm.

5   OECD, *Under Pressure*. chapter 4.

6   Ibid.

7   Hale Stewart, "Consumer Spending and the Economy," *New York
    Times*, September 19, 2010, https://fivethirtyeight.blogs.nytimes.
    com/2010/09/19/consumer-spending-and-the-economy/.

8   Nathaniel Meyersohn, "Family Dollar Will Close Nearly 400 Stores,"
    CNN, March 6, 2019, https://www.cnn.com/2019/03/06/investing
    /family-dollar-stores/index.html.

9   Tom Polansek and Humeyra Pamuk, "Trump Administration
    Proposed Rule Would Cut 3 Million People from Food Stamps,"
    Reuters, July 23, 2019, https://www.reuters.com/article/us-usa
    -trump-foodstamps/trump-administration-proposed-rule-would
    -cut-3-million-people-from-food-stamps-idUSKCN1UI0AH.

10 Center on Budget and Policy Priorities, "A Guide to Statistics on
    Historical Trends in Income Inequality," https://www.cbpp.org
    /research/poverty-and-inequality/a-guide-to-statistics-on-historica
    l-trends-in-income-inequality.

CHAPTER 7: GLOBALIZATION AND THE DIGITAL REVOLUTION

1   Suetonius, *The Twelve Caesars*, trans. Robert Graves (London: Penguin, 2007), 284. Another translation has Vespasian saying "Let me feed the mob" (Lionel Casson, "Unemployment, the Building Trade, and Suetonius, Vesp. 18," *Bulletin of the American Society of Papyrologists* 14, no. 1/2 [1978]: 43–51, https://www.jstor.org /stable/24518751?seq=1#page_scan_tab_contents).

2   Needless to say, Queen Elizabeth I only delayed the inevitable. It's interesting that a machine designed to automate sock-making touched off the Industrial Revolution (Wikipedia, "Stocking Frame," last modified August 28, 2019, https://en.wikipedia.org/wiki /Stocking_frame).

3   Ljubica Nedelkoska and Glenda Quintini, "Automation, Skills Use and Training," OECD Social, Employment and Migration Working Papers No. 202, March 6, 2018, http://pmb.cereq.fr/doc_num .php?explnum_id=4268.

4   Paul Davidson, "Automation Could Kill 73 Million US Jobs by 2030," *USA Today*, November 28, 2017, https://www.usatoday.com/story /money/2017/11/29/automation-could-kill-73-million-u-s-jobs-2030 /899878001/.

5   "Something's Not Right Here: Poor Working Conditions Persist at Apple Supplier Pegatron," China Labor Watch, October 22, 2015, www.chinalaborwatch.org/report/109.

6   Ibid.

7   Dane O'Leary, "Where Are Smartphones Made," Android Authority, August 5, 2016, https://www.androidauthority.com/where-smart- phones-are-made-707989/.

8   Allana Akhtar, "While CEOs Like Jack Ma and Elon Musk Praise Grueling Job Schedules, Employees around the World are Demanding Shorter Workweeks" Business Insider, April 16, 2019, https://www .businessinsider.com/jack-ma-defends-his-996-workweek-but -productivity-experts-disagree-2019-4.

9   Reuters, "JD.com boss Richard Liu Criticises 'Slackers' as Company Makes Cuts," Gadgets360, April 13, 2019, https://gadgets.ndtv.com /internet/news/jd-com-richard-liu-comments-on-996-work-culture -china-2022618.

10 Sarah Katz-Lavigne, "Demand for Congo's Cobalt Is on the Rise. So Is Scrutiny of Mining Practices," *Washington Post*, February 21, 2019, https://www.washingtonpost.com.

11 C.P. Baldé, V. Forti, V. Gray, V. Keuhr and P. Stegmann, *The Global E-Waste Monitor 2017: Quantities, Flows, and Resources* (Tokyo: United Nations University, 2017), https://collections.unu.edu/eserv /UNU:6341/Global-E waste_Monitor_2017__electronic_single _pages_.pdf.

12 "Gartner Says Global Smartphones Sales Stalled in the Fourth Quarter of 2018", Gartner, February 21, 2019, https://www.gartner .com/en/newsroom/press-releases/2019-02-21-gartner-says-global -smartphone-sales-stalled-in-the-fourth-quart.

13 Associated Press, "America Ships Electronic Waste Overseas," Redmond, November 19, 2007, https://redmondmag.com/articles /2007/11/19/america-ships-electronic-waste-overseas.aspx.

14 John Misachi, "Guiyu, China—The Largest Electronic Waste Site in the World," WorldAtlas, June 6, 2017, https://www.worldatlas.com/articles /guiyu-china-the-largest-electronic-waste-site-in-the-world.html.

CHAPTER 8: DUELLING GIANTS: THE TRADE WAR WITH CHINA

1 Evelyn Cheng, "Trumps Tariffs Backfire as EU Retaliation with Force American Icon Harley-Davidson to Build Overseas," CNBC, June 25, 2018, https://www.cnbc.com/2018/06/25/trump-tariffs-backfire -on-harley-davidson-after-eu-retaliates.html.

2 Reuters, "Harley-Davidson Strikes Deal to Build Smaller Bike in China," *Financial Post*, June 19, 2019, https://business.financialpost .com/transportation/harley-davidson-strikes-deal-to-build-smaller -bike-in-china.

3 Bruce Brown, "In Depth: Why Harley-Davidson Is Building Small Bikes for China but Not the U.S.," Digital Trends, July 5, 2019, https://www .digitaltrends.com/cars/harley-davidson-small-bikes-for-china/.

4 In 2018, the US trade deficit with China was $419 billion (U.S. Census Bureau, Foreign Trade, "Trade in Goods with China, 2019," https: //www.census.gov/foreign-trade/balance/c5700.html).

5 M. Szmigiera, "Personal Saving Rate in the United States from August 2018 to August 2019," Statista, last modified October 28, 2019, https://www.statista.com › personal-savings-rate-in-the-united -states-by-month).

6 Eric Rosenbaum, "1 in 5 Corporations Say China Has Stolen Their IP within the Last Year: CNBC CFO Survey," CNBC, March 1, 2019, https://www.cnbc.com/2019/02/28/1-in-5-companies-say-china -stole-their-ip-within-the-last-year-cnbc.html.

7   Joshua Gallu, "Trump Says He's Raising Tariffs on China After Its Retaliation," *Bloomberg*, August 23, 2019, https://www.bloomberg.com/news/articles/2019-08-23/trump-says-he-s-raising-tariffs-on-china-after-its-retaliation.

8   Zhou Xin, "Donald Trump Can Outgun China on Tariffs but Beijing Has Other Ways to Fight Back," *South China Morning Post*, June 19, 2018, https://www.scmp.com/news/china/diplomacy-defence/article/2151502/donald-trump-can-outgun-china-trade-tariffs-beijing-has.

9   Jackie Wattles, "Trump Encourage Boycott against Harley-Davidson," CNN, August 12, 2018, https://www.cnn.com/2018/08/12/politics/trump-harley-davidson-overseas-manufacturing/index.html.

10 "US-China Trade War: Deal Agreed to Suspend New Tarrifs," BBC News, December 2, 2019, https://www.bbc.com/news/world-latin-america-46413196.

11 US Census Bureau, "Trade in Goods with China, 2019."

12 According to the World Bank, in 2018, exports of goods and services represented 20 percent of China's GDP. By comparison, export of goods and services represented 12 percent of US GDP (https://data.worldbank.org/indicator/NE.EXP.GNFS.ZS).

13 Cary Huang, "US-China Trade War: Who Wanted the Deal the Most? Just Look at the Concessions Made by Both Sides" *South China Morning Post*, October 23, 2019, https://www.scmp.com/comment/opinion/article/3033940/us-china-trade-war-who-wanted-deal-most-just-look-concessions-made.

14 Arjun Kharpal, "Chinese Smartphones Sales Keep Falling," CNBC, March 13, 2019, https://www.cnbc.com/2019/03/13/china-smartphone-sales-keep-falling--thats-likely-bad-news-for-apple.html; and "Record Slump in China's Auto Sector Continues in September," *Bloomberg News*, October 12, 2019, https://www.bloomberg.com/news/articles/2019-10-12/historic-slump-in-china-car-market-continues-as-sales-drop-6-6.

15 Enda Curran, "How the U.S.-China Trade War Got to This Point," *Washington Post*, August 26, 2019, https://www.washingtonpost.com/business/how-the-us-chinatradewargot-to-this-point/2019/08/25/f54427da-c7b1-11e9-9615-8f1a32962e04_story.html.

16 David Reid, "5 Big Risks That the World's Fragile Economy Doesn't Need Right Now," CNBC, October 4, 2019, https://www.cnbc.com/2019/10/04/5-big-risks-that-the-worlds-fragile-economy-doesnt-need-right-now.html.

17 Dorcas Wong and Alexander Chipman Koty, "The US-China Trade War: A Timeline," China Briefing, November 5, 2019, https://www .china-briefing.com/news/the-us-china-trade-war-a-timeline/.

18 Office of the United States Trade Representative, "United States and China Reach Phase One Trade Agreement," December 13, 2019, https://ustr.gov/about-us/policy-offices/press-office/press-releases /2019/december/united-states-and-china-reach.

19 Like Ronald Reagan, President Trump sees an expanded role for the US military in space. In 2018, he directed the Pentagon to create a "space force"—a new, sixth military branch to oversee missions and operations in space—claiming, "We must have American dominance in space." ("The Trump Administration Is Establishing the United States Space Command to Advance American Interests and Defend Our Nation," White House Fact Sheet, August 29, 2019, https: //www.whitehouse.gov/briefings-statements/trump-administration -establishing-united-states-space-command-advance-american -interests-defend-nation/).

20 Matthew Johnston, "The Post-Soviet Union Russian Economy," Investopedia, June 25, 2019, https://www.investopedia.com/articles /investing/012116/russian-economy-collapse-soviet-union.asp.

21 Niall McCarthy, "Stalin Is Far More Popular than Gorbachev," *Forbes*, May 12, 2017, https://www.forbes.com/sites/niallmccarthy /2017/05/12/stalin-is-far-more-popular-with-russians-than-gorbachev -infographic/#d77ae816635a.

CHAPTER 9: TARIFF MAN

1   Steve Hendrix, "Truman declared and emergency when he felt thwarted. Trump should know: It didn't end well," *Washington Post*, January 11, 2019, https://www.washingtonpost.com/history /2019/01/08/truman-declared-an-emergency-when-he-felt-thwarted -trump-should-know-it-didnt-end-well/.

2   The American Institute for International Steel, a pro-trade advocacy group, estimates that about 142,000 Americans work in the steel industry. Those workers would stand to benefit from the tariffs (Patrick Gillespie, "U.S. Steel Is Bringing Back 500 Workers, but Tariffs Could Cost Thousands of Jobs," CNN, March 7, 2018, https://money.cnn.com/2018/03/07/news/companies/trump -tariffs-steel-jobs/index.html).

3 Chris Isadore, "When American Steel Was King," CNN, March 9, 2018, https://money.cnn.com/2018/03/09/news/companies /american-steel-history/index.html.

4 Jeff Ferry, "US Steel and Aluminum Tarrifs—the Right Move at the Right Time," The Hill, June 2, 2019, https://thehill.com/opinion /international/390375-us-steel-and-aluminum-tariffs-the-right-move -at-the-right-time.

5 "Presidential Proclamation on Adjusting Imports of Steel into the United States," White House Proclamation, March 8, 2018, https: //www.whitehouse.gov/presidential-actions/presidential-proclamation -adjusting-imports-steel-united-states/.

6 "Who Pays Trump's Tariffs, China or U.S. Customers and Companies?" Reuters, May 21, 2019, https://www.reuters.com /article/us-usa-trade-china-tariffs-explainer/who-pays-trumps -tariffs-china-or-u-s-customers-and-companies-idUSKCN1SR1UI.

7 Naomi Powell, "Trump Drops Steel and Aluminum Tariffs, Clearing Way for the USMCA," Financial Post, May 17, 2019, https://business. financialpost.com/business/trump-drops-steel-and-aluminum -tariffs-clearing-path-for-usmca.

8 Bruce Baschuk, "US Can Tariff about $8 Billion of EU Goods Over Airbus Aid," Bloomberg, September 25, 2019, https://www.bloomberg .com/news/articles/2019-09-25/u-s-can-sanction-nearly-8-bln-of-eu -goods-over-airbus-aid-kozigcr2.

9 Doug Palmer and Adam Behsudi, "Trump Holds Off on Auto Tariffs, but Threat Still Looms," Politico, May 7, 2019, https://www.politico.com /story/2019/05/17/donald-trump-auto-tariffs-1330014.

10 Reuters, "Here's Why US Importers and Consumers Pay Trump's Tariffs, not China," CNBC, August 2, 2019, https://www.cnbc.com /2019/08/02/heres-why-us-importers-and-consumers-pay-trumps -tariffs-not-china.html.

11 Cindy Wang, "World's Top Bicycle Maker Says the Era of Made in China is Over," Bloomberg, June 17, 2019, https://www.bbc.com /news/world-latin-america-46413196.

12 Chuck Devore, "Manufacturers Added 6 Times More Jobs Under Trump Than Under Obama's Last 2 Years," Forbes, February 1, 2019, https://www.forbes.com/sites/chuckdevore/2019/02/01/manufacturers -added-6-times-more-jobs-under-trump-than-under-obamas-last-2 -years/#3af92f8c5635.

13 Ibid.

14 Robert E. Scott, "Aluminum Tariffs Have Led to a Strong Recovery in Employment, Production, and Investment in Primary Aluminum and Downstream Industries," Economic Policy Institute, December 11, 2018, https://www.epi.org/publication/aluminum-tariffs-have-led -to-a-strong-recovery-in-employment-production-and-investment -in-primary-aluminum-and-downstream-industries/.

15 Jeffry Bartash, "At a 10-Year High, Wage Growth for American Workers Likely to Keep Accelerating," MarketWatch, March 8, 2019, https://www.marketwatch.com/story/at-a-10-year-high-wag e-growth-for-american-workers-likely-to-keep-accelerating-2019 -03-08.

CHAPTER 10: MAYBE WHAT'S GOOD FOR AMERICAN WORKERS ISN'T GOOD FOR GM

1 For McLaughlin's own account, see "How the Auto Beat the Horse: My Eighty Years on Wheels," *Maclean's*, October 1, 1954, http://archive .macleans.ca/article/1954/10/1/how-the-auto-beat-the-horse.

2 "McLaughlin Motor Car Company," Wikipedia, last modified September 4, 2019, https://en.wikipedia.org/wiki/McLaughlin _Motor_Car_Company#cite_note-19.

3 David Crane, "Canada-US Auto Pact," Canadian Encyclopedia (online), last edited June 12, 2017, https://thecanadianencyclopedia .ca/en/article/canada-us-automotive-products-agreement

4 Marti Benedetti, "Hard-charging Charles Wilson Ran GM—and then the Pentagon," *Automotive News*, September 14, 2008, https: //www.autonews.com/article/20080914/OEM02/309149916 /hard-charging-charles-wilson-ran-gm-and-then-the-pentagon.

5 As reported in "The Administration: Conflict of Interest," *Time*, January 26, 1953, http://content.time.com/time/magazine/article /0,9171,817757,00.html.

6 Jeff Rubin, "How Has Canadian Manufacturing Fared under NADTA: A Look at the Auto Assembly and Parts Industry," CIGI Paper No. 138, August 8, 2017, Centre for International Governance Innovation, https://www.cigionline.org/publications/how-has-canadian -manufacturing-fared-under-nafta-look-auto-assembly-and -parts-industry.

7 Ibid.

8 Ibid.

9 David Hunkar, "Manufacturing Labor Costs in Mexico vs. China,"

TopForeignStocks.com, May 12, 2018, https://topforeignstocks.com
/2018/05/12/manufacturing-labor-costs-in-mexico-vs-china/.

10 Kyle Linder, "10 Facts about Labor Unions in Mexico," Borgen
Project, July 26, 2019, https://borgenproject.org/10-facts-about
-labor-unions-in-mexico/.

11 David Welch and Nacha Cattan, "How Mexico's Unions Sell Out
Autoworkers," Bloomberg, May 5, 2017, https://www.bloomberg.com
/news/articles/2017-05-05/how-mexico-s-unions-sell-out-autoworkers.

12 Linder, "10 Facts about Labor Unions in Mexico."

13 Rubin, "How Has Canadian Manufacturing Fared under NAFTA?"

14 Reuters, "Ford Cancels a $1.6 Billion Mexican Plant and Adds
700 Jobs in Michigan," *Fortune*, January 3, 2017, https://fortune
.com/2017/01/03/ford-cancels-mexico-plant-trump/.

15 "The Growing Role for Mexico in the North American Auto Industry,"
Center for Automotive Research, July 2016, http://www.cargroup
.org/wp-content/uploads/2017/02/The-Growing-Role-of-Mexico-in
-the-North-American-Automotive-Industry-Trends-Drivers-and
-Forecasts.pdf.

16 In the United States, GM and Chrysler were given an $80 billion
bailout by American taxpayers, with the bulk going to GM, which was
America's largest car manufacturer. In Canada, the federal government, along with the Ontario provincial government, coughed up
$13.7 billion to keep GM's and Chrysler's Canadian plants operating.
Only $10.2 billion of that bailout was eventually recovered, leaving
Canadian taxpayers on the hook for $3.5 billion of the bailout
package (Mark Milke, "Crunching the Numbers on the 2009 Auto
Bailout," Fraser Institute, n.d., https://www.fraserinstitute.org
/article/crunching-numbers-2009-auto-bailout).

17 "WTO Upholds Auto Pact Ruling," CBC New, May 31, 2000, https:
//www.cbc.ca/news/business/wto-upholds-auto-pact-ruling-1.245894.

18 Rubin, "How Has Canadian Manufacturing Fared under NAFTA?"

19 "US Dollar Peso Exchange Rate: Historical Chart," Macrotrends, n.d.,
https://www.macrotrends.net/2559/us-dollar-mexican-peso-exchange
-rate-historical-chart.

CHAPTER 11: FROM FREE TRADE TO MANAGED TRADE: THE US-MEXICO-CANADA TRADE AGREEMENT

1 Rubin, "How Has Canadian Manufacturing Fared under NAFTA?"

2 Ibid.

3 Robert Fife, "They Stole the Company: Frank Stronach Accuses

Daughter Belinda of Betrayal," *Globe and Mail*, July 20, 2019, https://www.theglobeandmail.com/business/article-they-stole-the-company-frank-stronach-accuses-daughter-belinda-of/.

4 Dana Flavelle, "Magna Says No New Plants for Canada, *The Star*, May 8, 2014, https://www.thestar.com/business/2014/05/08/magna_says_no_new_plants_for_canada_cites_ontario_energy_costs.html.

5 "Canadian Manufacturer Magna, with 32 Plants in Mexico, Posts Record Quarterly Profit," MexicoNow, May 14, 2018, https://mexico-now.com/index.php/article/4030-canadian-manufacturer-magna-with-32-plants-in-mexico-posts-record-quarterly-profit.

6 Jie Ma and Maiko Takahashi, "Carmakers See $17 Billion Wiped Out by Trump's Mexico Threat," Bloomberg, May 30, 2019, https://www.bloomberg.com/news/articles/2019-05-31/japanese-automobile-stocks-drop-on-trump-s-mexico-tariff-tweet.

7 Alicia Siekierska, "I'm Worried about What's Going on in Canada: Magna CEO Concerned about Competitiveness" *Financial Post*, May 10, 2018, https://business.financialpost.com/transportation/im-worried-about-whats-going-on-in-canada-magnas-ceo-concerned-about-competitiveness.

8 Eli Watkins, "Peter Navarro Says There Is a Special Place in Hell for Justin Trudeau," CNN June 10, 2018, https://www.cnn.com/2018/06/10/politics/peter-navarro-justin-trudeau/index.html.

9 Chapter 11 was designed to provide a rule-based system for governing investment between the three countries, including the establishment of impartial tribunals to settle disputes with the government over actions that were deemed discriminatory.

10 Office of the United States Trade Representative, "United States-Mexico-Canada Trade Fact Sheet," n.d., https://ustr.gov/trade-agreements/free-trade-agreements/united-states-mexico-canada-agreement/fact-sheets/rebalancing.

11 Ibid.

12 Sean McLain and William Boston, "NAFTA Rewrite Is Mixed Blessing for Foreign Car Makers," *Wall Street Journal*, October 1, 2018, https://www.wsj.com/articles/nafta-rewrite-is-mixed-blessing-for-foreign-car-makers-1538403059.

13 David Welch, "GM Squeezed $118 Million from Its Workers, Then Shut Their Factory," *Los Angeles Times*, March 29, 2019, https://www.latimes.com/business/la-fi-hy-general-motors-lordstown-ohio-union-20190329-story.html.

14 Sean O'Kane, "GM Still Plans to Sell Lordstown Plant to EV Startup after UAW Strike," The Verge, October 17, 2019, https://www.theverge .com/2019/10/17/20919378/gm-workhorse-lordstown-plant-sale-uaw -strike.

15 Ole Moehr, "US-EU Auto Tariffs: What's at Stake?" Atlantic Council, August 28, 2019, https://www.atlanticcouncil.org/blogs/econographics /us-eu-auto-tariffs-what-s-at-stake-copy/.

16 Office of the United States Trade Representative, "Japan, Korea & APEC," n.d., https://ustr.gov/countries-regions/japan-korea-apec/japan.

17 This move also includes immediate plans to invest $749 million and hire 568 new workers at existing operations in Alabama, Kentucky, Missouri, Tennessee and West Virginia. The company also plans to hire another 450 workers at its Hunstville, Alabama, engine factory by 2021. Toyota intends to bulk up its production of the fast-selling SUVs and light trucks that currently dominate the US market (Chester Dawson, "Toyota Boosts US Spending Plan Almost 30% with an Eye on Trump," Bloomberg, March 14, 2019, https://www .bloomberg.com/news/articles/2019-03-14/trump-wary-toyota -boosts-u-s-investment-to-almost-13-billion).

18 I. Wagner, "Number of Employees in the U.S. Automotive Industry from 2007 to 2019, by Sector," Statista, August 9, 2019, https://www .statista.com/statistics/276474/automotive-industry-employees-in -the-united-states-by-sector/.

19 Dawson, "Toyota Boosts US Spending Plan Almost 30%."

20 Josh Rubin, "Plan to Save 300 jobs at Oshawa's GM Plant Gets Mixed Reviews," The Star, May 8, 2019, https://www.thestar.com/business /2019/05/08/plan-to-save-300-jobs-at-oshawas-gm-plant-gets-mixed -reviews.html.

CHAPTER 12: KEEPING CHINA OUT OF AMERICA'S BACK DOOR

1 Julian Bajkowski, "Turnbull Defends Australia Front Running Huawei 5G Ban," ITNews, March 6, 2019, https://www.itnews.com.au /news/turnbull-defends-australia-front-running-huawei-5g-ban-520199.

2 Robert Fife and Stephen Chase, "Five Eyes Spy Chiefs Warned Trudeau Twice about Huawei National Security Risk," Globe and Mail, December 17, 2018, https://www.theglobeandmail.com/politics /article-five-eyes-spy-chiefs-warn-trudeau-about-chinas-huawei/.

3 Thomson Reuters, "Chinese Envoy to Canada Warns of Repercussions if Ottawa Bans Huawei from 5G Mobile Phone Network" CBC News,

January 17, 2019, https://www.cbc.ca/news/politics/china-envoy
-warning-huawei-ban-1.4982601.

4   While large American wireless carriers have already cut commercial
    links with both Huawei and ZTE, both companies still have extensive
    sales with small rural carriers in the United States, who use their
    competitively priced switches and other telecom equipment. In Canada,
    Bell and Telus, both of whom use Huawei equipment, claim it would
    cost them at least $1 billion to replace it in their transmission networks
    (https://www.theglobeandmail.com/canada/article-canadian-political
    -parties-rallying-around-telecom-pricing-issue-as/).

5   Mike Blanchfield, "Beijing Attacks USMCA Clause Seen as Blocking
    Efforts to Expand Trade with Canada, Mexico," CBC News, October 5,
    2018, https://www.cbc.ca/news/politics/usmca-nafta-china-trade
    -1.4852269.

6   Betsy Klein, "Trump Expresses Openness to Using Huawei CFO as
    Bargaining Chip in China Trade Talks," CNN, December 12, 2018,
    https://www.cnn.com/2018/12/11/politics/trump-china-huawei
    -cfo/index.html.

7   Borzou Daragahi, "How a Tangled and Deadly Web of Global Corruption
    Spreading Out from Gaddafi's Libya Threatens to Topple Justin
    Trudeau," Independent, March 7, 2019, https://www.independent.co.uk
    /news/world/middle-east/canada-libya-snc-lavalin-scandal-corruption
    -gaddafi-trudeau-explained-a8821221.html.

8   Nathan Vanderklippe, "China Halts New Purchases of All Canadian
    Canola," *Globe and Mail*, March 22, 2019, https://www.theglobeandmail
    .com/world/article-china-ramps-up-tensions-bars-new-purchases-of
    -all-canadian-canola-and/.

9   Xiao Xu, "Tour Operators Report Sharp Drop in Chinese Government
    Tourists in the Wake of Huawei Dispute," *Globe and Mail*, April 11, 2019,
    https://www.theglobeandmail.com/canada/article-tour-operators
    -report-sharp-drop-in-chinese-government-tourists-in-the/.

10 Joanne Lee-Young, "Chinese Buyers Responsible for One-Third of
    Value of Vancouver Home Sales: National Bank," *Vancouver Sun*,
    March 24, 2016, http://www.vancouversun.com/business/chinese
    +buyers+responsible+third+value+vancouver+home+sales+national
    +bank/11804486/story.html.

11 Jeremy Luedi, "Chinese International Students Are Pumping Billions
    into Canada," True North Far East, n.d., https://truenorthfareast.com
    /news/chinese-international-students-canada-impact.

12 Office of the United States Trade Representative, "United States and China Reach Phase One Trade Agreement," December 13, 2019, https://ustr.gov/about-us/policy-offices/press-office/press-releases/2019/december/united-states-and-china-reach..

13 Nathan Vanderklippe, "Canada Risks Being Left Behind as China-US Trade Talks Advance," *Globe and Mail*, April 13, 2019.

CHAPTER 13: MAKING CHINA GREAT AGAIN

1   Karen Yeung, "Does China Have Enough US Dollars to Survive the Trade War," *South China Morning Post*, May 30, 2019, https://www.scmp.com/economy/china-economy/article/3012460/does-china-have-enough-us-dollars-trade-war-escalates.

2   "Malacca Strait Is a Strategic Chokepoint," Reuters, March 4, 2010, https://in.reuters.com › article › idININdia-46652220100304.

3   "Railway Boosts Economic Growth in Tibet," ChinaDaily, January 15, 2014, http://www.chinadaily.com.cn/business/2014-01/15/content_17236538.htm.

4   Chris Buckley and Steven Lee Myers, "China's Legislature Blesses Xi's Indefinite Rule," *New York Times*, March 11, 2018, https://www.nytimes.com/2018/03/11/world/asia/china-xi-constitution-term-limits.html.

5   Maria Abi-Habib, "How China Got Sri Lanka to Cough Up a Port," *New York Times*, June 25, 2018, https://www.nytimes.com/2018/06/25/world/asia/china-sri-lanka-port.html.

6   William Niba, "Kenya's Struggle with the Burden of Chinese Loans," RFI, March 1, 2019, http://www.rfi.fr/en/africa/20190102-kenyas-struggle-burden-chinese-loans.

7   Anisah Shukry, "China, Malaysia to Resume East Coast Rail for $11 billion," Bloomberg, April 12, 2019, https://www.bloomberg.com/news/articles/2019-04-12/china-agrees-to-resume-malaysian-east-coast-rail-for-11-billion.

8   In suspending the project, President Mohamad said, "When it involves giving contracts to China, borrowing huge sums of money from China, and the contract goes to China, and China contractors prefer to use their own workers from China, use everything imported from China, even the payment is not made here, it's made in China . . . that kind of contract is not something that I welcome." Subsequently, Malaysia was able to renegotiate better terms for the project, which is now going ahead (Shukry, "China, Malaysia to Resume East Coast Rail for $11 billion").

9 Hugh White, "Australia Must Prepare for a Chinese Military Base in the Pacific," *The Guardian*, July 15, 2019, https://www.theguardian .com/world/commentisfree/2019/jul/15/australia-must-prepare-for -a-chinese-military-base-in-the-pacific.

10 Stuart Lau, "Italy May Be Ready to Open Up Four Ports to China under 'Belt and Road Initiative,'" *South China Morning Post*, March 19, 2019, https://www.scmp.com/news/china/diplomacy/article/3002305 /italy-may-be-ready-open-four-ports-chinese-investment-under.

11 John Hurley, Scott Morris and Gailyn Portelance, "Examining the Debt Implications of the Belt and Road Initiative from a Policy Perspective," CIGI Paper No. 121, March 2018, https://www.cgdev .org/sites/default/files/examining-debt-implications-belt-and-road -initiative-policy-perspective.pdf.

12 Ben Blanchard, "China's Xi Touts More Than 64 billion in Belt and Road Deals," Reuters, April 27, 2019, https://www.reuters.com /article/us-china-silkroad-xi/chinas-xi-touts-more-than-64-billion -in-belt-and-road-deals-idUSKCN1S308Q.

13 John Boone and Kiyya Baloch, "A New Shenzhen? Poor Pakistan Fishing Town's Horror at Chinese Plans," *The Guardian*, February 4, 2016, https://www.theguardian.com/world/2016/feb/04/pakistan -new-shenzhen-poor-gwadar-fishing-town-china-plans.

14 "China's Silk Road Cuts through Some of the World's Riskiest Countries," Bloomberg, October 25, 2017, https://www.bloomberg .com/news/articles/2017-10-25/china-s-new-silk-road-runs-mostly -through-junk-rated-territory.

15 Cecilia Joy-Perez and Derek Scissors, "The Chinese State Funds Belt and Road but Does Not Have Trillions to Spare," American Enterprise Institute, March 28, 2018, https://www.aei.org/research-products /report/the-chinese-state-funds-belt-and-road-but-does-not-have -trillions-to-spare/.

CHAPTER 14: ON THE MOVE

1 John Cassidy, "Donald Trump Is Transforming the G.O.P. into a Populist, Nativist Party," *New Yorker*, February 29, 2016, https: //www.newyorker.com/news/john-cassidy/donald-trump-is -transforming-the-g-o-p-into-a-populist-nativist-party.

2 Jeff Rubin, "Canada Isn't So Different. It Could Go Populist Too," *New York Times*, October 21, 2019, https://www.nytimes.com/2019 /10/21/opinion/canada-free-trade-populism.html.

3   Sarah Marsh, "Polish Ambassador Urges Poles to 'Seriously Consider' Leaving UK," *The Guardian*, September 18, 2019, https://www .theguardian.com/politics/2019/sep/18/polish-ambassador-urges -poles-to-seriously-consider-leaving-uk.

4   Overall, EU mobile citizens accounted in 2018 for 3.9 percent of total EU resident population, which was 1.2 percentage points more than in 2008. When looking at absolute numbers, in 2018 the most numerous national groups of mobile EU citizens aged twenty to sixty-four were those from Romania (2,524,000), Poland (1,666,000), Italy (1,133,000), Portugal (824,000) and Bulgaria (562,000) ("EU Citizens Living in Another Member State: Statistical Overview," Eurostat, July 2019, Statistical Overview-Eurostat https://ec.europa .eu/eurostat/statistics-explained/index.php?title=EU_citizens _living_in_another_Member_State_-_statistical_overview#Key _messages).

5   Lucie Bednárová, "Employers' Chief: Juncker Won't Admit He Is Wrong on Posted Workers Directive," Euractiv, August 5, 2016, https://www.euractiv.com/section/social-europe-jobs/interview /german-employers-chief-we-are-against-the-posted-workers -directive-revision/.

6   Not surprisingly, African-Americans tend to support the immigrations policies often denounced by others as racist (David Seminara, "Op-Ed: Liberals Say Immigration Enforcement Is Racist, But the Group Most Likely to Benefit from it Is Black Men," *Los Angeles Times*, March 16, 2018, https://www.latimes.com/opinion/op-ed /la-oe-seminara-trump-immigration-reform-african-americans -20180316-story.html).

7   Timothy Hatton and Jeffrey Williamson, *The Age of Mass Migration: Causes and Economic Impact* (Oxford: Oxford University Press, 1998), 169.

8   Hellen Warrell, "Net Migration from EU to UK falls 70% since Brexit Vote," *Financial Times*, February 28, 2019, https://www.ft.com /content/960b4672-3b3e-11e9-b72b-2c7f526ca5d0.

9   Some have speculated that Russian intervention in Syria constitutes a "weaponization" of refugees, as expressed by General Phil Breedlove, NATO's Supreme Allied Commander for Europe and head of the US European Command (Lizzie Deardon, "Russian and Syria 'Weaponising' Refugee Crisis to Destabalise Europe, NATO Commander Claims," *Independent*, March 3, 2016, https: //www.independent.co.uk/news/world/middle-east/russia-and

-syria-weaponising-refugee-crisis-to-destabilise-europe-nato
-commander-claims-a6909241.html).

10 NATO officials claim that they made no such promise to Russia, but
their own documents prove otherwise. https://www.latimes.com
/opinion/op-ed/la-oe-shifrinson-russia-us-nato-deal--20160530-snap
-story.html.

11 Warrell, "Net Migration from EU to UK falls 70% since Brexit Vote."

12 Andrius Sytas, "Resettled in the Baltics, Refugees Flee for Wealthier
Lands," Reuters, November 28, 2016, https://www.reuters.com
/article/us-europe-migrants-baltics/resettled-in-the-baltics-refugees
-flee-for-wealthier-lands-idUSKBN13N0RY.

13 Jon Henley, "What Is the Current State of the Migration Crisis in
Europe," *The Guardian*, November 21, 2018, https://www.theguardian
.com/world/2018/jun/15/what-current-scale-migration-crisis-europe
-future-outlook.

14 Kim Hjelmgaard, "Trump Isn't the Only One Who Wants to Build a
Wall. These European Nations Already Did," *USA Today*, May 24, 2018,
https://www.usatoday.com/story/news/world/2018/05/24/donald
-trump-europe-border-walls-migrants/532572002/.

15 Paul Karp, "MPs Widely Condemn Fraser Anning's Final Solution
Speech," *The Guardian*, August 15, 2018, https://www.theguardian
.com/australia-news/2018/aug/15/mps-widely-condemn-fraser
-annings-final-solution-speech.

16 Susan Ormiston, "How thousands of asylum seekers have turned
Roxham Road into a de facto border crossing," CBC News, September
29, 2019, https://www.cbc.ca/news/canada/the-national-roxham-road
-immigration-border-1.5169249.

17 Peter Turchin, *Ages of Discord: A Structural-Demographic Analysis of
American History*. (Chaplin, CT: Beresta Books, Chaplin, 2016), 176.

18 Jose A. Del Real, "The Number of Undocumented Immigrants in the
U.S. Has Dropped, a Study Says. Here are 5 Takeaways," *New York
Times*, November 27, 2018, https://www.nytimes.com/2018/11/27/us
/illegal-immigrants-population-study.html.

19 "GDP Per Capita (current US$)," World Bank Data, 2019, https://data
.worldbank.org/indicator/ny.gdp.pcap.cd.

20 Ibid.

21 Ian Kullgren and Anita Kumar, "Trump Threatens Mexico with Tariffs
over Immigration," Politico, May 31, 2019, https://www.politico.eu
/article/trump-threatens-mexico-with-tariffs-over-immigration/.

22 Ibid.

23 "US Border: Mexico Announces 56% Migrant Drop after Crackdown,"
    BBC News, September 6, 2019, https://www.bbc.com/news/world
    -latin-america-49612597.

24 Stef W. Kight and Alayna Treen, "Trump Isn't Matching Obama
    Deportation Numbers," Axios, June 21, 2019, https://www.axios
    .com/immigration-ice-deportation-trump-obama-a72a0a44-540d
    -46bc-a671-cd65cf72f4b1.html.

25 Devin Dwyer, "Obama Warns Central Americans: 'Do Not Send Your
    Children to the Borders,'" ABC News, June 26, 2014, https://abcnews
    .go.com/Politics/obama-warns-central-americans-send-children
    -borders/story?id=24320063.

26 Jason Lemon, "Bernie Sanders Says U.S. Can't Have 'Open Borders'
    Because People Will Come "from All Over the World,'" Newsweek,
    April 8, 2019, https://www.newsweek.com/bernie-sanders-open
    -borders-poverty-world-immigration-1388767.

27 "The Number of International Migrants Reaches 272 Million,
    Continuing an Upward Trend in All World Regions, Says UN," United
    Nations Department of Economic and Social Affairs, September 17,
    2019, https://www.un.org/development/desa/en/news/population
    /international-migrant-stock-2019.html.

28 Neli Esipova, Anita Pugliese and Julie Ray, "More Than 750
    Worldwide Would Migrate If They Could," Gallup, December 10, 2018,
    https://news.gallup.com/poll/245255/750-million-worldwide-migrate
    .aspx.

29 "The International Migration Report, 2017 (Highlights)," United
    Nations Department of Economic and Social Affairs, December 18,
    2017, https://www.un.org/development/desa/publications
    /international-migration-report-2017.html.

CHAPTER 15: DÉJÀ VU

1 Still, Marx was a regular reader of the magazine ("Karl Marx:
   False Consciousness," The Economist, August 27, 2016, https:
   //www.economist.com/node/21705665/all-comments?page=2).

2 "Economic History of the United Kingdom," Wikipedia, last modified, November 12, 2019, https://en.wikipedia.org/wiki/Economic
   _history_of_the_United_Kingdom.

3 Jeffry A. Frieden, "International Investment and Colonial Control:
   A New Interpretation," International Organization 48, no. 4 (Autumn,

1994): 559–93. Unlike the U.S.'s trade imbalance, some of Great Britain's was willingly given back. India presented Britain with a "gift" of £100,000,000 as a contribution to the Empire's efforts in the First World War, in addition to as much again in goods, and more than a million troops (Santanu Das, "Responses to the War (India), International Encyclopedia of the First World War, last modified October 8, 2014, https://encyclopedia.1914-1918-online.net/article /responses_to_the_war_india).

4 Frieden, *Global Capitalism*, 16.

5 Ibid., 73.

6 John Darwin, *Unfinished Empire: The Global Expansion of Britain* (London: Bloomsbury, 2012), 185.

7 The common feature of both waves of globalization has been dramatic declines in transport costs. In the first wave, often referred to as the Age of Mass Migration from Europe, the advent of steam-powered shipping was vital, dramatically reducing both the cost and the time of transatlantic travel. Migration flows exploded, with the United States single-handedly receiving nearly 30 million migrants from Europe over the latter half of the nineteenth century and the first two decades of the twentieth century. Declining transport costs continued to be critical for the second wave of globalization that followed during the postwar period. With the advent of supertankers and containerships, the cost of shipping a ton of freight fell by three quarters over the course of the past century, while the cost of air passenger traffic fell by 90 per cent from 1930 to 2000 (Frieden, *Global* Capitalism, 395).

8 Freiden, *Global Capitalism*, 52.

9 Ibid.

10 Claudia Goldin, "The Political Economy of Immigration Restrictions in the United States 1890 to 1921" in National Bureau of Economic Research, *The Regulated Economy: A Historical Approach to Political Economy*, January 1994, 250.

11 Hatton and Williamson, The Age of Mass Migration, 164–169

12 Ron Abramitzky and Leah Boustan, "Immigration in American Economic History," *Journal of Economic Literature* 55, no. 4 (2017): 1311–45, https://www.ncbi.nlm.nih.gov › pmc › articles › PMC5794227.

13 The Hamilton Project, "Foreign Born Share of US Population, 1850–2017," October 9, 2018, https://www.hamiltonproject.org

/charts/the_foreign_born_share_of_the_u.s._population_has
_returned_to_its_late_19th.

14 Michael Bordo, "The Second Era of Globalization is Not Yet Over: An
    Historical Perspective," NBER Working Paper No. 23786, September
    2017, https://www.nber.org/papers/w23786.

15 World Trade Organization, "The Trade Situation in 2009–10," World
    Trade Report 2010, https://www.wto.org/english/res_e/booksp_e
    /anrep_e/wtr10-1_e.pdf.

16 "Trade (% of GDP), 1960–2018," World Bank, https://data.worldbank
    .org/indicator/NE.TRD.GNFS.ZS.

17 "Global Trade Growth Loses Momentum as Trade Tensions Persist,"
    World Trade Organization (press release), April 2, 2019, https://www
    .wto.org/english/news_e/pres19_e/pr837_e.htm.

18 Ken McAtamney, "Has Globalization Peaked," William Blair, March
    2018, https://sicav.williamblair.com/investing_insights/detail/6299
    /has-globalization-peaked.fs. See, specifically, the chart "Global
    Trade Volume Growth versus Industrial Production Growth"
    featured here.

19 The appellate body—the Supreme Court for global trade disputes at
    the WTO—has three judges now. Two will retire in December 2019,
    rendering the appellate body effectively non-functional.

20 Mario Ritter Jr., "Japan Raises Trade Tensions with South Korea"
    VOA Learning English, August 2, 2019, https://learningenglish.
    voanews.com/a/japan-raises-trade-tensions-with-south-korea
    -in-dispute/5026746.html.

21 "Mahathir, Soros and the Currency Markets," *The Economist*,
    September 25, 1997, https://www.economist.com/finance-and
    -economics/1997/09/25/mahathir-soros-and-the-currency-markets.

22 Daniel Greenwald, Martin Lettau and Sydney Ludvigson, "How the
    Wealth Was Won: Factor Shares as Market Fundamentals," NBER
    Working Paper No. 25769, April 2019, https://papers.ssrn.com/sol3
    /papers.cfm?abstract_id=3375822.

23 Kristen Myers, "Not Just Amazon: 60 Big Companies Paid $0 Taxes
    under Trump Law," Yahoo Finance, April 12, 2019, https://ca.finance
    .yahoo.com/news/companies-paying-zero-taxes-trump-law
    -155944124.html.

24 Paul Taylor, Cary Funk and Peyton Craighill, "Once Again, the Future
    Ain't What It Used to Be," Pew Research Center, May 2, 2006, https:

//www.pewresearch.org/wp-content/uploads/sites/3/2010/10
/BetterOff.pdf.

25 Roberto Stefan Foa and Yascha Mounk, "The Danger of
Deconsolidation: The Democratic Disconnect," *Journal of Democracy* 27,
no. 3 (July 2016): 5–17, https://www.journalofdemocracy.org/articles
/the-danger-of-deconsolidation-the-democratic-disconnect/.

26 Neil Howe, "Are Millennials Giving Up on Democracy?" *Forbes*,
October 31, 2017, https://www.forbes.com/sites/neilhowe/2017/10
/31/are-millennials-giving-up-on-democracy/#dedf8092be12.

27 OECD, *Under Pressure*.

28 Peter Turchin, *Ages of Discord: A Structural-Demographic Analysis of
American History* (Chaplin, Connecticut: Beresta Books, 2006), 61–74

29 Freiden, *Global Capitalism*, 209.

30 The Washington Consensus refers to the period after the fall of the
Soviet Empire, when the United States stood alone as the world's
only hegemon. Trade and (most of all) capital flows exploded as
globally integrated capital markets allowed speculators like George
Soros to invest huge sums of money into Thai or Malayan bonds or,
at the same time, bet against those countries' capital markets when
so inclined. Global but US-led institutions like the International
Monetary Fund exacted the same financial discipline on borrowing
developing countries that the gold standard had a century before.
Governments around the world were encouraged to privatize public
enterprises. Telecommunications, transportations and, most
importantly, banking were deregulated, freeing them not only
from government regulations but in some cases even government
oversight. The mixed-economy model based on a public-private
partnership of the economy that had defined much of the success
of the early postwar era was dismantled and replaced by a laissez-
faire version of global capitalism.

31 Eric Reguly, "Populist parties make gains in EU elections but fall
short of overturning political order," *Globe and Mail*, May 26, 2019,
https://www.theglobeandmail.com/world/article-pro-europe-parties
-prevent-a-populist-surge-in-the-eu-elections/.

INDEX

Hewlett-Packard, 146
Hockey Night in Canada, 192, 197, 205
Hoover, Herbert, 29–30
housing market, 94–95
Howe, Gordie, 192
Huawei, 107, 108, 125, 192–97, 199,
    203, 205
Hungary
    and EU migrant quota, 236–37
    fences along border, 237
    populism in, 281

immigration. *See* migrants/migrant
    workers; migration
Immigration Act (Johnson Reed Act)
    (US), 243
income
    globalization and distribution of,
        83–84
    shrinking middle-class share of, 58
income gaps
    among OECD economies, 82
    in China, 82
    between developed vs. developing
        countries, 78–79
    factory relocation and, 79
    globalization and, 82, 85, 248
    household, 84–85
    migration and, 245, 248, 249
    offshoring wealth and, 71
    one percenters and, 82–83
    and populism, 85–86
    between rich and poor within
        countries, 82
    and spending habits, 95–98
    and stagnant income, 86
    tax policy and, 68–69
    wealthiest and, 68–69
income growth
    middle class, 58–59, 60
    in OECD countries, 99
    production relocation and,
        80–81
    rich and, 59, 60, 99
    in US, 99–100

income redistribution
    capital gains and, 69–70
    in China, 82
    between vs. within countries,
        250–51
    falling impact of, 67–68
    Gini coefficients and, 68–70, 71, 82
    globalization and, 65
    international trade flows and, 77
    and middle class, 64–65
    offshoring wealth and, 71
    progressive taxation and, 68–70
    and social security, 62–63, 65, 277
    tax declines and, 67–68
    trade agreements and, 65
    transfer payments, 62–63, 67, 68,
        270–71
    from wages to profits, 85
income stagnation
    and debt loads, 94
    and home ownership, 95
    in US, 87–88
    See also wage stagnation
Independence Party (UK), 22, 229,
    230–31, 234
India
    economic growth, 78, 86
    Harley-Davidson factory, 114
    income gaps, 79
    middle class in, 86
    population, 78
    smartphone production, 107
Indian Motorcycle, 113
Industrial Revolution, 77, 79, 104
inflation
    and borrowing rates, 92
    and consumer demand, 98
    and economic growth, 98
    globalization and, 91
    oil prices and, 63
    price increases and, 145
    and stagflation, 63–64
    steel spending and, 130
    tariffs and, 145
    vanishing of, 91

JEFF RUBIN is a world-leading expert on trade and energy, and former chief economist and chief strategist at CIBC World Markets. He recently served as a senior fellow at the Centre for International Governance Innovation. His first book, *Why Your World Is About to Get a Whole Lot Smaller*, was an international bestseller, winner of Canada's National Business Book Award, and longlisted for the *Financial Times* and Goldman Sachs Business Book of the Year Award. His two other bestsellers are *The End of Growth* and *The Carbon Bubble*.